Teaching With
THE STUDY OF
ECONOMICS

Program

Text:	*The Study of Economics: Principles, Concepts and Applications,* 3rd ed. (1987)
Student Workbook:	*Working With The Study of Economics,* 3rd ed.
Teacher's Guide:	*Teaching With The Study of Economics,* 3rd ed.
Transparency Masters Booklet:	*Transparency Masters to accompany The Study of Economics,* 3rd ed.
Color Transparency Set:	*Color Transparencies to accompany The Study of Economics,* 3rd ed.
Testing Book:	*Testing From The Study of Economics,* 3rd ed.
Microcomputer Test-Generating System:	*EZ-Test: to accompany The Study of Economics,* 3rd ed.

For further information on the above
materials please contact the
Sales Service Department
The Dushkin Publishing Group, Inc.
Sluice Dock
Guilford, CT 06437
800-243-6532

In Connecticut, call collect: 453-4351

Teaching With

THE STUDY OF

ECONOMICS

Principles, Concepts & Applications

3rd Edition

Prepared by Turley Mings

Chapter Overviews; Teaching Suggestions;
Answers to Learning Objectives, For Thought,
and Study Questions; and Schematic Outlines

Teaching With The Study of Economics: Principles, Concepts & Applications
3rd Edition

Printed in the United States of America

International Standard Book Number (ISBN) 0-87967-639-6

First Printing

The Dushkin Publishing Group, Inc., Sluice Dock, Guilford, Connecticut 06437

Introduction

This book was designed to assist teachers in using *The Study of Economics: Principles, Concepts and Applications* by serving as a guide to the material in the text, providing answers to questions in the text, and suggesting teaching techniques and audiovisual materials that may be useful in the classroom.

The organization of this guide for each chapter begins with a chapter overview that briefly summarizes the content of the chapter, section by section. The overview is followed by suggested responses to the learning objectives given at the end of the introductory articles in the text. The purpose of the learning objectives is to alert the students to the important principles and concepts they should be aware of as they read the chapter. (The review exercises and practice test questions in the student workbook, *Working With The Study of Economics*, are keyed to these learning objectives, as are the questions in *Testing From The Study of Economics* and in the computer test-generating program, *EZ-Test: to accompany The Study of Economics*.)

Each section of the chapter is then discussed under the organizing questions that head the sections in the text. Suggested here are noted classroom teaching techniques, the use of appropriate overhead transparencies from the transparency masters booklet, and the relevant study questions for that section at the end of the chapter. Discussing the study questions in class can help to clarify, reinforce, and extend the students' understanding of the concepts. Where appropriate, the study questions ask the students to relate the concepts to their own experience or their own area. This helps to transform abstract concepts into concrete experience.

The discussion of each section concludes with a brief summary of the case application for that section and gives suggested answers to the "For Thought" questions. There are three "For Thought" questions for each application, and a consistent format has been followed for each set of questions. The first question is a concept recognition or simple application question that students should not have much difficulty in answering if they have read the material carefully. The second question is usually more difficult, a complex application or analysis type of question that requires students to make use of economic reasoning. The third question is an integrative/evaluation type question that calls for students to draw upon their own value systems and integrate their broader social understandings with the economic principles that they have learned in order to answer the question. The consistent pattern of the three "For Thought" questions is intended to help students understand that there are some questions in economics that have specific, unequivocal answers and other questions that have different possible answers, depending on the values assigned to different goals or the credence given to alternative assumptions. The first two questions of each set of "For Thought" questions fall under the heading of "positive economics" and are concerned with verifiable facts and logical reasoning. The third question is in the area of "normative economics," which involves value judgements about the way things ought to be, as well as economic analysis. The answers to those questions are "open" because different answers can legitimately be given, but whichever answer is given should be supported by the economic principles studied. The suggested answers given in this book include the rationales for supporting either side of the issue.

Following the treatment of the analysis sections of the chapter, there is a brief summary of the chapter Perspective. The Perspectives are one-page essays designed to enrich the learning material by giving an historical background on the chapter or presenting the contribution of an outstanding past or present economist.

This is succeeded by suggested answers to the study questions. The study questions can be employed in class discussions as suggested above, used for cooperative-learning questions in small group discussions, or assigned as homework. The exercises in analysis following the study questions at the end of each chapter are suggested assignments of a more extensive nature, many requiring outside research by the students.

After the study question answers there is a section giving annotated references to appropriate lessons from the video series, *Economics U$A*. The 28 program series was first shown over the Public Broadcasting System during the 1986–1987 school year. It complements *The Study of Economics* very well both in pedagogy and content. Like the text, it introduces the economic concepts by first putting them in the context of a real application. The applications in *Economics U$A* are largely historical, compared to the more contemporary applications in the text. Viewing the series provides the additional benefit of giving the students a good overview of U.S. twentieth-century economic history.

Whether you show the corresponding *Economics U$A* program before or after the student reads the text chapter is a matter of choice; there are advantages to either procedure. Some of the programs serve as a bridge from the content of one chapter to the content of the next chapter, as cited in the annotations. Generally, my preference is to show a program after the students have read the material in the text and follow it up with class discussion of how the program illustrated economic concepts they learned in the chapter. This provides helpful reinforcement.

For current information on where to order the videotapes and the supplementary teaching materials contact the Joint Council on Economic Education, 2 Park Avenue, New York, NY 10016—(212) 685-5499—or the Center for Economic Education in your area.

The coverage of the text chapters concludes with a summary of the additional case applications in *Working With The Study of Economics*. There is an application for each section of a chapter in the workbook as in the text and each application is followed by a set of three "For Thought" questions with the same taxonomy. The students are provided with the answers to the "For Thought" questions for applications in the workbook but not for those in the text. This provides for flexibility in how the teacher chooses to make use of the questions.

A major innovation for this edition are the schematic outlines for each section of the text chapters which appear in *Working With The Study of Economics* as well as at the end of this book and in the booklet of transparency masters. The students should be encouraged to use the schematic outlines both to preview the chapter sections before they read them and to review the material afterward for reinforcement. They are given directions how to use the schematic outlines in the introduction to the workbook as shown below.

If the students follow these directions it will help their learning process more than if they merely use the outlines to study for tests. You might want to make a different use of the schematic outlines by making transparencies of them for overhead projection to orient the students to the material in the chapter that you are covering.

The foregoing paragraphs describe the contents of the resource book. The balance of the introduction deals with my own philosophy and methodology in teaching introductory economics.

I believe that to learn and retain the principles of economics, the student must play an active or interactive role in the process, rather than merely a passive role as listener. Just as a student does not learn how to do algebra just by listening to or reading about algebra, so a student cannot effectively use economics without practicing it. Although introductory economics uses very little mathematics, economics is a problem-solving discipline and requires reasoning processes that students learn by doing, just as they learn to solve mathematical problems by doing them. Therefore, *The Study of Economics* and the student workbook contain a multiplicity of applications, questions, and exercises that give students a chance to actively practice economic reasoning.

Because I believe in an active student learning mode, lecturing in my introductory economics classes is restricted. *The Study of Economics* was written with the intention that it could be understood with a minimum of explanation by the teacher. This frees class time for interactive discussion between the class and the teacher or among the students in small groups. Such discussion is most valuable when it is focused—and that is the purpose of the "For Thought" questions following the applications and the study questions and exercises in analysis at the ends of the chapters.

Cooperative learning in small groups serves a number of purposes. First, it enables students to clarify the meaning of questions and terminology. Secondly, students act as peer tutors—when one student explains a concept to another student, it helps the learning of both. Another benefit of the small group work is that it gets the students to verbalize economics, which helps them master the unfamiliar terminology.

In a broader way, working in small groups to accomplish an objective—determining the correct answers to

How Can You Get the Most Out of Your Study Time?

SCHEMATIC OUTLINES — The schematic outlines in this workbook at the beginning of each section of a chapter show the relationships between the different concepts and give a brief explanation of their meaning. The outlines can increase your study time efficiency when used as follows:

AS A PREVIEW
Studies of how people learn show that you get more out of reading something if you have an idea in advance of what the reading is about.

Before you read a section in the textbook, look over the schematic outline of that section in this book. Do not try to understand everything in the outline. Concentrate on the headings and see how the different concepts relate to each other — which ones are parallel concepts, which are sequential, and which are subordinate concepts of others.

AS A REVIEW
After reading the section in the textbook chapter, go over the schematic outline again, this time more carefully to reinforce your learning of the concepts and better retain what you read in the textbook.

the questions—is a valuable socialization process which will help them in their future occupations. One study of why people are fired showed that a full 70% lost their jobs because they could not work effectively with the other people, not because they were incompetent. Only 20% were let go because of incompetency in the work itself. Also, students become more interested when they exchange ideas; the subject comes alive.

The best size for the groups is four students, although three to five works satisfactorily. In my classes I give the students approximately 20 minutes to discuss and arrive at consensus answers for the three "For Thought" questions following an application. Occasionally more time is needed, but if they have read the material in advance and their discussion is focused, 20 minutes is generally sufficient. One student in each group writes up the answers for the group, rotating the task among the students; each member of the group signs the paper; and it is turned in to be graded. (I use a simple grading system of 1 to 3 points depending on whether the answers are below, at, or above expectations.) I discuss the answers with the class immediately afterward.

According to the findings concerning learning theory, variety in learning activities is helpful. Another activity I have found useful is a periodic team quiz, scheduled just before tests. As a homework assignment, each student writes eight questions and answers dealing with the economic concepts to be covered on the test. In class they are arranged in teams of about five students, and the teams are paired off facing each other. Students alternate asking a student on the opposing team one of the prepared questions. One student keeps score. If the student to whom the question is directed gives the correct answer, the team scores a point. If that student cannot answer the question, any other student on the

team may volunteer to answer, but if the answer is not correct on that second try the team loses a point. This is to discourage second trys that are pure guessing. The value of the team quizzes is that they induce the students to review the material in advance of the tests and permit them to compare their understanding with that of the other students, enabling them to identify areas in which their understanding is weak.

Another consideration in effective learning is that the teaching materials be interesting. *The Study of Economics* attempts to make the subject interesting as well as understandable, and student feedback on the earlier editions indicates that it succeeds. Students obtain satisfaction from learning when they perceive the relevance of what they are learning to the world around them. The chapters' introductory articles and case applications were selected and written to interest students and show them the relevance of what they are studying. Teachers can supplement this by introducing new applications that are currently in the news. The practice students get from applying economic concepts to the cases in the text and workbook should enable them to transfer the analytical reasoning to new situations that are in the news.

Humor is also a useful device to stimulate interest and promote learning. The cartoon strip that follows each introductory article serves as a humorous bridge between the topic of the article and the explanation of the economic concepts in the body of the chapter. A point made with humor has a greater impact and longer retention. Besides, cartoons are fun. I hope *The Study of Economics* will put some fun into "the dismal science" for you and your students.

Turley Mings

Contents

Chapter 1

Economic Choices

Chapter Overview

This chapter covers the basic rationale of economics as a field of study arising from scarcity, the goals or objectives of economics, and the principal tools of this discipline used in economic reasoning. The introductory article provides a framework for examining these topics by discussing the African famine of 1985.

This subject provides a dramatic illustration of the scarcity of resources relative to needs and the consequent necessity for making choices about the use of resources. Agricultural production in Africa has been reduced by cutting down the forests to use for firewood and construction. The resulting loss of watershed diminished irrigation and increased erosion. In addition to these private trade-offs affecting agriculture, the policies of African governments have also reduced food production. The opportunity cost of armaments expenditures has been a loss of productivity increases in agriculture.

Decisions about the alternative uses of resources are made in the light of various economic and socioeconomic goals, which are discussed in the second section of the chapter. In analyzing the problem, various economic concepts (scarcity, trade-offs, opportunity cost) and models (production possibility frontier) are helpful, along with such factual tools as statistics, economic history, and the behavior of institutions.

Graphic models are particularly useful in teaching economics, especially line graphs. Since graphs are employed in chapter 1 and students may not be accustomed to working with them, it might be helpful to suggest or assign the appendix on graphs at the end of the textbook before covering this chapter. The guide to the appendix begins on p. 125 of this book.

The first organizing question in the chapter is "Why do we have to make economic choices?" In this section the concepts of scarcity, trade-offs, and opportunity cost are explained and a production-possibility-frontier diagram is used to graphically illustrate trade-offs and opportunity cost. The case application for this section is "Dieting—The National Pastime," which examines trade-offs and opportunity cost from the perspective of a non-economic but all too familiar problem.

The second organizing question is "What are society's economic goals?" Under this question the four primary economic goals—efficiency, price stability, full employ-

ment, and economic growth—are discussed in addition to some socioeconomic goals. The application, "Replaced by R_2D_2?" deals with the effects of the increasing use of production robots to replace human labor.

The third organizing question is "How does the study of economics help us make choices?" It covers the analytical tools of economic reasoning (concepts and models) and the factual tools (statistics, economic history, and institutions). The application, "Does It Pay to Go to College?", illustrates the use of a cost-benefit model and other tools of economics to examine this question.

Suggested Answers to the Learning Objectives

The knowledge acquired from this chapter should enable the students to:

1. Explain scarcity as an economic term.

    In economics, scarcity is a condition that exists when resources are insufficient to satisfy all wants and desires for goods and services. Whatever sells for a price is scarce and is considered an economic good.

2. Define and give examples of economic trade-offs.

    An economic trade-off is the choice between alternative uses for a given quantity of a resource. When forests are used for firewood and construction they are no longer available as watersheds. When governments allocate resources to armaments, there are less available for investment in agriculture. There is a double trade-off in overeating—the resources we consume in putting weight on and the resources we use in trying to take it off— that could be used for other things. When students allocate their time to studying, they have less time to work for income or to participate in leisure-time activities.

3. Explain opportunity cost.

    Opportunity cost is the value of the sacrificed alternative output when resources are used to produce a good or service. For example, when national resources are used to increase a country's military might, the opportunity cost is the other public or private goods that the resources could have been used for instead of armaments, such as increasing agricultural output.

4. List the four primary economic goals.

The four primary economic goals are efficiency, price stability, full employment, and growth.

5. Distinguish between purely economic and socio-economic goals.

   Purely economic goals are concerned with making the economy work as effectively as possible to maximize output and living standards. Socioeconomic goals are objectives which our culture considers desirable and which have significant economic dimensions.

6. Explain the fundamentals of economic models.

   Economic models are simplified representations of real-world situations showing the cause and effect relationships. They may show the relationships in the form of words, graphs, or mathematical equations.

7. Describe three types of facts used in economic analysis.

   Facts used in economic analysis include: statistics, which are numerical data on economic variables; economic history, which is the recounting of previous events and relationships between economic variables; and institutional behavior, which encompasses the policies and practices of institutions that affect the economy.

8. Explain the production possibility frontier.

   The production possibility frontier is a graphical representation of the different maximum output combinations of goods or services that can be obtained from a given amount of resources. One output is measured on the horizontal axis and the other on the vertical axis. A point on the PPF shows the quantities of the two outputs produced. If the trade-off is constant, the PPF is a straight line. If the opportunity costs are increasing, the usual case, the PPF is curved.

Why Do We Have To Make Economic Choices?

This section begins by explaining that the existence of scarcity is the reason why a science of economics is necessary. It emphasizes that in economics the term scarcity is relative rather than absolute. If there is no demand for something, it is not scarce—no matter how rare it is. A light-hearted example of something that is rare, but not scarce, is gophers. You might ask the class if they can suggest other examples.

Because of scarcity, we have to make choices about the use of our resources. When we have to choose there is a trade-off involved. The concept of trade-offs can be reinforced by Study Questions 1-3 on page 24 of the textbook.

When resources are allocated to armaments production, the opportunity cost to African countries is a sacrifice of increased food output. The opportunity cost concept can be reinforced by Exercise in Analysis 4 on textbook page 25, which could be used for class discussion rather than as a written exercise.

The production possibility frontier diagrams on pages 10 and 11 might present some difficulties for the beginning student who is unfamiliar with the use of graphs. This difficulty can be minimized by first going over the constructing and reading of line graphs explained in the appendix. Transparency masters are provided in a separate booklet so that you may reproduce overhead projections of Figures 1A, 4, and 5 from the appendix to assist in explaining what line graphs mean and how to use them.

If the students understand how to read line graphs, the transparencies of Figures 2 and 3 on textbook pages 10-11 can be used to compare changes in resource allocations on the PPF with constant costs in Figure 2 and the PPF with increasing costs in Figure 3. Color transparencies of these graphs are included in the transparency set available for the text.

Additional help in understanding the production possibility curves can be had by showing the first program in the videotape series *Economics U$A*, which is described below. The meaning of the PPF diagram can be further reinforced with Study Question 4, which follows nicely from the example in the videotape program.

Case Application: Dieting—The National Pastime

This application of the concepts of scarcity, trade-offs, and opportunity costs is less serious than the introductory story about famine in Africa, although dieting is a serious problem for many people. It is ironic that in this country so many resources are allocated to weight reduction while millions are underfed in Africa and elsewhere.

One type of trade-off in dieting is the trade-off between food gratification on one hand and self-image or health on the other. This application shows how a problem of major proportions for young people—their body image—which is not basically an economic problem, can nonetheless be examined with the tools of economic analysis.

Answers to the "For Thought" Questions

1. In economic terms, is food scarce in America? Is garbage scarce? How can you determine what is scarce and what is not?

   In economic terms, food is scarce in America. Although we grow more than enough to satisfy our domestic needs, it is not free. (The problems of overproduction in U.S. farming are discussed in the introductory article for chapter 5. Here it need only be noted that the resources used to produce food could be allocated to producing other things.) Food is scarce because there is a cost of obtaining it. Garbage, on the other hand, is not scarce because there is more of it than we have any need for. You can determine what is scarce by whether or not it has a price. Anything that is free or that you have to pay someone to take, as is the case with garbage, is not scarce.

2. What is an example of a trade-off in this case application? Where a dieter is concerned, are there different types of opportunity costs of a chocolate chip cookie? What are they?

   There are different types of trade-offs in this case, both direct and indirect. The normal types of trade-offs exist—resources allocated to food cannot be used for something else and resources allocated to diet books, medicines, equipment, and programs involve trade-offs. For a dieter, there is both the direct opportunity cost of purchasing a chocolate chip cookie and an indirect opportunity cost of the added calories from consuming it.

3. Is the annual $5 billion spending on losing weight justified? Why or why not?

   Open answer. The answer to this question is open because it depends upon one's value system and interpretation of the facts. It could be argued that the $5 billion a year spent on losing weight is justified because being overweight is hazardous to a person's health and people feel better about themselves when they are not overweight. On the other side, it could be argued that the $5 billion expenditure on dieting is not justified since it is largely wasted because most people are not able to maintain a weight loss, excessive weight loss can itself be damaging to a person's health, and the only program that works in the long run is adopting a lifestyle of balanced nutrition and exercise.

What Are Society's Economic Goals?

There are four primary economic goals discussed in this section—efficiency, price stability, full employment, and growth—and five socioeconomic goals—environmental protection, economic security, equity, justice, and freedom. Microeconomics is concerned principally with the goal of efficiency, while the other three primary goals come under macroeconomics. It might be useful to point out the interrelationships between different goals—sometimes goals are complementary and sometimes conflicting. This can be reinforced by Study Questions 6 and 7. A great deal of public controversy arises from the area of socioeconomic goals. This can be explored through Study Question 8 and Exercise in Analysis 2.

Case Application: **Replaced by R₂D₂?**

The current explosion in the use of industrial robots provides a case for exploring the impact of technology on our economic and socioeconomic goals. Up to 1986 there were less than 25,000 production robots in the United States, but the number is growing rapidly, especially in the automobile

industry. As a consequence, it is projected that they will replace as many as 1.3 million workers by the year 2000. It should be noted, however, that such technological developments also create new jobs. The effects of new technology are further explored in the Perspective on "The Industrial Revolution," (p. 49) and in the introductory article for chapter 14 on "The New Industrial Revolution," (p. 351).

Answers to the "For Thought" Questions

1. Which primary economic goals are served by the use of production robots?

   The primary goal which is most significantly served by the use of production robots is efficiency. Another important economic goal which production robots serve is growth. It could also be said that production robots, by holding down costs, contribute to price stability.

2. Does the use of robots involve a trade-off among different economic or socioeconomic goals? Which?

   The use of robots may involve a trade-off between the goals of efficiency and growth on the one hand, and full employment on the other hand. One socioeconomic goal it may involve is the sacrifice of economic security for the workers who are displaced by robots.

3. Do you favor or oppose a rapid increase in the use of robots to replace human workers? Why?

   Open answer. Students might favor a rapid increase in the use of robots to replace human workers because it would increase efficiency and economic growth and thereby result in higher living standards. They might oppose a rapid increase in the use of robots because this would put workers out of jobs, resulting in unemployment and the loss of economic support for workers and their families.

How Does the Study of Economics Help Us Make Choices?

This section gives the student an explicit view of the types of intellectual tools employed in the discipline of economics. It is useful to distinguish between theoretical and factual tools. The former make up the methodology of economics, and the latter provide the raw material for economic analysis. Most of the marginal glossary terms in *The Study of Economics* are examples of economic concepts. The production possibility frontier in this chapter is an example of an economic model. Another example is the cost-benefit model in the case application for this section. An understanding of the factual tools used in economics is reinforced by Study Questions 8 and 9 and by Exercise in Analysis 1. An additional look at the cost-benefit analysis model, which should be of interest to the student, is Exercise 3.

Case Application: Does It Pay to Go to College?

This application explores the question of whether the increase in the supply of college graduates since World War II has reduced the value of a college degree so much that it no longer pays a sufficiently high premium income to justify the costs of a college education. There is no definitive answer to this question because of the many uncertainties involved, such as the future college premium, the appropriate discount rate, and non-income variables. However, with reasonable assumptions about the unknowns, it appears that the return to education is comparable to the returns on other types of investment.

The application provides an opportunity for economic analysis employing the concepts of trade-offs and opportunity costs, the cost-benefit model, and some factual tools of economics.

Answers to the "For Thought" Questions

1. What factual tools of economic reasoning do you find in this application?

   The factual tools in this application include statistics, such as the data on the cost of a college education and the difference in earnings between college graduates and non-college graduates. They also include economic history in the relationship between the payoff of going to college in earlier years compared with the payoff today.

2. What theoretical tools of economic analysis do you find in this application?

   The theoretical tools in this application include concepts such as the opportunity cost of sacrificed wages and the trade-off between time and money. Another applicable theoretical tool is the cost-benefit model.

3. What additional non-monetary benefits of attending college might be included in a complete cost-benefit model of a college education? Are there non-monetary costs as well? In your view, would a complete cost-benefit model of a college education justify it or not? Why?

   Open answer. Non-monetary benefits of attending college might include the enjoyment of college life and activities, expanded cultural and intellectual interests and understanding, new friendships, and increased ability to adapt to future changes. The non-monetary costs of attending college might include the pressure and stress of college life, the postponement of marriage and family, and the sacrifice of leisure time.

Perspective: The Affluent Society

The Perspective provides a view contrary to the idea of scarcity as the overriding issue of economics. It presents the thesis of John Kenneth Galbraith that modern industrial economies have solved the problem of scarcity and that the important problems now are the composition and distribution of output and the conditions of worklife. This could be the basis for a stimulating class discussion of the question. It is a topic that is relevant to discussions in subsequent chapters concerning working conditions (pp. 196-198), income distribution (pp. 212-214), poverty (p. 219-221), and world poverty (pp. 466-472).

Answers to Study Questions

1. Give an example of a personal economic choice you have made recently. What was the trade-off, and why did you decide to make it?

   Open answer. Examples might be consumer purchases (the selection of one consumer item at the sacrifice of an alternative purchase), the decision about what job to take (the trade-off being an alternative employment or leisure time), or the decision whether to commute by private automobile or by public transportation.

2. Give an example of an economic choice made by society as a whole. How was the choice made? What trade-offs were involved?

   Open answer. One example might be whether to increase or decrease military spending. Other examples might be whether or not to construct a new freeway or to provide housing for the homeless. The trade-offs of public spending are the alternative public or private goods that could have been produced with the resources.

3. Why are trade-offs necessary in our modern economic system?

   Trade-offs are necessary because of scarcity. There are not enough resources to produce all of the things that people need and desire, both private and public. Consequently, if we devote more resources to production of one item, less of something else will be produced.

4. Points on a production possibility frontier, such as Points A and B in Figure 2, show the different combinations of two goods that could be produced with the available resources. Would it be possible to produce at a point inside, or at a point outside, the PPF curve? What would these points indicate?

   A point inside the PPF curve would indicate that not all of the available resources were being used in production. This is a situation of less than full employment. In this case, trade-offs are not necessary. More of one item can be produced without reducing the production of something else. It is normally not possible to produce at a point outside of the PPF curve because production capacity is not sufficient to produce such large amounts with existing resources and technology.

5. Some economic and socioeconomic goals are complementary; achieving one goal helps to achieve

another goal. What is one example where economic and socioeconomic goals are complementary?

Open answer. Examples might include: full employment helps to achieve economic security; economic growth helps to achieve economic equity; and efficiency helps to achieve price stability.

6. In other cases, there are conflicts between different goals; efforts to achieve one make it more difficult to achieve another. What is an example of a conflict between economic goals?

Open answer. Examples might include: achieving full employment makes it more difficult to achieve stable prices; achieving production efficiency may make it more difficult to have full employment; or measures to achieve price stability may reduce the amount of economic freedom.

7. How have some of the socioeconomic goals of our society been affected by government regulations of the development of private land?

Open answer. Federal environmental regulations and city zoning laws restrict the economic freedom of individuals to use their property as they desire.

8. What is one example of each of the three factual tools used in economic reasoning?

Open answer. Examples should include statistical data, economic history, and information about the way institutions function that affect the economy.

9. What are three institutions that affect you in some way? Explain how these institutions affect you.

Open answer. The institutions might include firms that are employers of the students, firms with which the students do business, government institutions such as schools or the post office, or legal institutions.

10. At the same time Africa was suffering mass starvation in 1985, there was such a surplus of grain produced in the United States that farmers were going bankrupt because they couldn't sell their grain for enough to pay their costs. How does this situation fit Galbraith's ideas in *The Affluent Society*?

This situation lends support to Galbraith's contention that we have solved the problem of production, and that the problem now is a distribution problem.

Integrating *Economics U$A* Programs

(For information on Economics U$A *see the introduction, p. v.)*

The corresponding program for this chapter from *Economics U$A* is the first one in the series, "Resources and Scarcity: What Is Economics All About?" This program directly reinforces the concepts in the first section of the chapter—scarcity, trade-offs, opportunity cost, and the production possibility frontier model. Journalist David Schoumacher narrates three situations in which trade-offs and opportunity

costs were involved: the trade-off between Alaskan wilderness recreation and mineral development, the World War II trade-off between "guns and butter," and the trade-off in the textile industry between worker health and efficient (low-cost) production.

Economist Richard Gill shows the production possibility frontiers for these trade-offs and explains why they show increasing opportunity costs. The PPF model that he discusses for the "guns vs. butter" trade-off in World War II provides students with a firm basis for answering Study Question 4.

The concepts in the second and third sections of chapter 1 are implicit in the program and can be brought out in class discussion. The economic objectives of our society can be reinforced by asking the students what goals discussed in the chapter are implied in the three applications (efficiency, full employment, and environmental protection, to name some obvious ones).

Ask the students to cite examples in the program of the use of the tools of economic analysis. Examples might include the PPF curve and the cost-benefit model; statistics (e.g.,180 million acres of Alaskan land protected from development, 42-43% of the nation's output allocated to the military at the peak of World War II, 300,000 workers displaced in the textile mills); history (e.g., gas shortages in the 1970s, depression of the 1930s, deaths from brown-lung disease in the textile industry); and institutions (e.g., Congress, environmental movement, War Production Board, textile industry, Amalgamated Clothing and Textile Workers Union, Supreme Court).

Case Applications in Student Workbook

(Answers are supplied to students in the workbook.)

Why Do We Have To Make Economic Choices?

Case Application: The Vanishing Land

The conflicting demands for the uses of one of our basic natural resources, land, provides an application of the terms scarcity, resources, trade-offs, and opportunity costs. It also lends itself to analysis using a production possibility frontier with agricultural output on one axis and non-agricultural output on the other axis. The PPF curve for land would be concave to the origin, like that in Figure 3 on page 11. Since some land is more productive for agricultural use and some more productive for urban, suburban, and industrial development, there are increasing opportunity costs to the trade-off of agricultural land for other uses.

Answers to the "For Thought" Questions

1. How is the problem of scarcity reflected in the above case application?

Society does not have sufficient land resources to satisfy all of the agricultural and non-agricultural needs for land. The sacrifice of agricultural land to satisfy urban and industrial needs is an example of the trade-offs that result from scarcity of all types of resources, including natural resources, labor resources, and capital resources.

2. What is the opportunity cost of a housing tract built where a cherry orchard stood?

The opportunity cost to society of building a housing tract in place of a cherry orchard is the sacrificed production of the cherry orchard. Consumers will no longer have the cherries that were produced by that orchard.

3. Do you think that disappearing agricultural land is a problem? If it is a problem, can you suggest any solutions?

The answer to this question is open-ended because there are different possible answers. On the one hand, disappearing agricultural land can be viewed as being a problem for society because food is one of our basic needs. A smaller amount of land on which to grow food could be expected to result in higher food prices. On the other hand, it could be argued that we have sufficient agricultural land available to meet all of our current food needs. In some cases we even have excess production of some crops, which results in low food prices for the farmers. Our greater need is for land to accommodate our growing cities and industries. This is shown by the fact that land used for urban and industrial purposes has a higher price than the same land when used for agricultural purposes. The opposing viewpoints may hinge on whether we are considering only present food needs or anticipating future needs and on whether we are considering only the food needs of the United States or those of the world. If the loss of agricultural land is considered a problem, possible solutions include land zoning, ordinances, favorable property tax treatment for agricultural land, and the farm subsidy program. Longer term solutions include increased farm productivity per acre, bringing submarginal land into production, and redesigning metropolitan areas for more vertical expansion.

What Are Society's Economic Goals?

Case Application: A Plastic World

This application shows the impact a new industry can have on the economy and on our economic and socioeconomic goals. The plastics industry has been a major growth industry. But it has put out of work many employees in older industries—steel, wood, natural fibers—and has created serious environmental problems.

Answers to the "For Thought" Questions

1. What economic goals has the plastics industry helped in achieving?

The expansion of the plastics industry in recent years has definitely contributed to achieving the goal of economic growth. It most probably also has contributed to achieving the goal of full employment, despite the job losses in the older steel, wood, and fibers industries, because of the jobs created in the industry itself and the jobs created by industries using plastic.

2. How has the growth of the plastics industry resulted in a trade-off of some economic or socioeconomic goals which are not being satisfied as well?

An increasingly troublesome trade-off resulting from the growth of the plastics industry is the environmental pollution from the accumulating plastics garbage on land and in the oceans. Another trade-off is the loss of economic security by those workers who have been laid off in the more traditional materials industries because of the competition from plastics.

3. Should growth of the plastics industry be retarded by restricting the use of plastics that are not biodegradable? Why or why not?

Open answer. On the environmental side, the answer is yes. If plastics garbage continues to accumulate in the environment, it will not only be aesthetically damaging and thus lower the quality of life, but it will be harmful to some animals, birds, and sealife. On the side of maximizing economic efficiency and minimizing costs, the answer is no. It is more costly to produce biodegradable plastics than standard plastics. It requires more resource inputs, and therefore we could not have as much consumption of other things as well as plastic.

How Does the Study of Economics Help Us Make Choices?

Case Application: Hot or Cold—Cost-Benefit Analysis

This case provides a numerical example of the application of cost-benefit analysis to a real-world problem. The problem is how to minimize costs for heating and cooling an office building. Would the cost of additional air conditioning and insulation be justified by the savings on energy costs? Are the direct money costs and savings the only consideration that should be included, or are there indirect benefits that should be included such as improved morale and productivity on the part of the firm's employees?

The application illustrates the use of economic concepts (the opportunity cost of the capital invested in the improvements), economic models (cost-benefit analysis), and factual tools of economics (statistics, history, institutional policies).

Answers to the "For Thought" Questions

1. What type of economic tool is a cost-benefit analysis?

   A cost-benefit analysis is a type of economic model.

2. Are there examples of three types of factual tools in this analysis? What are they?

   Statistics are one factual tool used in this analysis, such as the data on costs of improvements and savings on utility bills. History is also involved, such as the historical experience that utility bills rise at 10% a year. The institutional behavior of the firm is also involved, such as the policy that the company should provide good working conditions for its employees even if that resulted in reduced profitability.

3. Should the president of the company make the improvements even if it resulted in reducing profits?

Open answer. Many executives in businesses believe their principal responsibility is to maximize the profits of the company, what they refer to as "the bottom line." If the company is a corporation, they feel they owe it to the stockholders to earn as high a profit rate as possible, so long as they abide by legal and ethical standards. Other officers of firms believe company policies must take into account the welfare of its employees, the community, or society at large. They believe companies have social responsibilities as well as profit responsibilities. In any event, executives should consider long-run profits rather than short-run profits. Spending money to improve the comfort and health of the company's employees may improve the long-run profitability of the company.

Chapter 2

The Economic System

Chapter Overview

This chapter covers the need for and functions of an economic system, the various types of economic systems, and the basic elements of a market system. The introductory article describes an 1850s cattle drive delivering a herd of beef cattle from Oklahoma to New York City and compares that production method with raising cattle today.

The first organizing question is "Why Are Economic Systems Needed?" Modern beef production in the United States is a highly specialized operation. The western states specialize in beef production because they have an absolute advantage over places like New York City and a comparative advantage over places like rural New Jersey in producing beef for the eastern markets. The basis of this comparative advantage is the vast rangeland in the West which is not useful for other types of production. Specialization in modern beef production includes everything from veterinarians to nutritional specialists, feed lots, auction houses, slaughter houses, and various distribution activities before the meat arrives at the supermarket counter. Each of the links in the production chain is interdependent with all the others; and consumers, unlike those in the rural households in the 1850s, are dependent on such specialists for virtually all of their consumption needs. The case application for this section concerns "The Efficiencyburger," an examination of how specialization of production in the fast-food industry has increased efficiency.

The second organizing question is "What Basic Questions Must Every Economic System Resolve?" Economic systems must decide what outputs to produce with their limited resources, how to produce those outputs most efficiently, and for whom the outputs are being produced. The case application—"What Happened on the Way to the Nuclear Power Future?"—illustrates how events—nuclear accidents and escalating costs of nuclear power—have affected the resolution of the basic economic questions in energy production.

The third organizing question is "What Are the Principal Types of Economic Systems?" The three principal types of economies are market, centrally-directed, and traditional economies, but modern economic systems are mixtures of these basic types. The case application on "Free Enterprise in the Soviet Union" shows how a centrally-directed economy has been infiltrated by market influences.

The fourth organizing question is "How Does a Market System Resolve the Three Basic Economic Questions?" This section discusses how the allocating decisions are made in a market system through the operation of product and factor markets providing incentives and generating a circular flow in the economy of incomes and of real production. The case application explores further the question of providing for future energy needs with "Where Is Our Energy Future Now?"

Suggested Answers to the Learning Objectives

The knowledge acquired from this chapter should enable the students to:

1. Distinguish between absolute and comparative advantage.

   Absolute advantage exists when one producer is more efficient in the production of one good (can produce more of the good with the same amount of resource input) than a second producer, while the second producer can produce another good more efficiently than the first. Comparative advantage exists when one producer can produce two goods more efficiently than a second producer but has a greater efficiency advantage in one of the goods than in the other.

2. Explain why specialization based on absolute or comparative advantage results in greater economic efficiency and interdependence.

   Specialization is efficient because it enables labor and other resources to be concentrated on a single production task, which minimizes waste. Specialization based on absolute or comparative advantage results in greater economic efficiency because resources are applied to those production tasks in which they have the greatest ratio of efficiency relative to other producers. Specialization makes producers dependent on others for the goods which they don't produce.

3. Give examples of the three basic economic questions.

   An example of the answer to the "what" question illustrated in the introductory article was the decision by José and María Ruiz to raise short, heavy cattle that yielded large amounts of high quality beef. An example of an answer to the "how" question was their decision to keep the cattle on the ranch until they reached 450 to

500 lb and then truck them to feed lots. The resolution of the "for whom" question is illustrated by the fact that almost everyone can afford to buy some beef, but those with greater incomes can afford to eat beef more often and to eat higher quality cuts of meats.

4. Classify the factors (resources) as either land, labor, or capital.

   Land includes all natural resources such as agricultural land, forests, minerals, and the sea. Labor includes all human resources such as manual, clerical, technical, professional, and managerial labor. Capital consists of the means of production such as factories, office buildings, machinery, tools, and equipment. It may sometimes refer to the financial means to acquire the foregoing and employ land and labor resources.

5. Identify the three major types of economic systems and explain how they differ.

   The three major types of economic systems are market economies, centrally-directed economies, and traditional economies. In market systems, economic decisions are made largely by individuals and firms based on prices in the marketplace. In centrally-directed systems, economic decisions are made by a central planning agency based on production goals. In a traditional system, economic decisions are dictated by custom.

6. Explain how a market system resolves the three basic economic questions.

   A market system resolves the basic economic questions by a process in which buyers and sellers form a market for products and factors of production; income and profit incentives determine what will be produced, how it will be produced, and for whom the products will be produced.

7. Distinguish between goods and services sold in product markets and those sold in factor markets.

   When goods and services are sold to the final user, they are sold in product markets. When they are inputs into further production or distribution, they are sold in factor markets.

8. Diagram the circular flow of a market economy.

   The circular flow of a market economy is diagrammed as on page 45 of the textbook. Money flows in the inner circuit go from firms to households in the form of rent, wages, and interest payments, and from households to firms in the form of payments for purchases. Real flows in the outer circuit go from households to firms in the form of land, labor, and capital services, and from firms to households in the form of finished goods and services.

Why Are Economic Systems Needed?

This section explains how production is specialized and how this specialization leads to greater efficiency and lower production costs for goods and services. Labor and other resources are specialized in production according to their absolute or comparative advantage. Because students frequently have trouble with these concepts, it might be useful to engage in the following discussion: Ask a student who has a brother or sister to name something that the student does better than their sibling and something that the sibling does better than the student. If both things needed to be done, who would do which one? Obviously, it would be most efficient for each to do what they were most proficient at. This is the case of absolute advantage. Then ask the student to name a second thing he or she is better at than their brother or sister (or vice versa). In which of the two things does he or she have the greatest advantage? If the two things needed to be done at the same time, which sibling would perform which activity? Why? This inquiry provides the students with a clearer understanding of comparative advantage.

The concepts of absolute and comparative advantage are useful at this point to show that the specialization in production occurs not simply by chance, or even by choice, but is determined by the characteristics of the resources. However, the most important application of absolute and comparative advantage is found later in the understanding of international trade. They are brought up in that context in chapter 16, and the foregoing class discussion can be recalled to refresh the students' understanding of the difference between absolute and comparative advantage.

Specialization of production tasks results in interdependence among the various producers in the economy and interdependence between households and firms. This complicated network of interdependence in a modern economy makes necessary an economic system to coordinate the various parts effectively. The concepts of specialization and interdependence, and the complications it gives rise to, are reinforced by Study Questions 1 and 2.

Case Application: The Efficiencyburger

Fast-food operations such as McDonald's are dependent upon a high degree of specialization for their survival. In the 1700s Adam Smith used the case of a pin factory to illustrate the advantages of specialization in production tasks. Today, everyone has an opportunity to observe specialization in action in a fast-food restaurant operation.

Answers to the "For Thought" Questions

1. What economic principle did McDonald's adopt that was so successful that it was copied by others?

   McDonald's used standardization of their production operations and specialization of labor tasks to maximize efficiency.

2. How does the McDonald's operation reflect the relationship between specialization and interdependence?

   Each worker at McDonald's has a specific task and is dependent on the other workers to perform their tasks in filling customers' orders.

3. One objective of economics is to avoid waste, but McDonald's restaurants destroy hamburgers if not sold within 10 minutes. Is this a good idea? Why or why not?

   Open answer. Destroying food may be considered wasteful, especially in view of the starvation in Africa depicted in chapter 1. But McDonald's thinks it is a good idea to dispose of hamburgers that are not fresh and may not appeal to the customer. They find it less costly to destroy a certain amount of hamburgers than to reduce the efficiency of their production operation by preparing food to order.

What Basic Questions Must Every Economic System Resolve?

There are three basic economic questions which all economies must resolve. They can be characterized as allocation decisions. The first is the "what" question. This question concerns how the available resources should be allocated to the production of alternative types of goods and services. Since a nation's resources of land, labor, and capital are limited, it is necessary for the economy to determine for which outputs those resources will be used. The second basic question is the "how" question. This concerns the determination of production technology. There are usually alternative methods available for producing a particular good or service. Given a country's available resources and technology, what is the most efficient production method to use? The foremost aspect of this question is determining the most appropriate proportions of the amount of labor to the amount of capital equipment used in production. The third basic question is the "for whom" question. This concerns the allocation of the final output among consumers in the population; who gets how much of what is produced. A transparency of Figure 1 (p. 34) can be used to illustrate the allocation of resources in the economic system as the three basic questions are resolved in satisfying consumers' needs and wants. The "what," "how," and "for whom" questions are further explored in Study Questions 3, 4, and 5 at the end of the chapter. An additional look at what

constitutes the factors of production is found in Study Question 6.

Case Application: What Happened on the Way to the Nuclear Power Future?

One of the most significant allocation questions in the world today is how energy resources will be used and what form future energy production will take. This application shows how the original optimistic expectations for nuclear power have changed as a result of accidents and rising costs. Adequate supplies of energy are vital to economic well being. Nuclear power was seen as the successor to such non-renewable energy resources as petroleum, natural gas, and coal. However, the nuclear power industry is at a standstill in this country with no nuclear projects started since 1978. The early expectations that electricity produced by nuclear power would be so cheap that it would not be worthwhile even to meter it have not been realized . Because of high construction costs for nuclear power plants, the electricity generated by them has become prohibitively expensive. Consequently, we are not allocating more resources to the production of nuclear power.

Answers to the "For Thought" Questions

1. Which of the basic economic questions are involved in this case? In what way?

   The basic economic question most clearly involved in this case is the "how" question—the question of how electricity is to be produced. To a lesser extent it also involves the "what" question because the cost of producing electricity determines how much of it we will produce and consume. The resolution of the "for whom" question may also be affected, for example by the decline in employment and income in the nuclear power plant construction industry.

2. Using this case as an example, how does changing technology affect the "how" question?

   Changing technology affects the resolution of the "how" question by altering the relative costs of different production methods. The development of nuclear power technology initially caused a shift away from traditional methods of producing electricity by hydro-electric and fossil fuel plants . But as the nuclear power technology became more complicated to satisfy safety requirements, costs escalated to the point where it was no longer economically feasible.

3. Who should pay the costs of failed nuclear projects? The customers of the utility company? The stockholders or bondholders of the company? The government (taxpayers)? What are the advantages and disadvantages of putting the burden on each group?

2 The Economic System / 11

Open answer. Ordinarily, a public utilities commission allows the utility company to pass on all of its production costs to the rate payers. Customary regulatory practices would have the customers of the utility company pay for the failed nuclear projects in the form of higher electric rates on power produced by the company's existing plants. The customers, however, object to paying higher rates for mistakes in business judgment made by the utility company management. They maintain that the owners of the company should bear the risks of those decisions. Company management and the stockholders, on the other hand, claim that theirs is a regulated industry, and therefore the government has a responsibility to insure a fair return on the investment. Since the escalation of nuclear power construction costs was due in large part to stricter government safety regulations, they maintain that the government should be at least in part financially responsible. The advantage of having the utility customers pay the costs is that the rates reflect the total costs of the company, and future investment would not be discouraged. The disadvantage is that it may not be fair for the customers to pay for management's mistakes. The advantage of having the stockholders or bondholders pay is that is puts the burden on those who stood to make a profit from the investment. The disadvantage is that it would very likely discourage future capital investment in electric utility companies. The advantage of having the government pay is that it spreads the cost over a much larger number of people and it is the public at large that benefits from higher safety standards in nuclear power. The disadvantage is that it relieves those directly involved from paying the costs of mistaken decisions and shifts the costs to innocent taxpayers.

What Are the Principal Types of Economic Systems?

This section discusses the three principal types of economic systems—market, centrally-directed, and traditional—and points out that modern economies are mixtures of the various types. The discussion of the three principal types of economies is brief, giving only the essential differences. The basic elements of a market economy are discussed further in the next section of the chapter and in detail in subsequent chapters. Centrally-directed economies are covered in chapter 17 and traditional economies are discussed in chapter 18. Comparison of alternative types of economic systems is reinforced by Study Question 7.

Case Application: Free Enterprise in the Soviet Union

This application discusses the phenomenon of profit-making entrepreneurs operating in a controlled centrally-directed economy. There have long been reports of illegal private economic activity in the Soviet Union, but the wide extent and involved organization of the "underground economy" which has come to light is surprising. The application not only illustrates some of the difficulties encountered by authorities in operating a centrally-directed economy, but also raises ethical issues about the propriety of illicit private economic activity, which in our system would be referred to as the "black market," in planned economies.

Answers to the "For Thought" Questions

1. Is the underground economy in the Soviet Union a market economy, a command economy, or a traditional economy? How can you tell?

   The underground economy in the Soviet Union is a market economy because goods and services are produced in the underground economy in response to the high prices for which they can be sold.

2. Is "hustling" in the Soviet Union a production resource? How is it allocated?

   Yes, "hustling" in the Soviet Union is a production resource. It is a factor service that is part of the labor input in production. It is allocated according to the demand for it by the plants and their willingness and ability to pay for the service.

3. Would you approve or condemn the underground economy if you were a Soviet consumer? Why? How about if you were a government official? What effect does it have on the efficiency of the economy?

   Open answer. As a Soviet consumer, you might appreciate the ability to buy goods that are not available or services that entail long waits when obtained from government shops. But, on the other hand, you might have to pay a premium price for them, a price which you might not be able to afford. If you were a government official, you would probably condemn the underground economy because it violates the law and sabotages government production by diverting scarce resources from planned output. On the one hand, it increases economic efficiency by mobilizing labor activity that would otherwise not be producing and filling unmet consumer needs. On the other hand, it makes more difficult the fulfillment of the government's economic plan.

How Does a Market System Resolve the Three Basic Economic Questions?

The fundamental elements of a market system are discussed in this section, including the description of product and factor markets and the effect of profit incentives in stimulating production and distribution. The circular flow model is a simplified representation of the operation of a market system. It shows the circulation of money payments for goods and services from households to the business sector and the return flow of money payments from businesses to households in the form of wages, rents, and interest. There is a counterflow of real products and services for which the money payments are compensation. The real flows consist of the finished products supplied by businesses to the households and the labor, land, and capital services provided by the households to the business sector. The explanation of the circular flow model can be facilitated by a transparency of Figure 2 (p. 45), which is included in the color transparency set.

A more complete model of the economy—including the government, financial, and foreign sectors—is found in chapter 12. Study Questions 8 and 9 should reinforce the students' understanding of markets and factor incomes.

Case Application: Where Is Our Energy Future Now?

In view of the problems with nuclear energy, this application examines the alternative energy resources of coal and natural gas as successors to petroleum. The U. S. has vast supplies of coal, but its mining and use create environmental problems. Recent geologic findings of great potential natural gas reserves and technological developments in deep-well drilling have raised the possibility of a sizeable increase in natural gas production. Whether either of these resources or some other prove to be the principal source of our future energy supply depends upon the market conditions and incentives for development and production.

Answers to the "For Thought" Questions

1. Natural gas piped to a homeowner for heating a house is sold in what kind of market? Natural gas piped to a factory for heating its boilers is sold in what kind of market? Why can the same good be sold by the same supplier in two different types of markets?

   Natural gas piped to a homeowner for heating a house is sold in a product market. Natural gas piped to a factory for heating its boilers is sold in a factor market. The same good can be sold by the same supplier in two different markets if it is sometimes used as a final

product and other times as an input in the production of another good or service.

2. If the United States has vast reserves of both coal and natural gas, what will determine which of the two will replace petroleum as our principal source of energy?

   Our principal source of energy in the future will be determined by their relative costs of production and their suitability for our needs, including their relative pollution effects.

3. If natural gas is less polluting than coal when burned, should the government promote the use of gas and discourage the use of coal, or should the government leave the determination entirely to the marketplace? Indicate what forms government intervention might take and give the reasons for your answer.

   Open answer. The argument for government intervention to promote the use of natural gas rather than coal might be based on the government's responsibility to protect the environment and human health by minimizing air and water pollution. The government can regulate the maximum amount of pollution particles and chemicals that can be emitted from the smokestacks of coal-burning industrial plants and require the installation of pollution control equipment such as air scrubbers. Government intervention to promote the development and use of natural gas could take the form of tax subsidies for exploration and development of natural gas resources. The argument against government intervention could be based on the contention that the marketplace does a better job of determining what will be produced than does government. Such intervention in the private sector may result in unintended distortions in the economy which reduce efficiency. Also, government intervention has direct costs associated with it such as the cost of the bureaucracy itself and the cost imposed on private firms in meeting government regulations.

Perspective: The Industrial Revolution

The Perspective for this chapter is an introduction to the industrial revolution as an historical epoch that played a dominant role in shaping our present day economy. The emergence of factories for manufacturing created a great deal more specialization and interdependence in production. The industrial revolution had a major impact on the determination not only of how things were produced, but also on what was produced and for whom. The evolution of modern capitalism as an economic system is closely associated with the industrial revolution. The factory system, by separating the producing units in the business sector from the consuming units in the household sector, created interdependent relationships between the two sectors represented by the circular flow model. The suggestion at the end of the Perspective that we are in need of a "new industrial revolution" is followed up in the introductory article for chapter 14 entitled "The New Industrial Revolution." Study Question 10 asks the student to relate the industrial revolution to the three basic economic questions.

Answers to Study Questions

1. What is an example of a specialized job with which you are personally familiar? How is that job performed efficiently as a result of specialization?

   Open answer. Each student is likely to have had some work experience from which to draw when answering this question. The student should be able to discern in what way the job involves specialization of production activity and how that specialization was more efficient than if each worker attempted to perform the whole of the production operation.

2. Specialization and interdependence increase efficiency, but what disadvantage might result from interdependence? What is an example?

   Open answer. Disadvantages that might result from interdependence include the fact that when there is an interruption at one production stage, for example by a strike, production and income at all of the other stages in the process are also interrupted.

3. What are three examples of differences in the resolution of the "what" question in the United States today compared to five years ago?

   Open answer. Examples in 1987 might include compact disc players, laser printers, camcorders, more American-made automobiles, and less wheat production.

4. How has the increased use of production robots discussed in the Case Application in chapter 1 affected the resolution of the "how" question?

   The increased use of production robots has substituted capital equipment for labor in production processes.

5. What determines how much of the nation's output of goods and services is allocated to you?

   The amount of the nation's output of goods and services that is allocated to an individual depends on the individual's wealth and income.

6. What are some examples of each of the three major factors of production used in a business located in your community or in your state?

   Open answer. In an urban area, an example might be a local retail establishment which would use the land on which the business was located; the labor of the managers and clerks; and the capital, including the store building, cash registers and other equipment, and inventory of unsold merchandise.

7. How does tradition in the United States affect the resolution of any one of the three basic economic questions?

   Open answer. Tradition in this country plays some role in resolving each of the three basic economic questions. Our traditional tastes in food determine to some extent what agricultural commodities are produced. Traditional production methods are sometimes codified in labor union work rules, city building codes, or fair-trade laws to protect small businesses. Concerning the "for whom" question, there has traditionally been an earnings discrepancy between male and female salaries, which continues today despite legislative attempts to abolish it.

8. What is an example of a relatively well-organized market in your area? What is an example of a relatively unorganized market in your area?

   Open answer. Any market in which all of the potential buyers are in contact with all of the potential sellers is a well-organized market. Besides the securities and commodities markets, the banking system is a relatively well-organized market. Relatively unorganized markets would be those in which there is no close contact between potential buyers and potential sellers, such as the markets for used furniture and appliances.

9. Give an example of a factor market in which you have participated. What factor did you provide and what was the factor income called?

   Open answer. The most likely response will be that the student provided the factor service of labor and received the factor income of wages.

10. How did the industrial revolution affect the outcome of the three basic economic questions?

    The industrial revolution affected the outcome of the "what" question in a variety of ways. For one, the inventions of the steam engine, the textile machinery, and so forth, created entirely new goods to be produced. For another, the new production methods reduced the costs of textiles, metal products, and other factory products and thereby greatly expanded their markets. The construction of the factories themselves was a new type of production.

    As for its effect on the "how" question, that was the essence of the industrial revolution—radically changing the way things were produced. In the process, it also affected the resolution of the "for whom" question, creating a whole new class of capitalists whose income was due to manufacture rather than to ownership of land or to commerce. At the same time, it deprived some handicraft workers of a livelihood.

Integrating *Economics U$A* Programs

(For information on Economics U$A *see the introduction, p. v.)*

Program 2—"Markets: Do They Meet Our Needs?"—bridges the content of chapters 2 and 3. A good strategy is to show it at the end of the discussion of chapter 2 to reinforce the concepts in that chapter and to introduce the students to the demand-supply model in chapter 3.

The first application in the program deals with the booming housing market at the conclusion of World War II, following years of neglected housing construction in the depression and wartime periods. The demand to fill the housing needs was met by a new breed of mass-production builders such as William Levitt. The case illustrates the resolution of both the "what" question—resources allocated to housebuilding—and the "how" question—by means of new "assembly line" construction methods.

The housing case also shows how a market system gets needed goods produced—the profit motive incentives that motivated Levitt and the other builders. In addition, it demonstrates the relationship of factor markets—the labor market for carpenters—to the product market. It illustrates labor specialization of carpenters.

The second application concerns changes in the U.S. steel industry to meet foreign competition. It provides a good illustration of how new technology alters the resolution of the "how" question.

The third application—the income of baseball superstars—shows an extreme resolution of the "for whom" question. Star players such as Reggie Jackson command stratospheric salaries because of the limited supply of their particular skills and their ability to draw fans. Due to the great purchasing power their salaries give them, the economy produces a lot more goods and services for them than it does for most of us.

Economist Gill concludes each of the applications with an analysis of how demand and supply respond to the situation and determine prices in the marketplace.

Case Applications in Student Workbook

(Answers are supplied to students in the workbook.)

Why Are Economic Systems Needed?

Case Application: From Farm to City

This application discusses the transformation of the United States from a predominantly rural to a predominantly urban society. This change entailed a tremendous increase in specialization and consequent interdependence. The change

resulted in greater economic efficiency, but, as noted in the article, it also has exacted a price in the various social costs resulting from urban agglomeration.

Answers to the "For Thought" Questions

1. Are people more interdependent now than they were in 1790? Why?

   People are more interdependent now than they were in 1790 because there is more specialization of production. In 1790 most families were rural and produced nearly everything they needed: food, clothing, shelter, tools, etc. With industrialization and the movement to cities, families became dependent on others to supply their needs because they were now workers specialized in a particular type of production.

2. How does the growth of large metropolitan areas like BoWash, ChiPitts, and SoCal illustrate the principle of comparative advantage?

   The growth of large metropolitan areas illustrates the principle of comparative advantage because they are efficient at providing services and many types of products. They have a comparative advantage in the types of production that benefit from population concentration such as commerce, financial services, and communications. They are dependent on rural areas for those things that are not as easily produced in densely populated areas, such as food.

3. Would the United States be better off if it were still predominantly rural? Why or why not?

   Open answer. The answer to this question depends largely on people's value systems. If they think simpler lifestyles, knowing one's neighbors, and self-sufficiency are the most important attributes, they might prefer a more rural society. If they believe higher living standards, the availability of more goods and services, and economic growth are the most important characteristics, they might prefer urbanization of society.

What Basic Questions Must Every Economic System Resolve?

Case Application: Is Coal the Heir to the Energy Throne?

One of the most important allocation decisions the economy faces is determining what will be our primary energy source in the future. This application, which discusses coal as the primary alternative energy source to petroleum, illustrates what is involved in determining what, how, and for whom to produce. Whether to increase production of coal depends upon a number of factors including not only the direct costs of its production, but also the indirect costs of pollution from its use. Despite the vast amount of coal reserves available to the United States, it may not become our primary energy source if the pollution costs are excessive. This is an illustration of the various factors that can affect the "what" decision. An example of the "how" question is whether to develop tunnel mining of coal or strip mining. The "for whom" question is involved in the case in two ways: A large proportion of the increase coal output is for the European market, on the other hand, the increase results in more economic activity and rising income for the domestic coal mining areas. The increased income of these formerly depressed regions has provided them with purchasing power to acquire a great deal more goods and services.

Answers to the "For Thought" Questions

1. The decision whether to produce coal by underground tunneling or surface strip mining illustrates which type of basic economic decision?

   The decision between underground tunneling or surface strip mining illustrates the "how" decision—how to produce the coal.

2. What considerations enter into the "what" decision as regards the production of coal?

   The reallocation of our resources has resulted from petroleum prices that are higher than before the price increases of the 1970s and the increased costs of nuclear power and our heightened awareness of its dangers. These considerations have increased the attractiveness of coal as a substitute, and more resources are being devoted to coal production.

3. Should coal be substituted for nuclear power in the production of electricity, even if it results in an increase in air and water pollution? Why or why not?

   Open answer. Some people believe coal should be substituted for nuclear power in producing electricity, even if it results in an increase in air and water pollution, because nuclear power is dangerous due to the possibility of an accident and the problems of radioactive waste disposal. Others believe we should not use more coal to produce electricity if it increases air and water pollution because that results in damaging the environment, people's health, and the quality of life.

What Are the Principal Types of Economic Systems?

Case Application: Digging a Subway in Calcutta

This application illustrates the mixture of tradition and planning in the Indian economy. Traditional intensive labor production methods were used in constructing the Calcutta

subway by the government authorities that devised the project. This case suggests that there may be a logic in continuing to use traditional methods in some societies rather than switching to more modern techniques.

Answers to the "For Thought" Questions

1. The use of manual labor rather than mechanized equipment to dig the Calcutta subway is characteristic of what type of economic system?

   The use of manual labor rather than machinery is characteristic of traditional economies. The Calcutta subway is being dug in the fashion and with the implements that are traditional in India. The fact that it is a government project makes it characteristic of a mixed economy.

2. Manual labor is frequently used in place of machinery by private enterprise in India as well as by government. Why would private enterprise, which is not concerned about the unemployment problem, use manual labor?

   Private enterprise uses the production methods that are least expensive for the output obtained. If manual labor is cheaper than using machinery for the work to be done, which may be the case in India where labor is plentiful and capital scarce, private enterprise as well as government may use traditional rather than modern methods of production.

3. Do you think the Calcutta government should use unskilled workers to build the subway even if it slows down construction and in the end costs more than using mechanized equipment? Why or why not?

   Open answer. The answer to this question depends on how we evaluate the goals of efficiency versus full employment. If we make efficiency the overriding concern, the subway should be built by the method that minimizes total cost. On the other hand, if we consider providing jobs for unemployed workers as important or more important than maximizing production efficiency, the subway should be built by manual labor, even if that raises the total cost of construction.

How Does a Market System Resolve the Three Basic Economic Questions?

Case Application: The Shale Age—Not Yet

Two of the case applications for this chapter in the text discuss possible successors to petroleum as our primary energy source. This application discusses an additional possibility—that of oil shale. As with coal and natural gas, the potential energy resources of oil shale are enormous. Whether or not that potential is ever realized depends upon the solution to a number of problems, and the outcome will be resolved in the marketplace.

Answers to the "For Thought" Questions

1. Would shale oil be sold in a product market or a factor market? How can you determine which type of market it would be sold in?

   Shale oil would be sold in a factor market because it requires additional processing to refine it into finished petroleum products. Only when it is sold directly to a consumer in the form of gasoline, heating oil, motor oil, or other final products is it sold in a product market.

2. If the problems of adequate water supplies and rock waste disposal could be solved, would the oil companies go ahead with their shale oil projects? What would cause them to do so?

   The oil companies will proceed with the development of shale oil when the profit incentives are adequate. Since they have petroleum reserves in wells that are cheaper to exploit at the present time than the shale oil, they are not willing to risk large investments in the projects. Furthermore, bringing shale oil to market would reduce the value of their existing reserves in wells. Increases in oil prices or the development of shale oil by other companies or by the government would likely spur the oil companies to develop their lease holdings.

3. In view of the country's dependence on imported oil, much of it from the politically unstable Middle East, should the government step in to speed up the development of shale oil production on government lands? Why or why not?

   Open answer. One position is that energy is a critical need for the country, both for civilian and national defense purposes. If it is worthwhile for the government to finance a crash program to put a man on the moon, it is certainly worthwhile to do at least as much to solve our energy problems. The opposite position is that the government should keep out of the energy business because it would spend tax money wastefully and energy would cost more than if the development is left to private enterprise.

Chapter 3

Market Pricing

Chapter Overview

The concepts in this chapter are those the students are most likely to retain long after they have finished the course. If you ask someone who took an introductory economics course years ago what it was about, he or she probably will respond that it was about supply and demand. Without doubt, the market pricing model is the most useful tool in the study of economics. A question the early philosophers repeatedly wrestled with was "what determines the value of things?" Today's beginning economics student can easily solve that riddle simply by using the market pricing model.

A look at what happened to peanut butter prices as a result of a peanut crop failure opens this chapter's examination of what determines prices and what causes price changes. On one side of the market you have the households that consume peanut butter determining the demand, and on the other side of the market you have the peanut butter producers determining the supply. The first organizing question in the chapter is "What Forces Determine Prices in the Market Place?" In this section, hypothetical demand and supply schedules for peanut butter and the corresponding demand and supply curves are developed. It is then shown how functions of demand and supply jointly determine the market price for peanut butter and the quantity that will be sold. The case application "How Much is a Good Student Worth?" discusses how competition among universities for outstanding high school scholars has established a market price for high school academic talent.

The second section of the chapter examines "What Determines Demand?" The case application is "Pedal Power" which examines how the increased popularity of bicycling has affected the market for bicycles and accessories. The next section on "What Determines Supply?" explains how supply depends primarily upon production costs. The case application is "Jojoba: A Desert Weed That Smells Like Money" which examines why the desert jojoba plant is now being offered as a substitute for whale oil for a variety of uses.

The final section of the chapter concerns "Why Do Prices Change?" It examines how changes in the determinants of demand or the determinants of supply, or both, can change prices. In the market pricing model these changes are represented by shifts in the demand and supply curves. The case application "OPEC Takes a Lesson in Demand and Supply" shows how the rise in petroleum prices caused long-range changes in consumption habits and a shift in the demand for oil, resulting in a lower equilibrium price.

Suggested Answers to the Learning Objectives

The knowledge acquired from this chapter should enable the students to:

1. Explain the laws of supply and demand.

   The law of demand states that the quantity demanded of a good or service varies inversely with the price: the lower the price, the larger the quantity demanded; the higher the price, the smaller the quantity demanded. The law of supply states that the quantity supplied of a good or service varies directly with its price: the lower the price, the smaller the quantity supplied; the higher the price, the larger the quantity supplied.

2. List the determinants of demand.

   The determinants of demand are consumer tastes and preferences, income, the availability and prices of substitutes and complements, and the population constituting the market.

3. List the determinants of supply.

   The determinants of supply are the costs of producing the product.

4. Distinguish between short-run and long-run supply.

   Supply in the short run can be varied by changing the amounts of labor and raw material inputs, but it is limited by the production capacity of the existing plant and equipment in the industry. In the long run, the amount of plant and equipment can be altered to vary the supply more than in the short run.

5. Identify the causes of shifts in demand and how they affect market equilibrium.

   Shifts in demand result from either changes in consumer tastes and preferences, changes in incomes, changes in the availability or price of substitutes or complements for the product, or changes in the size of the market population. An increase in demand is shown by a shift outward in the demand curve, resulting in a movement up the supply curve to a higher equilibrium price.

6. Identify the causes of shifts in supply and how they affect market equilibrium.

Shifts in supply result from changes in the availability and price of factor inputs or other changes in production costs. An increase in supply is shown by a shift outward of the supply curve, resulting in a movement down the demand curve to a lower equilibrium price.

7. Explain why prices move toward an equilibrium price.

   Prices move toward an equilibrium price because of shortages or surpluses. If the price is below the equilibrium price there is a shortage which causes buyers to compete for the existing supply, thereby bidding up the price to the equilibrium. If the price is above the equilibrium price, there is a surplus which causes sellers to compete against each other to dispose of the product, bidding down the price to the equilibrium.

8. Distinguish between a change in demand and a change in quantity demanded.

   A change in demand means that at a given price more or less of the product would be purchased. This is indicated by a shift in the demand curve. A change in the quantity demanded means that more or less of the product would be purchased at a lower or higher price. This is represented by a movement along the demand curve.

What Forces Determine Prices in the Marketplace?

The peanut butter market is used here to illustrate demand and supply behavior and the determination of price. A hypothetical demand schedule of the number of jars of peanut butter that a family would purchase in a month at different possible prices is transformed into the family's peanut butter demand curve. It is then assumed that there are 9,999 other families in the community that have similar demand schedules for peanut butter. This is translated into the community's demand curve for peanut butter. The supply schedule of a single peanut butter producer and the resulting supply curve are developed, and then the market supply of four peanut butter producers. The community demand and market supply curves are then put on the same diagram. Their intersection point results in an equilibrium price of $1.25 per jar, at which price 30,000 jars a month are sold.

Transparencies of Figures 1–5 are useful in class explanations of demand, supply, and market equilibrium. If the students have trouble reading the market graphs, they should be referred to the appendix for help. Computer drill and practice programs, identified below, can be of assistance to students who continue to experience problems. Study Questions 1–6 provide students with practice in analyzing actual events in terms of the demand-supply model.

Case Application: How Much Is a Good Student Worth?

It may be unusual to think of a market for student academic talent with the universities as buyers and the students as suppliers; but because it is an unusual situation, it provides an opportunity to take a fresh look at the concepts in market pricing. It is an application which should have a relevance and interest to the students. Referring back to the discussion of markets in chapter 2, Study Question 8 in particular, it might be asked whether this is a relatively well-organized market or a relatively unorganized market.

Answers to the "For Thought" Questions

1. In the market for scholarly talent, what are the two sides of the market? Who is represented on the two sides of the market?

   The two sides of the market are the demand for outstanding scholars and the supply of such students. On the demand side are the colleges and universities that wish to enroll academic achievers and on the supply side are the students and their families that wish to get the best education for the least outlay.

2. What has happened to the equilibrium price for top high school scholars? Why?

   The equilibrium price for top high school scholars has increased because of a decrease in their supply. This has caused the colleges and universities to bid against each other for the short supply, thereby bidding up the equilibrium price.

3. Is the effort of college associations to regulate the recruitment of outstanding student scholars an unwarranted interference in the marketplace? Why or why not?

   Open answer. This regulation might be opposed as undue interference in the rights of individuals and businesses to engage in voluntary exchange. The regulation might be endorsed, on the other hand, as a means of preventing unscrupulous manipulation of students by high-pressure recruiters.

What Determines Demand?

The quantity of a good or service that consumers would purchase at the different possible prices depends upon their tastes and preferences, their incomes, the price and availability of substitutes and complements for the good or service, and the size of the market population. It may seem odd to the student that the price of the product is not one of the determinants of demand. The explanation for this is that demand refers to the quantities that would be purchased at all possible prices. The price of the product determines the quantity that will be demanded at that price, but it does not determine the whole demand schedule, which is what is meant by the term "demand."

A class exercise which can give the students an experimental understanding of demand is Exercise in Analysis 1. It allows the students to construct a demand schedule out of their own experience, drawing on their own tastes and preferences and other demand determinants. In this exercise the students are divided into groups (6–8 per group is a good number) and calculate how many times in total the students in the group would attend movies during a month at different ticket prices. Each student first makes a table of how many times he or she would go to the movies during the month depending upon the admission price. (If movie ticket prices in your area are typically more than $5, the range of prices for the demand schedule can be changed to vary from, say, $1 to $8 in increments of $1.) The number of times all of the students in the group would attend is then totaled for each admission price, and a community demand schedule and demand curve drawn up. When the students develop a community demand function out of their own experience, the abstract model becomes more concrete for them. The lesson can be reinforced by having the community demand curve for each group put on the blackboard. The different demand curves can then be compared for their similarities and differences. Ask in what ways they are similar. (Slope down to the right? Cover about the same range of quantities? Why?) In what ways are they different? (Tails of the curves differ? Some students would pay more to see at least one movie a month? Some would go more often at minimum prices? Why?) Have the students save their results for the first Exercise in Analysis at the end of chapter 4.

The concept of effective demand is reinforced by Study Question 7.

Case Application: Pedal Power

As part of the fitness fad of recent years, bicycling has attained increased popularity. As a result, the sales of bicycles and accessories has increased substantially. It creates an opportunity for examining what determines demand.

Answers to the "For Thought" Questions

1. Which of the determinants of demand have been responsible for the booming market in bicycles and accessories?

   The most significant determinant has been the change in tastes resulting from the increased popularity of fitness

activities. Another determinant which can be cited is increased incomes, which is suggested by the popularity of trendy bicycle accessories among Yuppies.

2. If higher import taxes increased the prices of bicycles, how would this affect the demand for cycle clothing? Why?

   This question introduces the effect on demand of a change in the price of a complementary good. Since cycle clothing is a complement to bicycles, an increase in the prices of bicycles would reduce the demand for cycle clothing.

3. Are the changes in the bicycle market, with a trend toward higher quality expensive bicycles and fashionable accessories, a good thing or a bad thing? Why?

   Open answer. It could be a good thing because it benefits the bicycle and accessory industries. Or it could be labeled bad because it has transformed a traditional healthy sporting activity into an expensive fad which may be too costly for some to afford.

What Determines Supply?

The determination of supply is more straightforward than that of demand. It is basically determined by the costs of production. Products will be put on the market if the price covers the production costs, including a normal profit return. The behavior of costs is thus the determinant of the amount supplied. Costs behave differently in the short run than in the long run because in the short run only the labor and raw materials inputs can be varied, while in the long run plants and equipment capacity can also be altered. The supply concept is reinforced by Study Question 8.

Case Application: Jojoba: A Desert Weed That Smells Like Money

The jojoba bush, which grows naturally in the desert, is now being cultivated for its oil, which is a good substitute for sperm whale oil in many uses. When it first became popular in substitution for the banned sperm whale oil, jojoba oil was very expensive because of the high costs of harvesting it from the natural desert growth. As systematic cultivation reduces production costs, more jojoba oil becomes available at lower prices.

Answers to the "For Thought" Questions

1. What period of time is the long run for increasing jojoba oil production?

The long run for increasing jojoba oil production is five years, the maturation time for the plant. The plants themselves are the capital investment which determines the long-run period.

2. How much did jojoba oil cost in the short run? Why was it so expensive? Why did it become cheaper in the long run?

    Jojoba oil cost over $7,000 in the short run because the supply was limited by the high costs of harvesting additional quantities of the wild bush. It became cheaper in the long run due to systematic cultivation that reduced production costs.

3. Investment in commercial jojoba farms was encouraged by especially favorable tax credits. Should jojoba farm investors be given special tax benefits? Why or why not?

    Open answer. In order to save the whales, the sale of sperm whale oil was prohibited. But the lubricants and other products made from it are important to our economy, and since jojoba oil is unique as a substitute for the whale oil, government subsidies for expanding its production by means of tax credits was considered good environmental and economic policy. On the other hand, if jojoba oil is so valuable, profit incentives for private industry should be sufficient to attract the necessary investment capital without taxpayers having to subsidize it.

Why Do Prices Change?

A change in demand is represented by a shift in the demand curve, and a change in supply is represented by a shift in the supply curve. What causes these shifts are changes in the underlying determinants of demand and supply. A change in one of the determinants of demand shifts the whole demand schedule. A change in supply results from a change in the availability and price of factor inputs in its production or a change in the technology of production.

Transparencies of Figures 6 and 7 are useful for demonstrating shifts in the demand and supply curves respectively. They show that a shift of one curve, say a change in demand, results in a movement along the other curve, a change in the quantity supplied, not a change in supply. A useful discussion is initiated by asking the class who is dissatisfied if the market price is below the equilibrium price, which may be the case just after an increase in demand or decrease in supply. The immediate response may be that when the price is "too low" the suppliers are unhappy. But closer examination shows that when a price is below the equilibrium price there is a condition of scarcity. If the good is scarce and people can't buy it, it is the consumers that are unhappy rather than the suppliers. In attempting to acquire the scarce good, they bid up the price to the equilibrium level. Conversely, when a price is "too high" the suppliers are unhappy because they

are stuck with unsold merchandise, and the price moves down to equilibrium.

The idea of market changes in the equilibrium price is reinforced by Study Question 9.

Case Application: OPEC Takes a Lesson in Demand and Supply

Because of the large increase in gasoline and heating oil prices in the 1970s, people changed their consumption habits by shifting to smaller cars and undertaking a variety of energy conservation measures. As a consequence, the steady rise that had previously occurred in energy consumption was capped, and a glut of oil developed at the high OPEC prices. This case illustrates how changes in supply, and the resulting price changes, can have long-run effects in shifting the demand curve. Such long-run effects are an exception to the general rule that supply does not determine demand and demand does not determine supply.

Answers to the "For Thought" Questions

1. What was the difference in the behavior of demand in the petroleum market of the 1970s and demand in the 1980s? What were the causes of the change?

    Despite increasing prices, petroleum demand in the 1970s remained high. In the 1980s, however, there was a decline in demand. The causes of the decline were energy conservation measures undertaken by consumers and businesses in a delayed response to the higher prices, combined with a downturn in the world economy.

2. What happened to the equilibrium price of petroleum in the 1980s? Was the change due to a supply shift or a demand shift or both? How would you show the change on a diagram?

    The decline in petroleum prices was due to decline in demand pursuant to conservation measures and a world recession and to an increase in oil production in non-OPEC countries. The change would be shown by a shift to the left of the demand curve and a shift to the right of the supply curve, resulting in a lower equilibrium price.

3. Should we limit our dependence on OPEC oil? Why or why not? If so, what measures should we use to limit it?

    Open answer. Proponents of limiting oil imports would like to reduce our dependence on foreign oil suppliers, punish the OPEC nations for their monopolistic pricing, and provide a stimulus to domestic petroleum exploration and production. Those who oppose cutbacks on oil from OPEC countries believe that the result would be a rise in the price of gas and heating oil, which would be inflationary. If we put restrictions or taxes on oil imports, it would cause the U.S. to use up its own reserves of this non-renewable resource at a faster rate, leaving us more vulnerable to energy shortages in the future. A better approach would be to increase conservation measures.

Perspective: Adam Smith's Marketplace

Adam Smith is an economist with whom everyone should be familiar since he has had such a great influence on our thinking, even today. The ideas that he has passed down to us include free enterprise unhindered by government intervention (*laissez-faire*), the advantages of specialization in production, free trade, and the allocative functions of markets, among many others. The Perspective for the preceding chapter sets the stage for a discussion of Adam Smith's ideas because his writing and influence grew out of, and were coincident with, the beginning of the industrial revolution. The ideas he expressed in *The Wealth of Nations* had a great deal to do with shaping the evolving industrial economy. His biography shows him to be of admirable character, but with some personality traits, such as his notorious absentmindedness, that might be considered rather "quirky."

Answers to Study Questions

1. "Retail Chain Stores Increase Sales of Tennis Balls." Does this headline reflect a change in demand for tennis balls? Explain.

    The headline might reflect an increase in the demand for tennis balls, or it might reflect an increase in the supply of tennis balls, resulting in a lower price and larger sales.

2. "Lobsters Found to Contain Harmful Levels of Mercury." How would this discovery affect your demand for lobster meat? Explain how some consumers might actually buy more lobster after the market adjusted to the news.

    People's demand for lobster could be expected to decrease. However, there might be some consumers who were not concerned about the levels of mercury in the lobster and would buy more after its price declined because of lower total demand.

3. "Cane Sugar Prices Rise Dramatically." How would this price rise affect the demand for beet sugar?

    The price rise for cane sugar would increase the demand for beet sugar because it is a close substitute.

4. "Record Number of Hockey Fans Paid Higher Prices." Explain how this situation could have occurred, and then use supply and demand curves to illustrate your answer.

    A record number of hockey fans might attend games even if the prices were higher if it was a winning team and there was an increased interest in hockey. On a

diagram this would be shown by a shift to the right of the demand curve.

5. "Pollution Curbs on Steel Mills Urged." What effect would this proposal to curb pollution have on the supply of steel? How would such a law affect the long-run planning for steel production?

    Pollution controls on steel mills reduce the supply of steel. Because laws requiring pollution control devices would increase the production costs of steel, long-run planning would project a lower level of steel production.

6. "New Auto Sales Off by 25%." What changes in demand and/or supply might have accounted for this headline?

    The decline in new auto sales might have been the result of a change in any of the determinants of demand, shifting the demand curve to the left, or it may have been a result of an increase in production costs, shifting the supply curve to the left.

7. If a friend said to you, "I really need a new car, but I can't afford one for at least six months," does your friend have an automobile demand in economic terms? What does demand mean in economic terms?

    The friend does not have an automobile demand in economic terms. There is a demand only when there is both the desire and the ability to purchase goods. If demand is not effective demand, backed by the purchasing power to buy the good, it does not affect the economy.

8. Is the time period that divides the short run from the long run in a particular industry different according to whether firms in the industry are increasing production capacity or decreasing production capacity? In the case study on jojoba oil production, does it take the same number of years to increase the quantity of jojoba beans grown as to decrease the quantity of beans grown?

    The period dividing the short run from the long run is generally different depending on whether production capacity is increased or decreased. Since the relevant period depends on the amount of time necessary to put new real capital into production or take it out of production, this depends on practical technical and financial considerations. It takes 5 years for a newly planted jojoba bush to produce harvestable seeds, but the bush continues to produce for 100 to 200 years.

9. What is the difference between a "change in demand" and a "change in the quantity demanded"? What is the cause of each? How is each represented on a diagram of the market?

    A change in demand means that consumers will buy more or less of the product at any given price than they would previously. A change in the quantity demanded means that consumers will buy more of the product because of a fall in the price or less of the product because of a rise in the price. A change in demand results from a change in any of the determinants of demand. A change in the quantity demanded results from a change in the price of the product. A change in demand is shown by a shift of the demand curve. A change in the quantity demanded is shown by a movement along the demand curve.

10. Adam Smith strongly believed that governments should not interfere in the marketplace. What examples of government interference in the marketplace do you find in this chapter?

An example of government interference in the marketplace in the introductory article is the government's price-support program for peanuts. Another example is the banning of the import of whale oil and other whale products, as are the government tax credits for commercial jojoba production. OPEC is an example of interference in the marketplace by foreign governments.

Integrating *Economics U$A* Programs

(For information on Economics U$A *see the introduction, p. v.)*

As noted in this segment for the previous chapter, the second program in the series, "Markets: Do They Meet Our Needs?," introduces the market demand-supply model in analyzing the applications in that program. The model is developed further in program 16, "Supply and Demand: What Sets the Price?" That program serves well as a bridge between this chapter and chapter 4.

The first application on the 1975-1977 California drought is an illustration of what happens when there is a drastic reduction in the supply of a vital resource—water. What effect did it have on the public's demand for water?

Economist Gill's analysis of the impact of the shortage on consumption habits introduces the concepts of utility and diminishing marginal utility, which are discussed in chapter 4 of the text.

The second application deals with the same subject as the last Case Application in the text chapter—the rise in oil prices in the 1970s and the market reactions which caused prices to come back down in the 1980s. As oil wildcatter William Rutter, Jr., states, "As soon as prices get high, producers want to produce a lot and consumers want to consume less. The law of demand and supply works."

Gill analyzes the changes with market diagrams that show the operation of the laws of demand and supply and how equilibrium prices are determined.

The third application concerning the market for designer jeans shows what happens when you have shifts in demand and supply. Gill discusses the determinants of demand. (Which one listed in the text does he not mention? The market population size.)

Ask the class what causes changes in a market, based on the examples shown in the program.

Case Applications in Student Workbook

(Answers are supplied to students in the workbook.)

What Forces Determine Prices in the Marketplace?

Case Application: The Grain Drain

This application deals with how a failure of the Soviet wheat crop resulted in a large increase in the demand for exports of U.S. wheat. This, in turn, resulted in a rise in domestic wheat prices and in the prices of bread and other wheat products. The application illustrates the fact that the demand for many products in markets abroad is related to the demand in the domestic market.

Answers to the "For Thought" Questions

1. What was the effect of the failure of the Soviet grain harvest on the demand schedule for American wheat?

   The failure of the Soviet grain harvest resulted in increasing the demand schedule for American wheat. Increased foreign demand was added to the domestic demand. This shifted the demand curve outward to the right.

2. Who caused the price of wheat to rise above $2 per bushel, the farmers, the Russians, or the American flour millers? Why?

   The increased Russian demand for wheat initiated the rise in the price of American wheat, but the Russians purchased wheat at a contracted price which was less than $2 per bushel. It was the American flour millers competing for the remaining supply that pushed the price of wheat above $2 per bushel.

3. After the rise in the price of flour and bakery products, it was argued that we should not have sold the wheat to the Russians, because it raised prices for American consumers. Do you agree or disagree? Why?

   One view was that we should not have sold the wheat to the Russians since it resulted in raising the price of a basic staple of the American diet and caused an increase in the cost of living. The opposite view, the one probably held by most economists, was that American farmers should be allowed to sell their wheat to the Russians or anyone else willing to pay the price. If the Russian wheat buyers outsmarted our negotiators and got the wheat at a bargain price, that's another question, and we should be more clever in the future. However, agricultural exports are very important to the farmer and to our economy in general and shouldn't be restricted in order to hold down the prices of agricultural products at home.

What Determines Demand?

Case Application: Upscale Munching

This application discusses the surge in popularity of expensive snack foods. It identifies two causes of this trend as the surge in the population size of the age group that indulges in snack foods most—the baby boomers—and the rise in their incomes as they obtain higher paying positions, as well as changing tastes and preferences.

Answers to the "For Thought" Questions

1. What determinants of demand have caused the popularity of gourmet snack products?

   The determinants of demand responsible for the sales of gourmet snack products are the increase in the population size of that market, an increase in incomes, and changing tastes and preferences.

2. What has caused a change in the effective demand of the baby boom generation and how has it affected the market for snack foods?

   The cause of the change in the effective demand of the baby boom generation is their entry into the labor force and advancement to higher paying jobs. The increase in their incomes has allowed them to indulge their tastes for higher quality snack foods.

3. Are the superpremium ice creams worth their extra cost? What factors need to be considered in answering this?

   Open answer. Some people might consider the superpremium ice creams overpriced, since regular ice cream that is much less expensive can be very tasty. Others believe that the superpremium is worth the extra cost not only because it tastes better but because it is made with less artificial additives and more natural ingredients. The factors that need to be considered are the tastes and preferences of the consumers, their incomes, and the price and availability of the substitute.

What Determines Supply?

Case Application: Black Walnut Worth Gold

This case discusses the "black market" for black walnuts. Rustling of valuable black walnut trees has become a serious problem. Black markets arise when supply is inadequate. There are proposals that other states follow the lead of

Missouri and enact laws which would help to eliminate the black market in black walnut.

Answers to the "For Thought" Questions

1. How does the rustling of black walnut trees affect the short-run supply of black walnut veneer?

   The rustling of black walnut trees adds to the short-run supply of black walnut veneer. It shifts the short-run supply curve outward to the right.

2. What effect does the length of time required for black walnut trees to mature have on the long run supply of black walnut veneer?

   The long-run supply curve for black walnut trees depends upon the length of growing time for the trees to reach maturity. With fertilizing and special care the long run can be reduced from 60 or 80 years to 30 years.

3. Should laws be enacted in other states to prosecute log buyers who purchase black walnut without knowing where it came from?

   Open answer. Perhaps laws such as the one in Missouri should be enacted to discourage rustling of black walnut trees grown by individuals or in our national parks. On the other hand, such laws may be difficult to enforce and they impose the burden of responsibility on log buyers, who claim that it's unfair.

Why Do Prices Change?

Case Application: Do Boycotts Work?

There is a good deal of disagreement over the effectiveness and fairness of boycotts. Consumer boycotts generally arise out of a feeling of frustration and are short-lived. The application examines how boycotts affect markets.

Answers to the "For Thought" Questions

1. Does a boycott cause a shift in the demand curve or a movement along the demand curve?

   If consumers respond to a boycott by reducing the amount of the product they would normally buy at any given price, the demand curve shifts backward to the left.

2. Does a boycott result in lower prices? Why?

   A boycott results in lower prices in the short run because the shift in demand causes sellers to move down their supply schedule to a lower price. However, in a competitive industry such as the cattle industry, the lower prices may cause a reduction in investment in the industry which shifts the long-run supply curve backward to the left, resulting in higher prices in the long run.

3. Are boycotts such as the one described in this application fair? Why or why not?

Open answer. From the consumers' point of view, boycotts are fair when the price of something goes up much more rapidly than the consumers' incomes, and they can't afford the higher prices. From the producers' point of view, boycotts are unfair because they may not be responsible for the higher prices which result from increased costs. To the producers, boycotts are a conspiracy which might force them out of business.

Chapter 4

The Consumer

Chapter Overview

This is the first chapter of the microeconomic section of the text. Microeconomics deals with the individual decision-making units in the economy, so it is appropriate to begin with a study of consumer behavior. Since consumption is the ultimate objective of economic activity, in a market economy the consumer is sovereign, determining what will be produced. The introductory article covers a consumer item which is of concern to young people—cigarettes. Although other age groups have reduced their consumption of cigarettes, there are still large numbers of young people, especially young women, taking up the habit. This article discusses the demand for cigarettes, where it comes from, and the marketing policies of the cigarette companies.

The first section of the chapter examines how consumers make decisions about spending and savings. An important concept developed in the section is price elasticity of demand. The case application is titled "Housing Woes" and discusses the demand for housing from the 1970s to the mid-1980s.

The second section of the chapter examines the basis of consumer decision making. Consumers try to maximize the amount of satisfaction (utility) they receive from spending their income. Consumer equilibrium is reached when consumers allocate their income in a way that achieves maximum total utility. "The Channel Race," the case application for the section, examines how consumers allocate their income to one or more cable TV services.

The third section deals with the need for adequate and accurate information in consumer decision making and the effect of advertising on utility. The case application, "That's No Alligator; It's a Chameleon," discusses the problem of counterfeit merchandise.

Suggested Answers to the Learning Objectives

The knowledge acquired from this chapter should enable the students to:

1. Define elasticity of demand and relate this concept to different products.

   Elasticity of demand is the relative size of the change in the quantity demanded of a good or service as a result of a small change in its price. Demand tends to be inelastic for goods that are necessities, for which there are no or few good substitutes, and which take an insignificant part of total spending. It tends to be elastic for luxuries, goods with many good substitutes, and those that are costly.

2. Differentiate between the terms perfectly elastic, unitary elasticity, and perfectly inelastic.

   Perfectly elastic is a demand condition in which the quantity demanded varies from zero to infinity when there is a change in the price. Unitary elasticity is a demand condition in which the relative change in the quantity demanded is the same as the size of the price change. Perfectly inelastic is a demand condition in which there is no change in the quantity demanded when the price changes.

3. Compute elasticity ratios and explain their applications.

   Elasticity ratios are computed by dividing the percentage change in quantity by the percentage change in price. Demand elasticity helps explain spending decisions by consumers and pricing decisions by producers. It is important in understanding market behavior and government policies.

4. Explain how consumer sovereignty is related to the allocation of resources.

   In a market economy, consumers decide what goods and services they will spend their incomes on. This, in turn, makes it profitable for entrepreneurs to produce those goods and services and to acquire the resources to produce them. In this way, consumer sovereignty determines the allocation of resources.

5. Explain spending and saving choices and define average propensity to consume and average propensity to save.

   People make their spending decisions based on their personal preferences and the prices of different goods and services in the marketplace. Their savings decisions are based on the largest returns they can get for the amount of risk they are willing to take. Average propensity to consume is the percentage of after-tax income which consumers usually spend on goods and services. Average propensity to save is the percentage of after-tax income which consumers usually save.

6. Explain the principle of diminishing marginal utility and show the relationship of marginal utility to total utility.

As successive units of a good or service are acquired, the utility diminishes because the first unit satisfies the most important and pressing needs for the good or service. Each successive unit provides a smaller amount of satisfaction. Total utility is the sum of the marginal utilities of each successive unit of the good or service consumed, as graphed in Figure 3 on textbook page 91.

7. State the conditions necessary for consumer equilibrium.

   Consumer equilibrium is achieved when consumers allocate their income in such a way that the last dollar spent on each good or service and the last dollar saved provide equal amounts of utility.

8. Explain the effects of product information and advertising on consumer choices.

   Adequate and accurate information about products can increase the ability of consumers to allocate their incomes in a way that maximizes their potential utility. Informative advertising can be useful in achieving this, but noninformative, repetitive, and deceptive advertising can reduce consumer utility by raising the prices of goods and services and by distorting consumer decision making.

What Choices Do Consumers Make?

Students, like everyone else, are consumers and want to get the most satisfaction they can out of the income they spend. The concept of elasticity presented in this chapter provides them with a structure for examining their own behavior. How we react to the change in the price of a good is explained by this concept. If a small reduction in the price causes us to increase our purchases of the good significantly, our demand for the good is elastic. The degree of elasticity is measured by dividing the percentage change in the quantity purchased by the percentage change in price. If students have a problem calculating percentages, the equation can be written as the amount of the change in quantity divided by the total quantity and the amount of change in price divided by the total price. For small changes in price, a reasonable approximation of elasticity is obtained from the equation:

$$\frac{Q_2 - Q_1}{Q_1} \div \frac{P_2 - P_1}{P_1}$$

This formula for obtaining the ratio of the percentage change in quantity and price is perfectly adequate for teaching the concept of elasticity. However, if you want to devote the time to teaching a more accurate but mathematically more sophisticated calculation, use the following elasticity ratio equation:

$$\frac{Q_2 - Q_1}{(Q_1 + Q_2) \div 2} \div \frac{P_2 - P_1}{(P_1 + P_2) \div 2}$$

The second equation gives a consistent measurement of the elasticity ratio, whether the price is increased or decreased, by using the midpoint of the quantity and price range in the denominators.

Demand elasticity ratios are negative numbers because price and quantity change in opposite directions. But the minus sign before the elasticity coefficient is ignored, and demand is characterized as elastic when the coefficient is greater than one *disregarding* the sign.

If you are going to have the students do Exercise in Analysis 1, which is a follow-up based on the data for students' demands for movie attendance developed in Exercise in Analysis 1 for chapter 3, you should give them one of the two above formulas to work with. In doing this exercise, the students will discover that elasticity tends to be large at higher prices and small at lower prices on the same demand curve. (In the next chapter there is another Exercise in Analysis—Exercise 3—based on this same data. Students should save the data in order to do that exercise.)

The transparency of Figure 1 is useful for showing the difference in elasticity for two groups of consumers for the same product. (It is also useful for making the point that the longer young people smoke, the tougher it is for them to break the habit). The transparency of Figure 2 compares the different degrees of elasticity. Reinforcement of the concepts covered in this section of the chapter can be found in Study Questions 1–7.

Case Application: Housing Woes

This application deals with one of our basic necessities, housing. But the decision to purchase a home is not only a consumption decision, it is also a savings decision. For most families, the largest part of their savings is the equity in their homes. For these reasons, probably the most important household choice is the housing purchase decision. This decision has been a difficult one in recent years because of the escalation in housing prices, high mortgage interest rates, and uncertainty about the future of the housing market.

Answers to the "For Thought" Questions

1. How did changes in the housing market reflect consumer sovereignty?

   The strong consumer demand for houses in the 1970s caused 18 million housing units to be constructed and escalated prices. The decline in demand in the 1980s reduced construction to a projected 16 million units and brought a halt to rising prices.

2. From the behavior of the housing market in the 1970s, can you draw any conclusions about the elasticity of demand for housing? How did the quantity demanded appear to be related to price changes? How can you explain this behavior of demand?

   The rapidly rising prices for housing in the 1970s did not reduce the quantity of housing demanded. Actually, rising prices stimulated increased demand for housing as a hedge against inflation. Housing demand appeared to be not just inelastic, but to violate the "law of demand" by sloping up to the right. But the analysis of demand behavior shows that the demand schedule was continuously shifting outward, so that successive observations of price-quantity equilibria traced out the upward sloping supply curve for housing.

3. Which is the better situation in the housing market, the rapid escalation of housing prices in the 1970s or the relatively static housing prices in the 1980s? Why?

   Open answer. For those who already own property or can invest in it, the rise of housing prices can be very profitable. But for renters and young people just starting out, inflated housing prices can put a severe squeeze on the budget. Housing booms create jobs in the construction industry, but to the extent that rising housing prices not only reflect inflation but help to cause it, stable prices are healthier for the economy.

How Do Consumers Make Choices?

A look at our buying attitudes and habits validates the principle of diminishing marginal utility. The concept is an intellectualization of something we are all familiar with in our own behavior. The same is true of the concept of consumer equilibrium. We all attempt to spend our income in the way that will maximize our total utility. We adjust our spending so the last dollar we spend on any item provides the same amount of satisfaction as the last dollar spent on any other item. This condition of consumer equilibrium can be expressed by the equation:

$$\frac{MU_1}{P_1} = \frac{MU_2}{P_2} = \frac{MU_3}{P_3} = \frac{MU_s}{\$}$$

This equation states that consumer equilibrium requires that the marginal utility of the first good divided by the price of that good equal the marginal utility of the second good divided by the price of that good. This, in turn, equals the marginal utility of the third good divided by the price of that good, which equals the marginal utility of all other purchases divided by their prices and also equals the marginal utility of savings for the last dollar saved. If you choose to introduce the students to this equation, hypothetical marginal utility values and prices for different consumer items can be

inserted into the equation to give the students an exercise in determining whether or not consumer equilibrium exists. For example, good 1 is hamburgers with a marginal utility of 10 and a price of $1.50; good 2 is records with a marginal utility of 50 and a price of $6; the third good is jeans with a marginal utility of 200 and a price of $30; and savings has a marginal utility of 5 for the last dollar saved.

The equation would be as follows:

$$\underset{\text{(hamburgers)}}{\frac{10}{\$1.50}} = \underset{\text{(records)}}{\frac{50}{\$6}} = \underset{\text{(jeans)}}{\frac{200}{\$30}} = \underset{\text{(savings)}}{\frac{5}{\$1}}$$

Does this represent consumer equilibrium? It does not because the marginal utility per dollar is higher for records and lower for savings than for other purchases. What changes in the consumer's spending pattern need to be made to move toward consumer equilibrium? Spending on records should be increased because that is where the marginal utility per dollar is higher, and savings should be reduced because that is where the marginal utility per dollar is lowest.

The transparency for Figure 3 shows a hypothetical consumer's diminishing marginal utility for cigarettes. Given what we know about the dangers of smoking, the whole utility function should probably be below the zero line, but not to an addicted smoker.

The concept of diminishing marginal utility is reinforced in the *Economics U$A* program described below.

Case Application: The Channel Race

An examination of consumer demand for cable TV channels provides a contemporary case for applying the concepts of total utility, marginal utility, and consumer equilibrium.

Answers to the "For Thought" Questions

1. How would adding a second movie channel to a cable subscription affect the subscriber's total and marginal utility from pay TV?

   Adding a second movie channel to a cable subscription would increase the subscriber's total utility from pay TV and decrease the subscriber's marginal utility.

2. What criteria would you use, in economic terms, in deciding how many premium cable channels to subscribe to?

   The criteria that you would use would be to add additional channels until the last additional channel provided a marginal utility per dollar of its cost that was just equal to the marginal utility per dollar spent on other goods and services.

3. Do you think that there is a danger that people might spend too much of their income on pay TV? Why or why not?

Open answer. In terms of maximizing the utility from their expenditures, there is little danger that people will spend too much of their income on pay TV since rational consumers will not spend more on a purchase unless it gives them as much added utility per dollar as their expenditures on anything else. A fear that people might spend too much on pay TV would be based on social or psychological considerations rather than economic considerations. If pay TV reduces human interactions with family and others and limits a person's scope of activities, it might prove to be detrimental.

How Can Consumers Make Better Choices?

There has long been a debate over the costs and benefits of advertising. One of the difficulties in determining the pros and cons of advertising is the failure to distinguish between informative advertising, which improves the functioning of markets and increases consumer satisfaction, and noninformative advertising. The latter adds to the cost of products but does nothing to assist consumers in making wise spending decisions, and sometimes may even be detrimental.

Study Questions 9 and 10 examine how the conditioning of consumers affects markets.

Case Application: That's No Alligator; It's a Chameleon

A growing problem in consumer economics is the proliferation of counterfeit goods. Overseas manufacturers have been imitating name brand products and affixing fake labels. Generally the imitation products are of lower quality and consumers do not get value for their money even if they may have paid a lower price. There are instances, however, of consumers knowingly buying an imitation, for example of an expensive Rolex watch, as one might buy imitation precious gems. This raises a situation in which the ethics of trading with counterfeit goods can be discussed.

Answers to the "For Thought" Questions

1. What consumer information is conveyed by a trademark?

   Information conveyed by a trademark includes the quality reputation of the manufacturer and the service support for the product which is provided.

2. How does counterfeiting of trademarks affect consumer utility?

   The counterfeiting of trademarks generally reduces consumer utility because it conveys misinformation about the product. With a misleading trademark, the

consumer cannot make accurate decisions to maximize utility.

3. Would you knowingly buy an imitation Apple computer made in Hong Kong if you could get it at a greatly discounted price, say one half the price of a legitimate Apple, and try it out before you bought it? Why or why not?

   Open answer. Some people might purchase the imitation Apple at such a large savings, expecting to get their money's worth in use from it. Others might be reluctant to take the chance, especially since follow-up service would not be available from the supplier. If the imitation had Apple markings on it, another consideration might be the ethics of purchasing a contraband product, the importation of which is illegal.

Perspective: Conspicuous Consumption

Buying goods and services to satisfy ego needs rather than material needs is an interesting aspect of consumer behavior. The phenomenon dates far back in history and is certainly not peculiarly American, but its prevalence among the *nouveau riche* of late nineteenth century America led an American economist to provide us with the most complete analysis of it. Thorstein Veblen was an outstanding economist, social philosopher, and educator, who studied the impact of conspicuous consumption.

Answers to Study Questions

1. What goods and services do you consider to be necessities in your own consumption? How do you differentiate between a necessity and a luxury?

   The goods and services traditionally classified as basic necessities are food, clothing, and shelter, along with medical care. As suggested in the introductory article, however, today there are additional goods and services that people may consider to be necessities in their own lifestyle which have not been traditionally classified as necessities.

   Traditionally, a necessity is defined as something which is necessary for life, all other things being luxuries. In modern society, however, transportation might be considered a necessity, since it is necessary to get to one's place of employment in order to earn an income to provide the other necessities. When you expand the concept of necessities this way, it becomes difficult to draw the line between what necessities are and what luxuries are.

2. What luxuries do you think would have a higher price elasticity of demand than others? Give three examples

and explain why you think they would have an exceptionally high elasticity.

Open answer. Luxuries with a high price elasticity of demand might include full-service gasoline (because apparently people are willing to do without gasoline service attendants if they can save a few cents per gallon with self-service), professional shoeshines (the rise in the price of shoeshines has nearly made the shoeshine stand an extinct institution in this country), and first class airplane seats (few people are willing to pay the extra cost of first class seats unless they are traveling on an expense account).

3. Besides salt and drinking water, what other items that you use regularly have an inelastic demand? Pick one of those items and explain why if its price went up 10% you would reduce your consumption of the item by less than 10%.

Open answer. Items with an inelastic demand might include soap, toothbrushes, and aspirin. For any of these, if its price went up by 10% purchases would probably decline by less than 10% because they are considered necessary for health and hygiene, they have few adequate substitutes, and they are all low in price and do not constitute a significant part of our budget.

4. If you were the owner of a business and trying to decide what price to charge for your product or service, why would the elasticity of demand be an important consideration?

Elasticity of demand would determine what the effect of a price change would be on sales and therefore on the revenue of the business.

5. A hamburger stand raised the price of its hamburgers from $2.00 to $2.50. As a result, its sales of hamburgers fell from 200 per day to 180 per day. Was the demand for its hamburgers elastic or inelastic? How can you tell?

The demand for its hamburgers was inelastic because the relative change in quantity sold was less than the relative change in price. The coefficient of elasticity was (-).40 using the first equation given above for calculating the elasticity ratio or (-).47 using the second equation.

6. Why would something that has many close substitutes tend to have an elastic demand?

If something has many close substitutes, a small increase in its price would cause many buyers to switch to a substitute, thereby greatly reducing the sales of the

product. *The relatively small change in the price would lead to a relatively large change in the quantity sold.*

7. If the average propensity to consume was 90% of after-tax income, what would the average propensity to save be?

The average propensity to save would be 10%.

8. How does tobacco company advertising affect the cigarette market? Does it influence the elasticity of demand for cigarettes? How?

Advertising affects the demand schedule for cigarettes by shifting it to the right. It shifts the supply curve to the left because it increases costs. As a result, the equilibrium price is higher. Advertising also increases the inelasticity of demand, causing the demand curve to be more vertical. It does this by convincing smokers that the consumption of tobacco is a necessity of their lifestyle.

9. Chemically, all aspirin is the same, but some aspirin sells for much more than other aspirin. Why do consumers often purchase the higher-priced aspirin when all aspirin is chemically the same?

Consumers have a tendency to purchase widely advertised name brands whether or not they are actually superior to less advertised brands. Apparently, many people have not heard or do not believe that generic or house brands of aspirin are the same as nationally advertised brands.

10. What are examples of purchases you have made because of the Veblen effect, the snob effect, and the bandwagon effect?

Open answer. Examples might include: Veblen effect—a pigskin jacket; snob effect—leather pants; bandwagon effect—a Walkman cassette player

Integrating *Economics U$A* Programs

(For information on Economics U$A *see the introduction, p. v.)*

In program 16 on "Supply and Demand; What Sets the Price?" economist Gill explains marginal utility and diminishing marginal utility in analyzing the public's response to water rationing during the California drought.

The effects of advertising on demand are illustrated by the designer jeans case when Jordache created a new market through the use of advertising. At first designer jeans had snob appeal, but "When everybody owned a pair of designer jeans, it lost its snob appeal."

Case Applications in Student Workbook

(Answers are supplied to students in the workbook.)

What Choices Do Consumers Make?

Case Application: Going to the Movies

This application examines how a couple responds to the rise in movie ticket prices by altering the number of times they attend the movies. It illustrates the type of consumer reasoning that results either in elastic or inelastic demand for goods and services.

Answers to the "For Thought" Questions

1. Do the Gardners consider going to the movies a necessity or a luxury?

   The Gardners consider going to the movies a luxury. This is indicated by their unwillingness to pay the higher ticket prices and by Martin's statement that if the price of groceries continues to rise they will substitute groceries for movie attendance.

2. From the application, does it appear that the Gardners' demand for theater movies is perfectly elastic, relatively elastic, relatively inelastic, or perfectly inelastic?

   It appears the Gardners' demand for theater movies is relatively elastic because they are substituting bicycle rides, picnics, and television in place of going to the movies.

3. Is $5 too much to pay for a ticket to the movies? What is your criteria for how much is too much?

   Open answer. The answer depends upon the individual's preferences for attending movies in comparison to other forms of leisure-time spending. If people rank movies very high on their preference scale relative to other types of activities, $5 may not be too much to pay for a ticket. If, on the other hand, there are substitute activities that cost less and provide almost as much satisfaction, $5 may be too high a price for a movie ticket. Another criteria is the amount of the individual's income. Those with high incomes may not consider $5 tickets too high, while those with lower incomes do consider it too high.

How Do Consumers Make Choices?

Case Application: Lifestyle and Consumer Choice

In this application, the relationship between changing lifestyles and changing consumer demand is examined. As lifestyles have changed in recent years, the markets for goods and services have become more dynamic. There may be rapid shifts in the amount of utility consumers derive from different types of purchases.

Answers to the "For Thought" Questions

1. Large cars can carry more passengers groceries, baggage, etc, than small cars. Does that mean that large cars have greater utility than small cars? Explain?

   Large cars do not necessarily have greater utility than small cars. The utility of an automobile depends not only on its carrying capacity, but also on such things as fuel efficiency, ease of parking, and the reflection of personal tastes and lifestyles. Those who do not need a car with a large carrying capacity may find that a small car has greater utility for them.

2. Does convenience have diminishing marginal utility?

   Convenience does have diminishing marginal utility. This is apparent both from consumer behavior and from economic analysis of the trade-offs of convenience. Although convenience foods have greatly increased in popularity, they have not entirely displaced other types of foods—which would have been the case if they did not have diminishing marginal utility. The popularity of gourmet cooking schools and the demand for fresh produce and meats proves that convenience foods have diminishing marginal utility. The more time we save from the use of convenience foods, the less valuable is the saving of additional time by further increasing consumption of convenience foods.

3. Convenience foods cost more than basic food products. During these hard economic times, can we afford the luxury of convenience foods? Why or why not?

   Open answer. The answer depends on the circumstances of the individual household. Many people have to cut back on the use of convenience foods because of tighter household budgets. In other cases, financial pressures have caused additional members of the household to enter the working forced, resulting in an increase in the necessity to resort to convenience foods, or to go out more for meals.

How Can Consumers Make Better Choices?

Case Application: Do You Have Time for Your Possessions?

This application raises the question whether all of the labor-saving and convenience gadgets that are now available are worth—not just their money cost—but all of the time required to shop for them, learn how to use them, care for them, protect them, and repair them when they break down.

Answers to the "For Thought" Questions

1. How do consumers normally find out about the availability of new products?

   The most common means by which consumers find out about the availability of new products is through advertising.

2. What information do consumers need that they do not generally have when purchasing convenience products that would help them make better choices?

   Purchasers could make better choices if they had information about the rate of failure and the frequency and cost of servicing the products that they buy.

3. Should producers be required to provide customers with information about the average number of repairs required on their appliances and the average cost of maintaining them? Why or why not?

   Open answer. It would certainly help consumers to make better choices if they had that information. (For a few things, such information is already required—e.g., refrigerator manufacturers are required to post on a refrigerator the average yearly energy cost of operating it; auto companies are required to post the average gas mileage of their models.) On the other hand, there is a cost involved in gathering, validating, and disseminating such information that would be passed on to consumers in a higher price for the product. Also, it would require government agencies to enforce the regulation—a cost to taxpayers.

Chapter 5

The Business Firm and Market Structure

Chapter Overview

This and the following chapter deal with what might be considered the core of microeconomics. It covers what is sometimes referred to as the theory of the firm. The introductory article deals with agriculture and the problems besetting farmers. The "farm problem" is not new, but it has taken on dimensions not seen since the depression of the 1930s.

The first section of the chapter discusses the different types of business firms and the economic functions served by businesses. The case application for the section, "Running With the Bulls," explains the functioning of the stock market. It shows why picking individual stocks is a gamble in a "perfect market." It also explains the contribution that the stock market makes to the performance of the economy.

The second section shows the behavior of a firm's costs and revenues and how that determines the price the firm will charge, the quantity it will produce, and its profits. The case application on "Rising Costs Hit Rock Concerts" examines the pricing decisions involved in rock group appearances.

The chapter's final section covers the different types of market structures from pure competition to pure monopoly and the differences in pricing behaviors, depending upon the type of market. The market for microcomputer software provides an enlightening case application on pricing in a new industry in "Hard Decisions for the Software Industry."

Suggested Answers to the Learning Objectives

The knowledge acquired from this chapter should enable the students to:

1. List the three main forms of business organization and cite the advantages and disadvantages of each.

   The three main forms of business organization are individual proprietorships, partnerships, and corporations. The advantages of individual proprietorships are that they are relatively easy and inexpensive to start and all of the rewards accrue to the owner. The disadvantages are that the financial, managerial, and other resources available to the firm are limited; the owner is legally responsible for the debts of the business; and if the owner dies the business is legally terminated. The advantages of partnerships are that they allow the pooling of capital and

managerial resources. The disadvantages are that if one of the owners dies the business is legally terminated, and each of the partners is individually liable for the debts of the business. The principal advantage of the corporate form of business organization is limited liability of the owners, which makes it possible to aggregate capital from large numbers of people, and also the firm as a legal entity is not dissolved when owners die or ownership changes. The disadvantages of the corporate form are that expense is incurred in obtaining a corporate charter; regulations are imposed on corporations selling stock to the public, such as public disclosure of finances and management; and a corporation tax is levied on the firm's profits.

2. Describe the four economic functions of business firms.

   The four economic functions of business firms are to identify consumer wants and determine what should be produced, to organize production and determine how goods and services should be produced, to allocate revenues to the workers and other factor inputs, and to increase production capacity by real capital investment.

3. Distinguish between fixed costs and variable costs.

   Fixed costs are those costs which are constant regardless of the level of output, such as depreciation on plant and equipment. Variable costs are those costs which depend upon the quantity produced, such as costs of labor and raw materials.

4. Show the relationship of total cost and total revenue to output.

   At zero output, the total cost is the amount of fixed cost. As output increases, total cost is the amount of fixed cost plus the amount of variable cost, as shown in Figure 4 on page 120 of the text. Total revenue is zero when output is zero and increases as output expands either at a constant rate as in Figure 3 on page 119 or at a decreasing rate as in Figure 9 on page 125.

5. Locate the break-even point and point of maximum profit.

   The break-even point is the level of output at which total revenue equals total cost. The point of maximum profit is the level of output at which total revenue exceeds total cost by the greatest amount.

6. Distinguish between normal profit and economic profit.

Normal profit is the rate of return on invested capital which could be expected in any type of business with a similar degree of risk. Economic profit is earnings in excess of the normal profit rate.

7. List the characteristics of purely competitive industries.

   Purely competitive industries are those in which there are such a large number of firms producing a standardized product that no single firm can noticeably affect the market price by changing its output, and which firms can easily enter or leave.

8. Explain the principle of diminishing returns.

   When a firm's output is increased by increasing inputs of the variable production resources while keeping one or more factor inputs fixed, the output per unit of inputs decreases due to diminishing returns.

9. Explain the short-run and long-run adjustments to changes in demand in a purely competitive industry.

   The short-run adjustment to an increase in demand would be an expansion of output from the existing plant capacity, which would be shown by a movement up the supply curve. The long-run adjustment to an increase in demand would be an increase in the production capacity in the industry, which would be shown by a shift to the right of the supply curve as shown in Figure 6 on textbook page 122.

10. Differentiate between pure monopoly, shared monopoly, and differentiated competition.

    Pure monopoly exists when there is an industry with a single producer. Shared monopoly exists when there is an industry in which there are a few producers of a standardized or differentiated product; the sales of each producer are noticeably affected by the pricing policies of the other firms in the industry. Differentiated competition is when there are a large number of producers of a differentiated product within an industry; the pricing policies of any one firm have a negligible effect on the sales volume of any other firm.

What Are the Forms and Economic Functions of Business Firms?

Figure 2 on page 107 of the text shows the numbers of firms and amount of total sales of the three types of business organizations for farming and other types of businesses. It shows that in non-farm businesses the greater number of firms do not account for a very large amount of total sales. The largest corporations, though relatively small in number, account for much more of the total sales than do the small proprietorships. In farming, on the other hand, the individual proprietorship is still the dominant form of business organization in sales as well as number of firms.

It might be noted that there is a parallel between the functions of business firms and the basic questions which

economies must resolve. The first function of a business firm, identifying consumer wants, corresponds to the economic question of "what" to produce. The second function, organizing production, corresponds to the question of "how" to produce. The third function, allocating revenues, corresponds to the question of "for whom" goods and services are produced. The fourth function of a business firm, to increase the stock of real capital, is related both to the "what" and "how" questions.

Study Question 1 reinforces the concept of the limited liability advantage of corporations compared to the other types of business organizations.

Case Application: Running With the Bulls

This application attempts to give the student a realistic picture of how the stock market works and the role it plays in the economic system. It draws on research which has shown that, because the stock market is a nearly "perfect" market, the relative prices of all stocks at any given moment are the best estimate of their worth. This makes it virtually impossible for anyone to consistently pick winning stocks in short term trading and explains the poor record of professional pickers who attempt to do so. It notes that the only "sure thing" in the stock market is insider trading, which is illegal. The book went to press before the Ivan Bosky case, the biggest insider trading scandal ever, broke in the news. That case, which is still being investigated as this is written, would make an interesting class supplement to this application.

After showing why short-term trading is more likely to enrich brokers than the investor, the long-term benefits of stock market investing using a "buy and hold" strategy and diversification are explained. In conclusion, the important role that the stock market plays in raising investment capital for business is examined.

Answers to the "For Thought" Questions

1. Are shares of ownership of most business organizations traded in the stock market? What types of businesses are traded there?

   Ownership of most business organizations is not traded on the stock market because most business organizations are individual proprietorships which do not issue shares of stock. Only the ownership of corporations is traded on the stock market.

2. Which of the functions of business firms are most affected by the stock market? How?

   The function of business firms that is most affected by the stock market is the function of real capital investment to increase production capacity. The existence of an efficient stock market makes it possible to raise large sums of equity capital for expansion and modernization of production facilities.

3. Should the Securities and Exchange Commission reduce the amount of speculation in the stock market by prohibiting investors from buying stock on credit, paying only a fraction in cash and pledging the stock as collateral on the balance owed? Why should such "buying on the margin" be allowed or why should it be prohibited?

Open answer. Buying on the margin enables investors to purchase more stock than would be possible if they were restricted to cash purchases. It could be argued that this creates a more dynamic market and makes more investment funds available to businesses. On the negative side, it encourages speculation and may make the market unstable. Excessive speculation through buying on the margin can cause booms and busts in the market unless it is properly regulated by the Securities and Exchange Commission.

What Determines a Firm's Profits?

This section uses the example of a chicken farm to explain production costs, revenue from sales, and the determination of profits. It works through a numerical example of the farm's operations and discusses what is meant by a normal rate of return and economic profits. Employing a purely numerical example in this section allows the student to become acquainted with cost and revenue concepts before dealing with them in graphic form in the following section.

Study Question 2 aids in understanding the concept of capital depreciation by exploring why it differs in different types of industries. Study Question 3 reinforces the distinction between accounting profits and economic profits.

Case Application: Rising Costs Hit Rock Concerts

The economics of rock concerts are an application of the theory of the firm model that will be of interest to students. For superstar groups like the Grateful Dead and the Rolling Stones, concerts are frequently loss leaders for their record album sales; but for the average rock group, concerts are a money-making business like any other.

Answers to the "For Thought" Questions"

1. What are the fixed costs shown for a rock concert? What are the variable costs?

The fixed costs of the rock concert are the guarantee to the performers, the arena rental, insurance, the cost of sound and lighting systems, and radio and newspaper advertising. The total fixed costs are $71,550. The variable costs include ushers and other personnel, ticket

agency commissions, and state taxes for a total of $3.75 per ticket sold.

2. About how many tickets would the promoter have to sell at $15 each to cover the above costs of a concert?

The promoter would have to sell 6,360 tickets at $15 each to cover the listed costs of the concert. A simple way to calculate this is to subtract the variable cost per ticket sold from the ticket price and divide the net of $11.25 into the total fixed costs.

3. If the promoter could only count on selling enough tickets to cover those costs, do you think it would be a good idea to go ahead and put on the concert? Why or why not?

The only circumstances under which it would be a good idea for the promoter to put on the concert if the revenue only covered the listed costs, with no provision for a normal rate of return on the promoter's up-front investment of capital or compensation for the time and effort put in by the promoter in organizing the concert, would be if the promoter got non-monetary satisfactions out of doing it. There is an example of this being the case when Apple Computer cofounder Steve Wosniak staged rock festivals which he in fact subsidized with his own money.

How Does Industry Market Structure Affect Price and Output Decisions?

Firms in all types of markets attempt to maximize profits, but different types of industries have different market conditions and differing constraints on their choices. The price/output outcome is dependent upon the type of market in which the firm operates.

The first type of industry considered is one that operates in a purely competitive market. In this type of market a single firm can increase output without having to lower the selling price. Consequently, total revenue rises at a constant rate with increasing production, as shown in Figure 3 on textbook page 119. Costs, on the other hand, because they are determined by the technology of production and not by the type of market in which the product is sold, behave similarly in different types of industries. They are composed of fixed costs and variable costs, as shown in Figure 4 (p. 120).

When the revenue and cost functions are combined, as in Figure 5 (p. 121), they indicate profits at different levels of output. As shown in Figure 5, this farm can make profits operating at any level of output between the lower and upper break-even points. The level of output at which the farmer's profits are maximized is 31,600 bushels with an economic profit (over and above the normal rate of return on capital) of $18,000.

However, because there is easy entry into purely competitive industries, above normal profits do not last due to expanded production in the industry. The market adjustment is shown in Figure 6 (p. 122), and the long-run equilibrium situation for a purely competitive firm is represented by Figure 7 (p. 123) in which total revenue just covers total costs at the optimum output level.

The situation is different in monopolistic industries in two ways. First, total revenue behaves differently because the monopolist must reduce prices to sell more output. The total revenue function is shown in Figure 9 (p. 125), rising to a maximum and then declining as output is increases. It might be useful to have the students construct the total revenue curve for movie ticket sales based on the group demand curves tabulated for Exercise in Analysis 1 of chapter 3, as suggested in Excercise in Analysis 3 for this chapter.

The most important difference between the situation of a purely competitive firm and a monopolistic firm is that the monopolist's profits can be sustained by restricting output and maintaining a price that returns a monopoly profit, as in Figure 10 on textbook page 126.

The other two types of market structures, shared monopoly and differentiated competition, have outcomes that fall between the extremes of pure competition and pure monopoly.

Study Question 4 brings out the difference in revenue behavior when firms sell in purely competitive markets and when they are monopolistic. Study Question 5 calls for the student to examine the relationship between marginal cost and marginal revenue and the changes in profits. Study Question 6 reinforces the concept of diminishing returns. Study Question 7 emphasizes the importance of the effects of free entry in competitive markets. Study Question 8 brings out the minimizing cost result of competitive markets. Study Question 9 reinforces the classification of industry market structures. Study Question 10 shows the effect of market structure on advertising costs.

Case Application: Hard Decisions for the Software Industry

This application illustrates the uncertainty that affects markets which are not either purely competitive or purely monopolistic. Pricing policies in the microcomputer software industry were quite erratic in its formative years. Firms initially adopted seemingly arbitrary prices, but as experience and competition evolved they gravitated toward more conventional pricing. One firm even conducted an experiment to determine what price would return the greatest revenue. Since fixed costs for development are the major component of software costs, maximizing total revenue is the significant consideration for a producer.

Answers to the "For Thought" Questions

1. What type of market structure exists in the software industry? How can you tell?

As with many new industries, the microcomputer software industry engendered quite a large number of small firms during its formative years, as many as 3,000. The large number of firms and the marketing behavior characterized it as an industry with differentiated competition. This period was followed by a shakeout in the industry from which emerged a few major suppliers of each software product for each computer. The market then took on the characteristics of a shared monopoly, with the different producers reacting to each other's pricing policies.

2. Is a software company likely to price its programs near the price that maximizes total revenue? Why? Diagram the total cost and total revenue situation of a hypothetical software producer and show whether maximum profit output is close to maximum revenue output. (It is unnecessary to put in quantity and revenue figures. Only the relative positions of the TR and TC curves are necessary.)

A software company is likely to price its programs near the price that maximizes total revenue because the greater part of its costs are the fixed costs of developing the program and only a minor part are the variable costs of producing the disk. Since variable costs are relatively insignificant, total profit is maximized close to the output which maximizes total revenue. This is shown on a diagram where the total cost curve is nearly horizontal and the total revenue curve is an inverted bowl shape. The maximum profit spread between cost and revenue is close to the highest point on the total revenue curve.

3. Do you think that more firms should experiment with charging various prices for a product to find the effect of different prices on their total revenue? Would there be disadvantages in doing this? Why?

Open answer. It might be beneficial for a firm to experiment with different prices to discover its maximum revenue point. However this procedure is expensive, retailers do not appreciate constantly changing prices, and it tends to confuse customers.

Perspective: The Evolution of the Modern Corporation

Although they are small in number compared to proprietorships, corporations dominate our economy—if not our whole society. This domination has occurred in a relatively short span of time, and the trend is continuing and even accelerating. The Perspective shows how this situation evolved.

Answers to Study Questions

1. Why isn't it a good idea to join in a partnership if you do not know the other partners very well? Does the same consideration apply to buying shares in a corporation?

   It is not a good idea to join in a partnership if you do not know the other partners very well because of the risk involved. If one of the partners in a partnership—through malfeasance or incompetence—makes the company liable to creditors or other claimants, you can be held personally responsible for those liabilities. The same consideration does not apply to buying shares in a corporation because of the provision of limited liability for stockholders.

2. Why would the capital equipment of a firm in a dynamic industry such as electronics depreciate more rapidly than in an industry such as textile manufacturing?

   The capital equipment of firms in dynamic industries depreciates rapidly because of the rapid changes in technology of production. New capital equipment can quickly become obsolete. In more static industries, technological changes are not so rapid, and the capital equipment can be profitably employed for a longer time span.

3. What is the difference between accounting profits and economic profits?

   Accounting profits are the net returns after subtracting direct costs from revenues. Economic profits are the returns after subtracting all costs, both direct and implicit costs, from revenues. Implicit costs would include the managerial time put in by the owner and imputed interest costs of the capital the owner invested in the business.

4. Why does the total revenue of an egg farm rise at a constant rate with increasing sales, while the total revenue of a monopolistic firm rises at a decreasing rate, reaches a maximum, and then declines with increasing sales?

   Because there are so many egg farms, the production of any one farmer cannot have an appreciable effect on the market price. Therefore, each farmer has a perfectly elastic demand for the output of that farm, and increasing output of the farm can be sold at the same price per dozen eggs. The total revenue of the farm rises at a constant rate. A monopolistic firm, on the other hand, must lower prices to sell more output because of facing a downward sloping demand curve. As prices are reduced on increasing outputs, total revenue rises at a decreasing rate up to the point where the elasticity of demand is unitary, and further increases in output beyond that point result in falling total revenue.

5. If a firm increases its output beyond the level where MR = MC, what happens to its profits? Why?

   If a firm increases its output beyond the level where MR = MC its profits will fall because it adds more to its total costs by producing additional units than it adds to its total revenue from the sale of those units.

6. Why is a firm more likely to encounter diminishing returns in the short run than in the long run?

   A firm is more likely to encounter diminishing returns in the short run because in the long run all factor inputs can be increased. When none of the factor inputs is fixed, all factors can be increased proportionately and output may rise at a constant rate rather than at a diminishing rate.

7. Why do economic profits tend to disappear in pure competition in the long run?

   Economic profits tend to disappear because their existence attracts new entry into the industry, which increases the supply and reduces the market equilibrium price to the level of normal profits.

8. Why do purely competitive firms in the long run have to operate at the level of output that minimizes their average cost while monopolists do not?

   Purely competitive firms are forced to operate at the level of output that minimizes their average costs because they otherwise could not sell their products at a competitive price. Other firms or new entrants into the industry would undersell them. Monopolists, on the other hand, are not forced by market competition to produce at the lowest possible cost and sell at the lowest possible price.

9. What are examples of firms in your area that represent each of the four types of industry structure? If there are not any firms that correspond exactly to one or more of the four types, what firm comes closest to the industry type?

   Open answer. Typical examples of pure competition would be in agriculture, while examples of differentiated competition would be consumer light industries and personal services. Typical examples of shared monopoly would be consumer durables and heavy industry producers' goods, and typical examples of monopoly would be public utilities.

10. What are three examples of industries in which advertising expenditures appear to be especially large? Are these industries purely competitive, monopolies, shared monopolies with standardized products or with differentiated products, or differentiated competition industries?

    Open answer. Industries with large advertising expenditures include automobiles (shared monopoly with differentiated products), soft drinks (shared monopoly with differentiated products), and fast foods (differentiated competition).

Integrating *Economics USA* Programs

(For information on Economics U$A *see the introduction, p. v.)*

The appropriate program for this chapter is program 17, "Pure Competition and Inelastic Demand: Can the Farmer Make a Profit?" The first application in the program examines the roots of the farm problem in the expansion of agricultural production to meet the food demands of World War I. This led to overproduction after the war and depression in the farm economy during the 1920s. Economist Gill presents a demand-supply analysis of long-run changes in a competitive industry such as agriculture.

The second application deals with the dairying industry and shows the effects of inelastic demand for a product. The final application describes the evolution of government farm price support programs from the 1930s to the postwar period.

Case Applications in Student Workbook

(Answers are supplied to students in the workbook.)

What Are the Forms and Economic Functions of Business Firms?

Case Application: The Progressive Bike Shop

This application discusses the formation of a small business selling and servicing bicycles. It shows some of the considerations used in determining what type of business to establish.

Answers to the "For Thought" Questions

1. What form of business organization was the Progressive Bike Shop?

   The Progressive Bike Shop was a partnership. Pat's parents invested in the business for a percentage return of the net earnings. This made them partners in the business. (Technically, it was a limited partnership, since they did not take an active role in running the business.)

2. What economic functions did the Progressive Bike Shop perform?

   The Progressive Bike Shop performed all four economic functions of a business. Pat and Mike decided what goods and services would be offered in the economy by establishing a bicycle sales and service firm. Deciding to rent the storefront location in the inner-city was an example of determining how goods and services would be provided. Relegating how the net receipts would be divided up affected the allocation of purchasing power by resolving the "for whom" question, which was also affected by providing their retail services to the campus

community. *Finally, the renovation of the store premises represented an increase in the economy's real capital investment.*

3. Do you think locating the shop in a deteriorated neighborhood was a good idea? Why or why not?

   Open answer. Locating the bike shop in a deteriorated neighborhood may have been a good idea from a business standpoint because of the low rent overhead which reduced the costs of operation and because the neighborhood population contained an age group of potential customers. From a socioeconomic standpoint, it was a good idea because it helped to revitalize a rundown area. On the other hand, it might not have been a good business decision if the store's marketing area did not have sufficient purchasing power to provide adequate sales revenues for the firm to succeed. If the business failed, it would have been bad for the neighborhood as well as for the owners.

What Determines a Firm's Profits?

Case Application: The Fortunes of the Progressive Bike Shop

This application continues the case study of the bicycle shop introduced previously. The costs and revenues incurred by the firm are examined, including the implicit costs of the contributions by the owners.

Answers to the "For Thought" Questions

1. Was the $13,200 cost of the merchandise a fixed cost or a variable cost?

   The $13,200 cost of the merchandise was a variable cost because it was directly related to the volume of sales.

2. What economic costs of operating the Progressive Bike Shop were not included in the $21,600 given as the total cost?

   Economic costs not included in the $21,600 total costs were the compensation to Pat and Jeff for the labor time they put in the business and a normal return on the $3,000 of their capital investment in the business.

3. Was it fair for Pat's parents to get 20% of the net receipts for their $7,000 investment in the business? Why or why not?

   Open answer. Pat's parents put up over two-thirds of the capital invested in the business. They were entitled to a return on their investment. Such small businesses are risky investments and they stood a chance of losing their $7,000. Therefore, 20% of the net receipts might be a fair return. However, the way the net receipts were calculated, they were greatly overstated. If Pat and Jeff *had been paid a salary out of the receipts for the time they put into the business, the firm would not have shown a profit during its first year of operation. It might have been more fair if the return to Pat's parents' investment was calculated on the basis of net earnings after compensating Pat and Jeff for their time.*

How Does Industry Market Structure Affect Price and Output Decisions?

Case Application: Wheat Farmers in Debt

This application illustrates problems of the farmers. Some of their difficulties stem from the fact that agriculture is a purely competitive industry. Being unable to control the prices of their products, farmers are subject to the vagaries of weather and fluctuating demand and supply conditions.

Answers to the "For Thought" Questions

1. What type of market structure is the industry in which Gus Bailey is engaged?

   Gus Bailey is engaged in a purely competitive industry because there are large numbers of wheat farmers producing a standardized product and there is relative ease of entry into the industry.

2. How does the application illustrate that, under purely competitive conditions, economic profits tend towards zero?

This application illustrates that under purely competitive conditions economic profits tend towards zero because profitable crop conditions result in more wheat being planted, and the increased supply reduces the price. The price decline results in profits disappearing.

3. Do farmers deserve government subsidies or other special assistance not afforded to other industries? Why or why not?

Open answer. Farmers are engaged in a business which provides a necessity of life but which is subject to varied unpredictable conditions over which they have no control. The unstable effects of weather, insects, and crop diseases are magnified by the unpredictability of prices in the competitive markets for farm products. The uncertainties of farming combined with its importance to our economy have been justifications for government farm price support programs. These programs have been attacked for misallocating resources by encouraging the production of unneeded crops, for contributing to inflation by artificially raising food prices, for subsidizing mainly the large farmers who are already wealthy and don't need government assistance, and for bureaucratic waste.

Chapter 6

Industry Concentration and Conduct

Chapter Overview

This chapter covers the degree of monopolistic concentration in American industry and the problems it gives rise to. Foreign competition has undercut the monopoly power of such industries as automobiles and steel, but aggregate concentration continues to increase. The introductory article discusses the numerous large mergers that have occurred in recent years, many of them hostile takeovers. The intrigue involved in these megamergers has an air of soap-opera melodrama about it. But it is serious business, involving billions of dollars, and could have serious consequences for the economy.

The first section of the chapter explains how the degree of market concentration is measured and the extent of aggregate concentration. The case application for the section, "Big Boy Blue Come Blow Your Horn," describes how IBM came to dominate its market.

The second section of the chapter examines the causes of concentration in industries. The case application examines the motivations for and the outcome of the merger fever that has affected the corporate world. The final section covers the consequences resulting from monopolistic practices. The case application concerns the effects of concentration in the U.S. automobile industry on pricing practices and industry behavior until it was forced to change by foreign competition.

Suggested Answers to the Learning Objectives

The knowledge acquired from this chapter should enable the students to:

1. Define and apply market concentration and market concentration ratio.

   Market concentration is based on the number of firms in an industry and the share of the market held by the largest firms. The concentration ratio is the percentage of total sales accounted for by the largest four firms in an industry (alternatively, by the largest eight firms). The extent of market concentration is determined by whether an industry has a concentration ratio of more than 50%, which classifies it as a monopolistic industry; or a ratio of less than 25%, which classifies it as competitive; or whether it falls in between.

2. Explain the difference between market concentration and aggregate concentration.

   Market concentration measures the degree to which the largest firms in a specific industry dominate the sales in that industry. Aggregate concentration does not refer to individual industries, but rather to the percentage of total sales of all industries which is accounted for by the largest firms in the country. There is a standard measurement for market concentration—the concentration ratio—but there is no standard measurement for aggregate concentration.

3. Describe the three different types of mergers and their effects on concentration.

   A horizontal merger is the joining of two firms that produce the same good or service, or close substitutes. A vertical merger is the joining of two firms in which the output of one firm is an input of the other firm. A conglomerate merger is the joining of two firms that do not produce the same good or service, or close substitutes, or output at different stages of the same production process. Horizontal mergers directly increase market concentration ratios, and vertical mergers are likely to result in increased market concentration. Conglomerate mergers may not increase market concentration, but do increase aggregate concentration.

4. List four barriers to entry and explain the consequences of each.

   Control of the supply of resources by a firm excludes other firms from the market by denying them the necessary raw material inputs for production. Patents and copyrights prevent other firms from entering the market by legally preventing them from producing and selling a particular product. Large capital requirements for investment in plant and equipment bar new firms from an industry because they are not able to accumulate sufficient financing. Economies of scale exclude firms from entering an industry because of the cost advantage held by the established firm.

5. Describe predatory business practices.

   Predatory business practices are actions by firms designed to injure a competitor. These include price discrimination, sales below cost, kickbacks, and malicious interference with a competitor's operations or product.

6. Explain the four consequences of high concentration in industries.

   One of the consequences of high concentration is monopolistic pricing, which sets the price above the cost of production. This results in monopolistic profits for the producer and a reduction in purchasing power for the consumer. A second consequence of market concentration is misallocation of resources. This results in reduced output and reduced employment of productive factors in industries with monopolistic control of the market and diverts more resources into competitive industries, causing a larger-than-optimum output. A third consequence of market concentration is that producers do not operate at the most efficient level of output to minimize the average costs of production, and a fourth is that pricing and output decisions tend to accentuate the cyclical instability of the economy.

How Monopolistic Is American Industry?

The theoretical types of market structures described in the preceding chapter are here examined to determine their degree of concentration in American industry. The conclusion is that roughly one-third of all industries are competitive, roughly one-third monopolistic, and roughly one-third somewhere between. With respect to aggregate concentration, the petroleum and automobile firms dominate American industry, as indicated by Table 2 on page 139 of the text. The idea of a concentration ratio is made more concrete for students by Study Questions 1 and 2.

Case Application: Big Boy Blue Come Blow Your Horn

International Business Machines became the nation's most profitable company by its domination of the market for mainframe computers, capturing 67% of the domestic market in the 1970s. It is now attempting to expand, in part by acquiring other companies, into the telecommunications business where it is confronting AT&T in head to head competition.

Answers to the "For Thought" Questions

1. If the mainframe computer business were considered a separate industry, how would it be classified on the basis of market concentration? Why?

   It would be classified as a shared monopoly, since IBM alone accounts for over 50% of sales in the industry.

2. What effect has IBM's expansion into telecommunications had on aggregate concentration? How?

It has increased aggregate concentration. IBM, one of the country's largest businesses, has acquired additional firms as part of its effort to expand into telecommunications.

3. Is it beneficial for IBM and AT&T to attempt to expand their activities into the areas dominated by the other? What economic benefits may result from this development? What drawbacks might there be?

   Open answer. Benefits that might derive from competition between IBM and AT&T in the telecommunications industry include the possibility of rapid technological innovation in the industry, competitive pricing to establish market share, and a reduction in the share that each firm held as a near monopolist in its own industry previously. The drawbacks that might result are that competition between the two giant corporations may eliminate the possibility of smaller firms surviving in the industry, and subsequently the two dominant firms could share the market and avoid price competition.

What Are the Causes of Concentration in Industry?

The most apparent reason for concentration in industry is mergers such as those described in the introductory article. When economic profits continue to exist in monopolistic markets, however, there must be barriers that prevent new competitors from entering the market to take advantage of the attractive profits. Mergers, barriers to entry, and predatory business practices are covered in this section. Study Questions 3 and 4 will help students understand the different categories of mergers. Study Question 5 brings out the differing effects on the economy of mergers in already concentrated industries, compared to mergers in competitive industries. Study Question 6 raises the possibility that in some instances mergers might benefit market structure.

Case Application: Does One and One Make Three? Is a Merger of Two Firms Worth More Than They Were Worth Separately?

The near tidal wave of merger acquisitions in recent years has made a major contribution to increasing concentration in industry. This application discusses the motivations for business takeovers and the consequences for the firms involved and for the economy as a whole.

Answers to the "For Thought" Questions

1. What type of merger is represented by the R. J. Reynolds acquisition of Nabisco Brands? Why?

The merger of R. J. Reynolds and Nabisco represents a conglomerate merger because the two firms produce in different industries.

2. How might mergers affect the barriers to entry?

Mergers are likely to increase barriers to entry by creating firms with larger capital assets and more market power. This would make it more difficult for new firms to enter the industry in competition with the established firms. This is particularly true in industries where advertising is a major consideration in the market. Larger firms can take advantage of economies of scale in their advertising expenditures which smaller firms cannot match.

3. Have takeovers gone too far? Should Congress impose curbs? Should the Securities and Exchange Commission have tighter regulations, for example, on leveraged buyouts? What actions should or should not be taken and why?

Open answer. Opinion is growing that takeovers have gone too far and that Congress should impose curbs and/or the Securities and Exchange Commission should tighten up regulations, such as making the issuance of "junk bonds" more difficult. Those who advocate such actions believe that the only beneficiaries of these takeovers are the speculators, that the takeovers are detrimental to the businesses involved, and that they absorb too much of the available investment capital. Those who oppose restrictions on takeovers maintain that a takeover can replace inefficient management of a business with more efficient executive control and that even the threat of possible takeover keeps management on its toes, which benefits the stockholders. They hold that this is an important ingredient in an efficient, dynamic economic system.

What Are the Consequences of Concentration in Industry?

Most people object to monopolistic firms because they charge unnecessarily high prices and make "unfair" monopoly profits. The economic analysis in this section shows that there are some other, less widely recognized disadvantages of monopolistic industries—such as misallocation of resources, inefficient production, and contributions to economic instability. Study Question 8 provides the student with the opportunity to use the theory of the firm pricing model. Study Question 9 examines the controversial acquisition of foreign direct investment in this country in terms of its effect on market concentration and conduct.

Case Application: Automobile Industry Shifts Gears

The automobile industry, arguably the most important of our industries in its overall impact on the economy, became more and more concentrated over the years as different makers failed or merged with other firms. When the industry was reduced to four producers, with General Motors dominating the field, it became a complacent and relatively unresponsive industry. It was shaken out of its lethargy by growing import competition, especially from the Japanese. In recent years the industry has been undergoing some revolutionary changes in management practices.

Answers to the "For Thought" Questions

1. What are indications of monopolistic pricing in the past behavior of the American automobile industry?

Indications of monopolistic pricing include price leadership, extensive advertising expenditures and other non-price competition, and the failure of firms in the industry to cut prices when there were conditions of oversupply in the market.

2. How has the pricing/output behavior of automobile firms affected economic stability? Explain.

The automobile industry has contributed to economic instability by attempting to hold the price line on their products during recessions and lagging sales, choosing instead to cut back production and lay off workers.

3. Is competition from Japanese and other foreign car producers a good thing or a bad thing? Why?

Open answer. Competition from imports has forced American automobile producers to be more responsive to consumer desires, to improve the quality of their products, and to increase production efficiency by automation and changed management practices. As a result, automobile buyers get more for their money. On the other side, competition from foreign imports has taken jobs from U.S. autoworkers and threatens to put the weakest of the American car firms out of business altogether.

Perspective: An Imperfect World

This Perspective introduces students to an outstanding economist and world-famous figure who has the added distinction of having been one of the few women in a traditionally male-dominated profession. Joan Violet Robinson established her credentials early in her career as a theoretical economist, and then went on to challenge economic orthodoxy. She continued in the forefront of critical analysis well into her later years. Study Question 10 asks the student to reexamine the meaning of pure competition by explaining why it was considered a special case by Robinson.

Answers to Study Questions

1. According to Table 1 (p.138), what is the most highly concentrated industry in America? What are the firms that constitute the concentration in that industry?

   The most highly concentrated industry is motor vehicles and car bodies, with a concentration ratio of 93%. Although there are 254 firms in the industry, most of them are small producers of specialty products, and the industry is dominated by General Motors, Ford, and Chrysler.

2. What are three businesses in your locality that are in industries with very low concentration ratios nationally (see Table 1)? Do any of them have a high degree of market concentration in their own marketing area? How can you tell?

   Open answer. Students may cite local printers, dairies, or bakeries as examples of firms in industries with low concentration ratios nationally. Depending on the concentration of population in the particular area, however, there may not be very many of these firms in the industry serving that market. If so, the industries would have a high degree of market concentration in their own marketing area.

3. Which of the following mergers would be horizontal, which vertical, and which conglomerate?

   The answers are: a) vertical; b) horizontal; c) vertical; and d) conglomerate.

4. What large mergers have been reported in the news within the past year? Were they horizontal, vertical, or conglomerate mergers?

   Open answer. Mergers, both hostile and negotiated, are repeatedly in the news. A notable merger that occurred after the text went to press was that between Chrysler and American Motors.

5. How does the merger of two oil companies differ in its effect on the economy from the merger of two printing companies?

   The merger of two oil companies has a significant effect in increasing monopolistic market conditions in the petroleum industry and increasing aggregate concentration in the economy as a whole. The merger of two printing companies would not have a significant impact in increasing monopoly either in the national printing market or in aggregate concentration, although

   it might result in a significant increase in local market concentration.

6. Under what conditions could a merger improve competition in a market?

   A merger could improve competition in a market if it joined two small and relatively weak firms in an industry dominated by a few large firms.

7. If patent laws help create monopolies, why are they not repealed? What useful purposes do patent laws serve?

   Patent laws are considered desirable because they encourage the invention of new products and innovations in producing existing products.

8. How do monopolies manage to keep prices higher than they would be in a competitive market? Why do they not raise their prices even higher?

   Monopolies manage to keep prices higher than they would be in a competitive market by restricting the supply. They do not raise the prices even higher because that would necessitate reducing supply even more, and the reduction in revenue (MR) would be greater than the reduction in production costs (MC).

9. Has investment by Japanese firms in automobile production facilities in the U.S. improved the allocation of resources? What are the reasons for your answer?

   This question is related to, but more focused than, the third question in the last Case Application of the chapter. Whatever the objections to foreign investment in one of our basic industries, it is likely that Japanese investment in the U.S. automobile industry has improved the allocation of resources by making the industry more competitive, improving technology and management practices in the industry, and giving the consumer more choice.

10. Why is pure competition a "special case" in economics?

    Pure competition is a special case in economics because it represents an extreme situation of a large number of sellers and buyers of a standardized product that can individually have no appreciable affect on market prices. Since it also implies an absence of government intervention in the market, there are few real-life examples of pure competition, even in agriculture. That is why Robinson considered it a special case.

Integrating *Economics U$A* Programs

(For information on Economics U$A *see the introduction, p. v.)*

The most appropriate program for this chapter is program 20, "Oligopolies: Whatever Happened to Price Competition?" Oligopolies are the type of shared monopolies in which there is no formal agreement among the firms in the industry, as there is with cartels. But even without formal agreements, there is not much price competition. The application on the evolution of the automobile industry shows how General Motors managed to avoid price competition with Ford and succeeded by using product differentiation and advertising. Gill shows that the result in the industry was prices, costs, and profits that were too high. The electrical equipment industry conspiracy case illustrates the lengths oligopolies will go to in avoiding price competition, in this case even to the extent of committing felonies.

In discussing the first application in the program recommended for the next chapter, "Monopoly: Who's In Control?" (program 19), Gill analyzes why the problem with monopolies is that output is too low and prices and profits are too high.

Case Applications in Student Workbook

(Answers are supplied to students in the workbook.)

How Monopolistic Is American Industry?

Case Application: Rent-a-Kidney Business: Dialysis for Profit?

This application discusses a small industry in which there is a high degree of concentration. Because it is a life-or-death situation for people who need the services of the industry, the government has become involved.

Answers to the "For Thought" Questions

1. How would you classify the home dialysis equipment industry with respect to the type of market structure in the industry?

   The home dialysis equipment industry is a shared monopoly. One firm sells almost 50% of all home equipment sold.

2. Does the hospital-based dialysis service industry have the same market structure as the home dialysis equipment industry? How can you judge from the information in the application whether the two industries operate in the same type of market?

   The hospital-based dialysis service industry does not have the same market structure as the home dialysis equipment industry. National Medical Care, the largest firm, has only 16% of the hospital-based business. Consequently, it can be concluded that the largest four firms have less than 50% of the industry sales.

3. The government dialysis program has increased the profitability of firms such as National Medical Care. Is this justified? Why or why not?

Open answer. The government program to pay the costs of dialysis treatment has made it possible for people to receive the treatment who otherwise would have died from kidney disease. It could be argued that such humanitarian programs should not be tainted with large profits being siphoned off by private industry. Others would argue that the private firms provide the service more economically than the government would if dialysis services were provided directly by government agencies. Furthermore, it is not unusual for firms doing business under government programs to make high profits because such programs are frequently in new areas of technology and involve high business risks, as for example the defense industries.

What Are the Causes of Concentration in Industry?

Case Application: Winning Strategies

This application discusses the strategies which are being proposed by business consultants to help firms increase their market shares. Some of the winning strategies proposed verge on predatory business practices.

Answers to the "For Thought" Questions

1. Would one of the business consulting strategists be likely to recommend price discrimination as a way of taking business away from rivals? Why or why not?

   The business consulting strategists would not be likely to recommend price discrimination as a way of taking business away from rivals because price discrimination is illegal.

2. Which of Professor Porter's three strategies would be most appropriate for a firm with significant economies of scale?

   The strategy of Professor Porter which would be most appropriate for a firm with significant economies of scale would be the "overall cost leadership" strategy. This strategy would be the most appropriate when there are sizeable economies of scale because the larger the sales of the firm, the lower would be the cost of each unit produced. This would enable the firm to undersell its competitors and drive them out of the market.

3. What strategies to drive competitors out of business do you consider fair, if any?

   Open answer. One attitude is that anything is fair in love, war, and business. Survival of the fittest is a fundamental part of the free enterprise system. The contrary opinion is that there have to be rules of behavior in business because otherwise it is not the most efficient firms that survive but the most unscrupulous. One business strategy which has come under increasing attack is that of influencing government regulations to prevent new firms from entering the industry.

What Are the Consequences of Concentration in Industry?

Case Application: Rx Profits

An industry in which prices have risen most rapidly is the health care industry. There are different reasons for this rapid price rise, but one factor was the monopolistic character of health care services. Whatever the justification for limiting competition in the field (e.g., protecting the quality of health care services), it contributes to higher costs.

Answers to the "For Thought" Questions

1. How does the American Medical Association foster monopolistic pricing in health care?

   The American Medical Association fosters monopolistic pricing by discouraging doctors from competing in the prices for their services—specifically not allowing advertising.

2. What were the consequences of monopolistic pricing in the health care field?

   The consequences of monopolistic pricing in the health care field were a rapid rise in health care costs that contributed to inflation and increased costs of government and employer health plans. It also resulted in some people in need of health care being priced out of the market and an excess of physicians in some specialities and in some large metropolitan areas.

3. Which is the better system for delivery of health care— fee-for-service in which the patient (or employer or insurance company) pays for each treatment or health maintenance organizations which collect a fixed monthly premium per subscriber? Why?

   Open answer. The medical establishment believes in a fee-for-service health care system because doctors have a greater interest in their personal patients, and the doctor-patient relationship is important to good care. Many patients prefer to be able to choose the doctor that treats them. The advocates of HMOs maintain that it is a more efficient and more equitable system which keeps down costs and provides health care for more people.

Chapter 7

Government and Business

Chapter Overview

The government's role as producer and regulator in the private sector is the subject of much debate, and this chapter examines the ways in which the government intrudes in this sector. The introductory article deals with the forced divestment by AT&T of local telephone service companies.

The first section of the chapter follows up the preceding chapter's discussion of industry concentration and the problems which arise because of monopolistic markets. It discusses the antitrust laws that have been passed to deal with monopoly and the regulation of such natural monopolies as the public utilities. It concludes with a discussion of the recent moves to deregulate many industries. The case application covers the controversy over how vigorously the antitrust laws should be enforced.

The chapter's second section deals with the government's role as a producer of goods and services. The case application concerns local public transit systems and their problems.

The last section of the chapter covers the government agencies which regulate various aspects of economic activity such as consumer, worker, and environmental protection. Its case application looks at the problem of acid rain.

Suggested Answers to the Learning Objectives

The knowledge acquired from this chapter should enable the students to:

1. Explain the purposes of the Interstate Commerce Act and the Sherman, Clayton, and Celler-Kefauver Acts.

   The Interstate Commerce Act ended the monopolistic and discriminatory practices of the railroads and set up the Interstate Commerce Commission to regulate the railroad industry and enforce the provisions of the act. The purposes of the Sherman Act were to prevent monopoly and monopolistic practices in industries over which the federal government had jurisdiction. The Clayton Act made the antimonopoly provisions of the Sherman Act enforceable by specifying what anticompetitive actions were illegal (such as the

   acquisition of stock in competing companies and price discrimination that injured competition). The Celler-Kefauver Act retarded the movement toward increased concentration by prohibiting certain types of mergers.

2. List the causes of natural monopoly and indicate what industries fall under that classification.

   Natural monopolies exist when the economies of scale are so extensive that a single firm can supply the whole market more efficiently than could two or more firms. The public utilities fall into this classification.

3. Explain how public policy deals with natural monopolies.

   Government bodies enfranchise a single firm to service a particular area, and they set up public utility commissions to regulate the pricing and services provided by the firm in order to prevent exploitation of its monopoly position.

4. Discuss the positive and negative aspects of regulation.

   By regulating prices and services, the government can prevent monopolistic firms from exploiting their monopoly power. This is the reason for regulating natural monopolies. Regulation of other industries was intended to foster competition. The difficulties of public utility regulation are ensuring both adequate service to consumers and a fair return to the investors. Regulation of some other industries in practice actually restricted competition.

5. Explain the reasons for and the consequences of deregulation.

   One of the purposes of deregulation was to achieve a more rational allocation of the nation's resources. Another was to introduce competition into industries where it had been stifled by the regulatory agencies. The consequences have been more competition and lower prices in some industries such as airlines and a readjustment of relative prices for different services in such industries such as communications. Other consequences have been that some firms were forced to shut down or merge, workers lost their jobs or suffered pay cuts, and sometimes customers were inconvenienced.

6. Identify the kinds of goods and services that constitute collective goods, and explain why the government provides them.

    Collective goods are goods and services which are so valuable to the public that they justify their costs, but which are not profitable for the private sector to provide. The government provides them because their total benefits to society as a whole are greater than their total costs.

7. Describe the concepts of external economies and external costs.

    External economies occur when third parties receive benefits from a good or service for which they make no payments. External costs are costs imposed on those other than the producer or purchaser of a good or service.

8. Explain how external economies and external costs are dealt with through government actions and internalization.

    External economies are provided for by government provision of goods and services with external economies as public goods or by subsidies for their production. External costs are internalized either by requiring those causing the external costs to stop creating those costs or requiring them to pay for the amelioration of the costs.

What Does the Government Do to Regulate Monopoly?

The problems posed by monopolistic markets have spurred much government antitrust legislation since the latter part of the nineteenth century. The various antitrust laws have been able to prevent pure monopoly (except in the case of natural monopolies) but have been unable to prevent increased concentration. A major policy issue today is whether more must be done to limit the degree of market concentration, and if so, what. In the case of natural monopolies, public utility regulation has long provoked controversy between the utilities and the rate payers.

Study Questions 1 and 2 reinforce the students' knowledge of antitrust policies and laws. Study Questions 3, 4, 5, and 10 deal with the concepts of natural monopoly, public utilities, and utility regulation.

Case Application: How Much Trustbusting? —And Who to Bust?

The Justice Department under President Reagan took a much less vigorous approach to the enforcement of antitrust laws than had earlier administrations. It did not attempt to prevent mergers between large, successful firms and did not even object to horizontal mergers that obviously increased

industry concentration. It called for changes in the antitrust laws to weaken them. This move was opposed by consumer groups, the National Small Business Association, and some members of Congress.

Answers to the "For Thought" Questions

1. What are three laws that the Reagan administration did not enforce as vigorously as previous administrations?

    Three laws that were not as vigorously enforced were the Sherman Antitrust Act, the · Clayton Act, and the Celler-Kefauver Anti-merger Act.

2. What are three examples of industries, other than the automobile industry, in which competition from foreign firms is effective in holding down domestic prices? What are three examples of industries in which it is not? Why is foreign competition not a market force in the latter industries?

    Industries in which foreign competition helps to hold down domestic prices include the clothing industry, the electronics industry, the steel industry, the footwear industry, the watch industry, and the photographic equipment industry, among others. Industries in which foreign competition is not effective include automobile repair and other such service industries, food service, entertainment, public utilities, and advertising, among others. Foreign competition is not a force in these industries because they can only be provided locally or because, as in the case of industries like advertising, foreigners are not in a position to service the market.

3. Should Section 7 of the Clayton Act be repealed? Why or why not?

    Open answer. If one accepts the argument that American firms need to be unrestrained in size in order to compete effectively with foreign competition in the domestic market and in markets overseas, one might favor repeal of that section in the Clayton Act. If one believes, on the other hand, that foreign competition is not a sufficient deterrent to monopolistic practices in many American industries or that shared monopoly on an international scale might be the result, one would oppose weakening of antitrust legislation.

Why, in a Market Economy, Does the Government Produce Goods and Services?

In market economies consumer demand acts through the marketplace and profit incentives to determine what will be produced. However, we find there are widespread exceptions to this rule when governments provide goods and (especially) services. This section examines the nature of and reasons for these exceptions to the market allocation of goods and services. It discusses what types of goods and services are collective goods, the reasons for collective goods, and how their existence affects equity.

Study Questions 6, 7, and 8 reinforce the concept of collective goods and examine different aspects of why they exist Study Question 9 reinforces the concept of external economies.

Case Application: City Transit Lines Get Their Tickets Punched

Urban public transit is a common example of a collective good. This application presents many of the questions and problems associated with such collective goods. Should such goods be provided? For what purposes? How should they be paid for?

Answers to the "For Thought" Questions

1. Why are city transit systems a collective good?

   City Transit systems are a collective good because they are subsidized by government to provide a service that would not be provided by the private sector, at least not as extensively.

2. What are the external economies of metropolitan public transportation?

   The external economies of metropolitan public transportation include the stimulus to downtown businesses which the transportation service provides, the increased employment in the region which is possible because commuters can use the transit system, and the increased property values of areas served by the system.

3. Should the deficits of mass transit systems be covered by higher fares, by state and local subsidies, or by federal subsidies? Why?

   Open Answer. The deficits of mass transit systems should be covered by higher fares if our goal is to cover the costs by user fees and reduce the amount of collective goods in the economy. They should be covered by state and local subsidies if our goal is to maintain a certain level of public transportation services and have them paid for by the region where the external economies are generated.

   They should be paid by federal subsidies if our goal is to provide an equitable distribution of public transportation services around the country, regardless of the different areas' abilities to pay, and provide a high level of public transportation services.

What Is the Role of Government in Protecting Consumers, Workers, and the Environment?

In the 1970s, the federal government undertook a much wider role in regulating business firms with the establishment of the National Highway Traffic Safety Administration (1970), the Environmental Protection Agency (1970), the Occupational Safety and Health Administration (1971), and the Consumer Product Safety Commission (1972). The establishment of these various agencies was based on the assumption that the marketplace did not provide adequate protection for consumers, workers, and the environment.

Exercise in Analysis 3 helps make current the students' knowledge of regulatory agencies.

Case Application: Environmental Murder

Environmental protection is a comparatively recent activity undertaken by the federal government. There is a consensus that protecting the environment is important, but at the same time there is wide disagreement over how rigorous that protection should be. The imposition of higher antipollution standards normally involves an increase in costs for producers and consumers. The question that needs to be resolved is how much environmental protection we are willing to pay for. This application focuses on the controversial current issue concerning acid rain.

Answers to the "For Thought" Questions

1. What external costs are produced in the electric power industry? Why are they considered external costs?

   The main external cost of the nonnuclear electric power industry is air pollution, especially that resulting from burning high sulphur content coal. (The external costs associated with nuclear electric power production were discussed in the case application for the second section of chapter 2.) They are considered external costs because they impose a cost burden on persons other than the electric power company and its customers. Acid rain, for instance, imposes a cost on the general public in destruction of forests and water habitats in recreational areas, hurting businesses dependent on the recreation industry, and raising the prices of timber products.

2. How can external costs in the industry be internalized?

   External costs are internalized by forcing the electric utility companies to take preventive measures to reduce or eliminate air pollution. These measures include the use of expensive low-sulphur coal and/or installation of air scrubbers for smoke stacks.

3. Should the electric utility companies be required to install expensive antipollution equipment before the exact cause of the environmental damage is known, or should action be delayed until cause and effect relationships are proven? Why?

   Open answer. The answer to this question depends on how one compares the value of a clean environment to the cost of antipollution measures. Those who feel strongly about environmental protection believe that the cost of cleaning up air pollution is well worth the price. Those who are more concerned about rising utility rates and a higher cost of living, especially perhaps for low-income groups, might argue for more proof that costly antipollution measures are actually needed before requiring them.

Perspective: The Interstate Highway to Serfdom

The title of the Perspective is a play on words of *The Road to Serfdom*, the best known book of Friedrich Hayek. Hayek is opposed to almost all of the government activities described in this chapter. The Perspective presents his philosophy and his position on the issues.

Answers to Study Questions

1. In what ways did monopolistic practices in the late nineteenth century frustrate the functioning of a free market?

   In market economies, goods and services should be produced whenever the prices that consumers are willing to pay are sufficient to cover the costs of production. The practice in monopolistic markets, however, is to restrict production in order to raise the price above the costs of production, thereby frustrating the function of the market.

2. How did the various laws passed by the federal government deal with the monopolistic abuses of certain industries?

   The laws passed by the federal government lessened the degree of concentration, prevented specific anticompetitive practices, and established agencies to regulate and prevent monopolistic behavior.

3. Would you agree or disagree with the statement, "Once a natural monopoly, always a natural monopoly"? Why?

   Industries that were natural monopolies at one time, because the existing technology made such monopolies more feasible, may someday not be natural monopolies because of technological innovations. Long-distance telephone communication is one example, as is rail transportation which lost its monopoly with the development of highway transport. Even electric power production may be moving away from monopoly control as a result of new technology in small-scale electric power production.

4. How are natural monopolies, such as utility companies, prevented from indulging in monopolistic practices?

   Public utility commissions have been established to regulate the prices and the services natural monopolies provide.

5. Why should investors in utility companies be guaranteed a fair return on their investments? How would a fair return be determined?

   Investors in utility companies should be guaranteed a fair return on their investments to assure that investment capital will continue to flow into the industry for replacement, modernization, and expansion of utility services. A fair return is a normal profit rate—that rate of return which equals the expected profitability of other investments with a comparable degree of risk.

6. Have you used any public goods (services) in the past week? What are they? Could you have gotten them from the private sector?

   Open answer. Answers might include riding the bus, attending school, or going to the public library. In some cases, similar services could have been obtained from the private sector, but usually at higher and possibly prohibitive costs. Private taxis are a substitute for public buses, private schools for public schools, and the purchase of books and periodicals for the use of libraries.

7. Why does the government subsidize public transportation when most people don't use it?

   The government subsidizes public transportation because it has external economies that benefit people who do not ride it. These external economies include a reduction in traffic and parking congestion, a reduction in the expenditures needed for expanding highway capacity, reduction in air pollution, and commercial economic benefits to businesses served by it. Such subsidies also contribute to the goal of greater equity, since the poor make extensive use of public transit.

8. What would happen if the government got out of the lighthouse business? Would lighthouses be provided by private industry?

   If the government did not build and maintain lighthouses, it is difficult to believe private industry would find it profitable to do so. There would be no feasible way to collect users' fees without some authority enforcing their collection, which would thus involve the government.

9. What are some external economies derived from goods or services that you have benefited from, but have not used or paid for yourself?

   Open answer. Examples might include automobile mufflers (on other motorists' cars) and lawns around neighbors' houses (keeping down the dust and increasing the attractiveness of a neighborhood).

10. Prior to the 1970s, it was common practice for utility companies to give discounts on quantity consumption by large users of electrical power, thus promoting increased power consumption. Today, utility companies give their lowest rates to their smallest consumers—thereby promoting conservation of electrical power. Why do you think this reversal of policy has taken place?

The earlier policy of giving discounts for large consumers of electrical power was based on the assumption that the economies of scale in the electric power industry would result in lower production costs per unit of power with increased consumption. Today, increased power consumption requires construction of expanded production facilities that have much higher construction costs than did earlier plants and equipment. This would raise the average costs of production. Also, with the increased relative scarcity of energy resources, expanded consumption drives up energy prices.

Integrating *Economics U$A* Programs

(For information on Economics U$A *see the introduction, p. v.)*

Program 19 on "Monopoly: Who's in Control?" contains applications reinforcing part of the content in this chapter. The first application shows how public resentment against the monopolistic practices of John D. Rockefeller's Standard Oil trust prompted the passage of the Sherman Act in 1890. The second application deals with the subject of the chapter introductory article, AT&T. It explains the rationale for natural monopolies and how new technology—microwave communications in this case—can eliminate the basis for an existing natural monopoly.

Another program, 26, on "Public Goods and Responsibility: How Far Should We Go?," asks the same question asked in the second section of the chapter—"Why must government provide goods and services instead of private industry?" In answering the question it reviews the reasons for the establishment of the Tennessee Valley Authority. Analyst Gill provides the rationale for public goods. You may or may not want to show the rest of the program depending on your time considerations. The main thing it accomplishes is to raise the question of how much of public goods we are willing to pay for. This question is probably better left for discussion in connection with chapter 15 on Public Finance after having covered income distribution and poverty in chapter 9 and government revenues, expenditures, deficits, and the national debt in chapter 15.

A third program in the series is relevant for the third section of the chapter, program 21 on "Pollution: How Much Is a Clean Environment Worth?" The first application

examines the problem of pollution of Lake Superior by mine tailings. Gill explains "negative externalities of production," i. e., external costs. He shows how social costs may differ from production costs, and why, when this happens, the market solution to allocation turns out not to be the best solution. The second application deals with the Clean Air Act and the establishment of the Environmental Protection Agency. This is followed by a cost-benefit analysis of the problem and Gill's explanation of how the external costs were internalized.

Case Applications in Student Workbook

(Answers are supplied to students in the workbook.)

What Does the Government Do to Regulate Monopoly?

Case Application: Water, Water, Everywhere, and Not a Drop (That's Fit) to Drink

The nationwide problem of polluted water supplies is exemplified by the case of the Boston suburbs of Dedham and Westwood where the water provided by the local water company was too polluted to even do the washing with, much less drink. The solution was the establishment of a public utility district to buy out the water company and upgrade the facilities.

Answers to the "For Thought" Questions

1. In what way is the move toward stricter regulation of water utilities contrary to the trend in government policies?

   The trend in government policies in recent years has been to decrease the role of government in the business sector.

2. How did the fact that there was only one company supplying water to Dedham and Westwood result in the problems they were having in obtaining satisfactory water?

   The fact that there was only one company supplying water to Dedham and Westwood meant that, even though the citizens were extremely unhappy with the water they were getting, they had no choice but to buy it. Since a water utility is a natural monopoly, there was no competition to force an improvement in the service.

3. Should government intervene to insure the purity of water supplies, whatever the cost? Why or why not?

   Open answer. Water is essential to life, and the purity of our water supplies is important to us. We look to government to protect the interests of the public, especially where natural monopolies are concerned. On the other side of the question is the argument that we cannot afford absolute purity of water or practically anything else. (Besides, there is no such thing as completely pure water unless it is distilled, and distilled water is not recommended for drinking on a regular basis because it lacks the minerals our body needs.) The market is a better regulator of business than the government. If people are dissatisfied with the water from the tap, they can purchase bottled water.

Why, in a Market Economy, Does the Government Produce Goods and Services?

Case Application: Should the Government Be in the Railroad Business?

This application examines how the government got into the business of operating railroads—Amtrak and Conrail—and whether or not it should get out of the railroad business.

Answers to the "For Thought" Questions

1. Can the government subsidy of Amtrak be justified in terms of equity? Why or why not?

   The government subsidy of Amtrak cannot be justified in terms of equity because it is not primarily lower income people who take advantage of the government subsidies to rail passenger traffic.

2. Are there external economies associated with passenger rail transportation? With freight rail transportation? If so, what are they?

   There are external economies associated with rail passenger and freight traffic. Rail transportation is more energy efficient and less polluting than highway or air transportation. Railroads reduce congestion on the highways, reduce the need for petroleum, reduce air pollution, and reduce the crowding of airports and flight paths. In addition, they help towns that are too small for an airport to compete for business and to remain viable places to live because of convenient transportation.

3. Should the government dispose of Amtrak or Conrail or both? Why or why not?

   Open answer. The arguments for the government to dispose of Amtrak and Conrail are that the government should not be in competition with other transportation suppliers, that private business does a better job of resolving the allocation questions than government agencies, and that the government can save the money it spends on subsidies to Amtrak and can obtain a substantial amount of money from the sale of Conrail. The arguments against disposing of them are: the reason the government took them over in the first place was because as private railroads they were neither serving the public well nor making profits; the

government has invested a great deal in upgrading them; ridership on Amtrak is increasing and the government subsidy diminishing; Conrail is returning a profit to the government; and railroads are an essential component of a nation's transportation system, with substantial external economies, that many communities and individuals would sorely miss if they were terminated.

What Is the Role of Government in Protecting Consumers, Workers, and the Environment?

Case Application: Declaration of Air Pollution Emergency

In 1975 in an area northeast of Pittsburgh, Pennsylvania, air pollution reached a dangerous level requiring emergency action. This case describes the measures taken to meet the emergency. It raises the question of what needs to be done to prevent such emergencies from recurring. This illustrates the concept of external costs, the method of internalizing those external costs, and the results of doing so.

Answers to the "For Thought" Questions

1. What external costs were associated with steel production in Allegheny County?

   The external costs associated with steel production in Allegheny County included air pollution, which resulted in many health problems, and decreased visibility which interfered with traffic.

2. What would the U.S. Steel Corporation have to do to internalize the external costs of its steel production operations? What would happen to the price and quantity of steel production when external costs are internalized? Explain your answer by a graph of demand and supply.

   In order to internalize the external costs of its steel production operations, the U.S. Steel Corporation would have to install fabric filters for electric arcs, high-energy wet scrubbers for open-hearth and basic-oxygen furnaces, and electrostatic precipitators for smokestacks. This would increase production costs, which would raise the price of steel and reduce the quantity of steel production. This can be shown on a demand-supply diagram by a shift of the supply curve to the left. The equilibrium price on the new supply curve is higher and the equilibrium quantity lower than on the previous supply curve.

3. Should U.S. Steel be forced to internalize its external costs even though that would result in increased unemployment in the Pittsburgh area? Why or why not?

   Open answer. Those who believe reducing air pollution and the effects it has on health and safety are the most important considerations would favor forcing U.S. Steel to internalize its external costs. Those who believe unemployment is the most important consideration would not.

Chapter 8

Labor

Chapter Overview

Labor is the most important of the factor resource inputs. Most people sustain themselves with income from labor. This chapter examines the determination of labor income—wages and salaries—and other conditions affecting jobs. (The determination of the other factor incomes—rents, interest, and profits—is covered in the following chapter.) The introductory article discusses the controversial topic of immigration (legal and illegal), its effect on jobs and its contribution to the output of goods and services.

The first section discusses the labor market forces of demand and supply and other influences on wages such as minimum wage laws and labor unions. The case application discusses how the sharp decline in the number of young workers entering the labor force (a "baby bust" generation instead of a "baby boom" generation) will affect wages and other employment conditions.

The second section of the chapter discusses the activities of labor unions and their effects. The case application concerns the move to establish two-tier pay systems.

The chapter's third section examines workers' employment objectives and needs, both monetary and nonmonetary. The case application looks at how the composition of the job market is expected to change between now and the end of the century.

Suggested Answers to the Learning Objectives

The knowledge acquired in this chapter should enable the students to:

1. Explain what determines the demand for and supply of labor and how demand and supply influence wages.

   The demand for labor is derived from the demand for the product which labor produces. It also depends upon the productivity of labor—the higher labor's productivity, the higher will be the demand for it. The supply of labor in total depends upon the size of the population and the proportion of the population which participates in the labor force in a given society. The supply of labor in a particular occupation depends upon the qualifications required for that occupation and the amount of education and training necessary to meet those qualifications. Just as demand and supply
   determine the prices of products, so the demand for and supply of labor determine wage rates.

2. Describe the effects of minimum wage laws.

   Minimum wage laws protect workers from being exploited. They can influence how goods are produced and may reduce the availability of certain types of jobs.

3. Discuss how mechanization affects labor demand and wages.

   Mechanization replaces labor with equipment. This displaces workers and causes a fall in their wages. On the other hand, by reducing the costs of production, mechanization can increase the market for the product and increase the total jobs available. By raising labor productivity, it leads to higher wages for labor as a whole.

4. Explain what labor unions do and describe the laws that affect union activities.

   Labor unions bargain collectively for their members concerning wages, working conditions, grievance procedures, fringe benefits, and the reform of hiring and firing practices. The basic law legitimizing unions is the National Labor Relations Act (Wagner Act). Some states have right-to-work laws that prohibit union shop provisions in collective bargaining agreements requiring all workers to join the union.

5. Explain what "sticky" wages are and discuss their impacts in labor markets.

   Wages tend to be "sticky" because they do not fall readily even when unemployment is rising. Union contracts reinforce the resistance to lowering wages. The consequence is that when demand falls in an industry there is a greater decline in production and employment in the industry than would be the case if wages were more flexible, reducing production costs.

6. List the differences between the different types of strikes and boycotts.

   A strike is a collective refusal by employees to work. A sympathy strike is a strike by employees in one union to show support for striking workers in another union. A general strike is a strike by all workers in a given geographical area regardless of occupation. A wildcat strike is a strike that is not authorized by the union organization. A primary boycott is a refusal to purchase or handle the products of a firm undergoing a labor conflict. A secondary boycott is a refusal to patronize or handle the goods of a firm that does business with a struck firm.

7. Explain what jurisdictional disputes are and why they are becoming increasingly important to unions.

   Jurisdictional disputes are conflicts between two or more unions over which one shall represent a specific group of workers. They are becoming more important to unions because the decline in union members in heavy industry has caused unions to look to other sectors to recruit members.

8. Describe the principal concerns of workers regarding their jobs.

   The principal concerns of workers regarding their jobs are job security; income, including fringe benefits; vacation, holiday, and personal leave time; health, safety, and pleasant working conditions; and the amount of psychic satisfaction derived from the job.

What Determines Wages in a Market Economy?

This section explains the various factors that affect the labor market—the demand for the goods or services produced by labor, the productivity of labor (and how that productivity is affected by technology and capital investment), minimum wage laws, and labor unions.

Study Questions 1 and 2 call for the student to analyze the demand side of the labor market. Study Question 3 examines the difference in the behavior of labor supply compared to the supply of other things. Study Question 4 analyzes the relationship between wage changes and productivity changes and the effects on product prices. Study Questions 5 and 6 analyze the effects of minimum wage laws on employment and labor unions on productivity.

Case Application: "Baby Bust" Generation Replacing "Baby Boom" Generation

This application examines the career problems of the members of the "baby boom" generation as it is reflected in the supply side of the labor market. Because the succeeding generation is substantially smaller, the oversupply in the labor market may change to a situation of scarcity.

Answers to the "For Thought" Questions

1. How has the baby boom generation affected the supply of labor? How has it affected the demand for labor?

   As the baby boom generation entered the labor market, it created a bulge in the supply of labor. While it also increased the demand for labor because of the
increased population consumption, the demand effects were more spread out (over time and over different work experience levels) so the demand effect did not offset the increased supply of labor enough to prevent an oversupply for that generation's age group.

2. What effect will the declining number of baby bust workers entering the labor force have on the amount of investment in capital equipment by companies? How will this affect workers' wages? Why?

   The decline in the number of new workers entering the labor force will cause companies to increase their investments in capital equipment as a substitute for labor. This investment will cause workers' wages to rise above present levels because the net value of labor will increase due to higher productivity.

3. Speaking as a member of the baby bust generation, do you see any economic problems arising from the small size of that generation? If so, what are the economic problems?

   Open answer. The small size of the baby bust generation has already created problems in certain sectors of the economy, such as the baby food and children's clothing industries. Potentially injurious effects on the economy in the future might include a shortage of manpower at the experience level for that generation. This shortage will benefit wages for those workers but reduce economic efficiency.

What Do Labor Unions Do?

This section covers the effects of unions on the labor market. It begins with a discussion of the National Labor Relations Act and collective bargaining. It also discusses the effect of wage demands on the labor market and the types of job actions employed by unions to enforce their demands.

Study Question 7 reinforces the student's understanding of the difference between labor market adjustments with flexible wage rates and labor market adjustments with rigid wage rates. Study Question 8 reinforces the understanding of the types of job actions employed by unions.

Case Application: Labor "Caste System" Creates Problems

The imposition by employers of two-tier pay systems has become very controversial. It surfaced during the 1981–1982 recession when unemployment levels were exceptionally high and labor unions were in a weak bargaining position. It was put forth as a way for U.S. firms to reduce labor costs and become more competitive with foreign producers. It generally provided that newly hired employees would be paid at a lower wage rate than that established for current employees in the collective bargaining agreement. Some unions reluctantly agreed to this "give back" as a lesser evil than further layoffs or a general wage cut. When economic conditions improved, the unions pressed for elimination of the two-tier pay schedules.

Answers to the "For Thought" Questions

1. Why did firms adopting two-tier wage systems have to get the agreement of the union in order to do so?

    It was necessary for firms to get union agreement to institute a two-tier wage schedule because it was not provided for in the existing collective bargaining agreement. If the employer had unilaterally imposed such a system, the union could have filed an unfair labor practices complaint with the National Labor Relations Board.

2. How does the two-tier wage system affect the labor market? How would you diagram the determination of wage rates and the number of workers hired under a system of two-tier wages?

    The two-tier wage system increases the number of workers hired in labor markets where it exists. Because the marginal labor cost is lower for workers hired at the lower wage rate, employers are willing to hire a larger number of workers. This would be shown on a diagram of the labor market by indicating the point on the demand curve for labor that shows the number of workers hired at the original wage rate and adding to that the additional number of workers that would be hired at the lower wage rate.

3. Is a two-tier wage system a good idea? Why or why not?

    Open answer. Supporters of the two-tier wage system argue that it creates more employment opportunities than would otherwise exist, reduces production costs and prices, and enables American firms to compete with foreign producers. Those opposed to the system claim that it creates resentment on the part of the lower paid workers, causing friction among workers on the job, and that it is misused by employers to get rid of senior employees on the higher wage track in order to replace them with lower paid new hires.

What Do Workers Want?

Discussions of the labor market and unions are generally focused on wages and salaries. However, workers are interested in much more than the monetary rewards connected with their jobs. There is evidence that they are more concerned about job security than about pay, and job satisfaction is an important aspect of work.

Study Question 9 has the student analyze the differences among high-wage and low-wage industries as shown in Table 1 on page 196 of the textbook. This consideration brings in the concept of industry concentration

covered in chapter 6. Study Question 10 considers what is currently happening in the labor movement.

Case Application: **Where Jobs Are Going in the 1990s**

This application discusses the changes in the composition of the labor force—the shift from agriculture and manufacturing occupations to white-collar and service jobs—that has been occurring and looks at the projected occupational distribution for 1995.

Answers to the "For Thought" Questions

1. If you are interested in job security, what types of occupations should you consider? What types should you avoid?

    The greatest job security will be in the expanding professional and technical fields where the largest demand will be in coming years. Agricultural and manufacturing jobs have little security, as do most jobs that require no training or skills. Occupations that may be displaced by technological change are also insecure.

2. Many former blue-collar workers who were laid off as a result of employment declines in heavy industry found that wages in the available white-collar and service jobs do not pay as much as they were previously earning. Why are their earnings not as great in those jobs?

    One reason is that there was more investment in capital equipment in heavy industry, making labor more productive. Another reason is the greater power that labor unions exerted in the blue-collar industries, obtaining "monopoly" returns for their workers. A third reason is the relatively more pleasant working conditions in the white-collar and service occupations, resulting in a larger supply of willing workers at lower wages.

3. Less than half of the auto workers and steelworkers, although among the highest paid workers, would choose the same line of work again. Why do you think there is such widespread dissatisfaction among employees in those occupations?

    Open answer. Likely reasons are the lack of job security in recent times and the unpleasant, sometimes dangerous, working conditions. Also, the way U.S. workers in those industries were used in earlier periods provided them with little job satisfaction, which may still be the case in many instances.

Perspective: **The Haymarket Affair**

The clash between labor demonstrators and police in Chicago's Haymarket Square in 1886 was an event that achieved worldwide notoriety. It was a milestone of labor union history because the railroading of the labor organizers in the subsequent trial generated a great deal of sympathy for the union movement. Many of those active in the labor movement today are still sensitive to the persecution of the union movement in its earlier years.

Answers to Study Questions

1. How would an increase in the demand for a product affect the wages of workers in that industry? Why?

    An increase in the demand for a product would tend to raise the wages of workers in that industry because, since the demand for labor is derived from the demand for the product, it would shift the demand in the labor market to the right, thus raising wages (unless the supply of labor in that industry is perfectly elastic).

2. What effects does the use of more capital equipment have on the productivity of labor in a particular industry? How can increased investment in capital equipment sometimes result in less demand for labor and at other times result in more demand for labor?

    The use of more capital equipment increases the productivity of labor. Increased capital equipment may substitute for labor and result in a decline of employment in the industry, especially if the demand for the product is inelastic. However, if the increased use of capital equipment reduces production costs and the demand for the product is sufficiently elastic, an increase in industry sales may result in more labor being needed in the industry despite the substitution of capital for labor.

3. For most things, a higher price results in a larger quantity being supplied, but higher wages for labor have led to shorter workweeks. How do you account for this?

    The reason why higher wages result in shorter workweeks is because workers make trade-offs between larger income and more leisure. When increased real wages raise living standards above a certain level, workers take further increases in their living standards in the form of more leisure time.

4. What should happen to product prices if, all other things being equal, wages increase in direct relationship to productivity? What would happen to product prices if wages increased and productivity did not?

    If wages increase in direct relationship to productivity, all other things being equal, prices would remain constant. If wages increased and productivity did not, product prices would be expected to rise.

5. How do minimum wage laws affect youth employment? What would be the effects of reducing or abolishing minimum wage laws for people under 20?

    The results of minimum wage laws are the subject of some controversy, but there is evidence that the laws reduce job opportunities for young, inexperienced workers. Reducing or abolishing minimum wage laws for people under 20 could be expected to increase job opportunities for those people. However, the extent to which this would be due to an increase in the total number of jobs available or a substitution of workers under 20 for those over 20 is uncertain.

6. In what ways might labor unions affect the rate of technological development?

    Labor unions could, and have on occasion in the past, slow the rate of technological development in some industries by contract restrictions on substituting capital for labor (so-called "featherbedding"). But those cases are the exceptions. The general rule is that union demands for higher wages accelerate the rate of technological development by stimulating firms to substitute capital for the increasingly expensive labor input.

7. What is the difference between the neoclassical assumptions about wage adjustments and the assumptions of contemporary economists?

    The neoclassical economists assumed that wage rates were flexible and that when there was a surplus of labor at existing wage rates, the wage rate would fall to an equilibrium level at which all labor would be employed. Contemporary economists recognize that wage rates tend to be sticky in the downward direction, and that a surplus of labor may exist for a long period of time without wage rates declining.

8. In what ways can union members legally support their demands for higher wages and better working conditions?

    The legal ways in which union members can support their demands for higher wages and better working conditions are strikes and primary boycotts.

9. What differences between U.S. industries result in some being high-wage industries and others being low-wage industries?,

    The major differences between high- and low-wage industries are the degree of monopolistic price-setting power the firms hold in their industries and the strength of the unions in enforcing wage demands in the industries' labor markets. These differences are accounted for by the extent of industry concentration in the product markets and the relatively inelastic demand for labor in the labor markets.

10. What new directions is the labor movement taking in the United States? What are the potential benefits or the potential dangers of these changes?

    The labor movement in the United States is assuming a more active role in decision making in firms. There is joint labor-management decision making through the appointment of union representatives to the boards of directors of some companies. The potential benefits of this development are increased cooperation, leading to increased efficiency and more worker satisfaction. The potential dangers are that the labor movement might be co-opted and that a bureaucratic stalemate will replace the dynamic labor-management interaction of the past.

Integrating *Economics U$A* Programs

(For information on Economics U$A *see the introduction, p. v.)*

The appropriate program for this chapter is 22, "Labor and Management: How Do They Come To Terms?" Its first application deals with the same topic as the chapter's introductory article—immigrant labor—but in a historical context. It discusses the role immigrants played in the labor movement early in this century, specifically concerning the emergence of the International Lady Garment Workers Union. Economist Gill examines the impact of unions on working conditions and wages. He compares the determination of wages in the labor market without unions to the outcome with unions. He shows how it results in a trade-off between higher wages and the number of jobs.

The next application illustrates the effect of new production technology on jobs and wages with computerized typesetting displacing members of the typesetters union, creating labor strife in which both sides can lose if it is badly handled. Gill illustrates the cases of successful and unsuccessful adaptation to changing technology by means of diagrams.

The final case concerns the successful cooperation between the auto workers union and Chrysler to prevent the company's collapse in the 1970s. It shows some of the reasons for the move toward more worker involvement in management.

Case Applications in Student Workbook

(Answers are supplied to students in the workbook.)

What Determines Wages in a Market Economy?

Case Application: Coal and Black Gold

This application illustrates a common dilemma confronting labor unions. Is it preferable to have a maximum number of workers employed in the industry, even at low wages, or is it better to force technological innovation by demanding higher wages and end up with fewer workers in the industry, but with those workers enjoying a higher standard of living? The choice of the United Mine Workers under John L. Lewis was to opt for higher wages for the miners with fewer job opportunities in the industry.

Answers to the "For Thought" Questions

1. In terms of the principles of derived demand, how do you explain the loss of jobs in coal mines after 1941?

   The loss of jobs in coal mines after 1941 can be explained in part by the substitution of petroleum for coal. Since the demand for coal miners is derived from the demand for coal, the substitution of petroleum for coal in many uses reduced the number of jobs available in coal mining.

2. What was the relationship between the efforts of John L. Lewis to raise the wages of coal miners and the increase in surface strip mining, using giant shovels to scoop out the coal deposits?

   The success of John L. Lewis in raising the wages of coal miners made labor in coal mining relatively more expensive than investment in capital equipment. This created a cost advantage for strip mines which use more heavy equipment and less labor.

3. Do you agree with the attitude of John L. Lewis concerning employment in coal mining? Why or why not?

   Open answer. Before John L. Lewis became president of the United Mine Workers, the wages, living standards, and working conditions of coal miners were very poor. Many died from blacklung disease, mine accidents, overwork, and poor nutrition and health care. Many generations grew up living under these conditions. Lewis believed it was better for the children of miners to be forced to seek jobs elsewhere than to continue in the mines under such circumstances. For those who remained in mining, the union succeeded in greatly improving their living standards and working conditions. The opposition to Lewis' union activity maintained that miners were free to seek other work any time they chose to, and taking away their bread and butter by forcing many mines to close due to the high labor costs was not beneficial for the miners, mine owners, other businesses which depended on the mines, or coal users.

What Do Labor Unions Do?

Case Application: Strike Three—They're All Out

The strike called by the Major League Players Association in the 1981 season generated a great deal more media coverage and public controversy than does the average strike. Because it interrupted "America's favorite pastime," and involved public celebrities, the strike's justification and issues were widely discussed.

Answers to the "For Thought" Questions

1. One of the baseball club owners is also the owner of a large brewery. Would it have been legal for the striking players to urge fans not to buy the owner's beer until the strike was settled? What would this action be called?

   Such action would not have been legal. It would have been a secondary boycott, since the players were not on strike against the brewery.

2. In baseball, players negotiate salaries individually with management. Why don't workers in other industries bargain the same way?

   The great majority of workers cannot bargain individually with management because they are easily replaceable. As individuals, they have no negotiating power.

3. Some fans felt that the baseball strike should not have been allowed. Do you think there are some strikes that should be prohibited? Which ones? Why?

   Open answer. The cases in which there is most widespread agreement about the unacceptability of strikes are those which involve the public's health and safety. These would include strikes by the military forces, policemen, firemen, or other workers providing vital services. Some would extend the prohibition of the right to strike to all public employees, including teachers. Government bodies have passed such laws, but they have proven to be difficult to enforce. Those who oppose restrictions on workers' rights to strike believe that without the threat of a strike to back up labor's demands, the workers will have no power to improve their working conditions.

What Do Workers Want?

Case Application: Quality of Work Life

This application reviews recent developments instituted to increase worker involvement in making decisions in the workplace. These programs are aimed at increasing efficiency and employee morale.

Answers to the "For Thought" Questions

1. Firms with quality-of-worklife programs have seen decreases in the number of grievances filed by workers. Which needs of workers are being met by such programs?

   The programs are meeting the psychic needs of workers to feel that they are valued employees.

2. In quality-circles, a team of workers determines who should do what particular tasks and how the work should be scheduled. The team shares information on how best to do each operation. How might this affect the psychic rewards the workers get?

   The right of the group to make autonomous decisions about production and scheduling provides increased psychic rewards to the workers because they have a part in making the decisions that affect their jobs.

3. Although there are few firms with majority worker ownership, many companies have profit sharing or stock option plans for their employees. Can workers be both employees and part owners without a conflict of interest? Explain your answer.

   Open answer. U.S. labor unions have traditionally been leery about worker participation in ownership. They have taken the position that even though only a small fraction of the worker's income may come from the ownership of shares in the company, the worker may be dissuaded from taking an aggressive position in labor-management negotiations. For example, workers may be reluctant to vote for a strike for higher wages, even though the wage is a much more significant part of their income, if the strike reduces company profits and the workers' dividends from shares that they own in the company. In recent years, however, union opposition to profit participation by workers has lessened, and profit-sharing plans are sometimes a part of contract settlements.

Chapter 9

Income Distribution

Chapter Overview

There are two ways of looking at the distribution of income. One is to look at its functional distribution—that is, how income is distributed among the different factor inputs. The other way is to look at its personal distribution, the distribution according to income size and groupings. The introductory article concerns the differences in income between the sexes. Women's incomes have improved in some areas, but the growing number of households headed by women have family incomes less than half the level of families headed by men. The proposal to establish "comparable worth" pay standards for jobs held by men and women has generated a great deal of controversy.

The first section of the chapter examines the distribution of income according to functional income shares and personal income distribution according to income classes. The case application concerns the issue of rent control.

The second section sets forth the causes of inequality in income distribution. The case application looks at the lifestyles of "average" millionaires.

The third section defines poverty and examines what groups lie below the poverty line. The case application deals with how some members of one poverty-stricken group, the American Indians, have acquired a great deal of wealth.

The chapter's final section covers the various programs and proposals for raising people out of poverty. The case application examines America's contemporary "underclass."

Suggested Answers to the Learning Objectives

The knowledge acquired from this chapter should enable the student to:

1. Define the different income shares that make up the functional distribution of income.

   The factor shares are rent (which is a payment for the use of land), wages or salaries (which are payments for labor services), and interest (which is the payment for the use of capital).

2. Identify the unique characteristics of the determination of rent compared to the determination of other sources of income.

   Rent is the payment for a factor which has a perfectly inelastic supply. Consequently, the level of rent depends entirely upon the demand.

3. Describe how the personal distribution of income is measured, how it has changed over time, and how the distribution is shown on a Lorenz curve.

   The way of measuring the distribution of personal income is to divide income recipients into five classes ranging from the lowest 20% to the highest 20%. Changes in income distribution over time are shown by comparing the percentage of total income received by each class of income receivers in different years. During the 1960s income became more equally distributed. Since then it has become more unequal than it was in 1960. The Lorenz curve graphically displays income distribution by showing how the actual pattern of income distribution compares with a distribution pattern of perfect equality.

4. List the causes of unequal distribution of personal income.

   The causes of unequal distribution of personal income are differences in productivity, opportunity, and asset ownership.

5. Explain how poverty is defined and list those socioeconomic groups that have a high incidence of poverty.

   Poverty is defined as an income level below three times the amount of a family's economical food budget. Groups that have a high incidence of poverty are families with female heads of household, black and Hispanic families, households including children, and those in the southern states.

6. Distinguish between programs which try to reduce poverty by increasing economic opportunities and those which try to reduce poverty by supplementing real income.

   The programs to reduce poverty by increasing economic opportunities include the equal employment opportunity provisions of the Civil Rights Act of 1964, affirmative action programs, and job training programs. Programs to reduce poverty by supplementing real income include

58

food stamps, Aid to Families With Dependent Children, Medicaid, and housing subsidies.

7. Explain how the negative income tax works.

    The negative income tax would provide government transfer payments to families below a specified income level; the payments would increase progressively the lower the family's income was.

How Is Income Distributed?

Chapter 8 covered the way in which wages are determined in the labor market. The first part of this section examines the determination of rent, interest, and profits. As Figure 1 on page 210 of the text shows, wages and salaries account for almost three-fourths of factor incomes. Although rents are the smallest factor share, the concept of economic rent is important analytically because it explains what determines prices when supplies are perfectly inelastic. This is true not only of land but anything else, including labor.

Profits are not considered a payment to a factor of production as are wages, rents, and interest. (The income from managing a business is considered a type of labor income.) Alternative ways of looking at profits are examined.

The section also examines personal income distribution. The table on page 213 of the text gives the income distribution according to income levels for selected years from 1960 to 1984. Figure 3 shows the inequality of income distribution for 1984 in graphic form.

Study Questions 1 and 2 help the student to understand the economic analysis of "proprietor's income." Study Question 3 reinforces the concept of economic rents. Study Question 4 brings out the relationship of interest rates to capital investment. Study Question 5 is an exercise in reading and interpreting the statistical data in the table of personal income distribution.

Case Application: Rent Control

Rent control is a very controversial issue. This application focuses on the social problems and the economic analyses. Further understanding of the issue can be gained from the Perspective at the end of the chapter.

Answers to the "For Thought" Questions

1. Why do rents tend to be higher in central cities than in the suburbs, despite the fact that population in the suburbs has grown more rapidly than in the cities?

    Rents tend to be higher in central cities than in the suburbs because the supply of land is more inelastic.

There is a greater elasticity of the supply of land for urban development on the edges of the suburbs; therefore, rents are lower.

2. For most types of goods and services, a reduction in supply costs is followed by a decrease in price. Why isn't this necessarily true for rent? Why would a reduction in property taxes, for example, not necessarily lower rents?

    A reduction in supply costs, for example a reduction in property taxes, would not necessarily lower rents because the supply of land is fixed and a lowering of supply costs does not make more of it available. Therefore, the level of rent depends entirely upon demand.

3. Are you in favor of or opposed to rent control measures? What considerations should you take into account?

    Open answer. Those who are in favor of rent controls believe that the increases in rent which have resulted from housing shortages are unfair, that the high rents exclude lower income groups from housing in metropolitan areas, and that high rents do not result in a significant increase in the supply of available housing. Those who are opposed to rent stabilization measures believe that such controls make the housing shortage worse by discouraging investment in new housing as well as maintenance and rehabilitation of older housing, are difficult and costly to administer, and are an intervention in private business which is unfair to landlords.

What Causes Unequal Distribution of Income?

There are obviously many diverse reasons why some people are rich and some people are poor. This section groups the reasons in three categories: differences in productivity, in opportunity, and in asset ownership. These categories are not mutually exclusive, since differences in opportunity generally result in differences in productivity. But the disparity in productivity may result from a variety of causes other than opportunity, such as capital investment in a particular industry. The question of differences of opportunity can be discussed in the light of the introductory article concerning income inequality between the sexes and in relation to the disparities in income according to race.

Study Questions 7, 8, and 9 reinforce the student's understanding of the causes of unequal distribution of income.

Case Application: Lifestyles of the Rich and Non-Famous

This application shows that the most common source of wealth of American millionaires today is a small business. The "ordinary" millionaire does not typically pursue a lavish lifestyle, indulging in a lot of conspicuous consumption. They do, however, wield a great deal of economic power. The way that the "super-rich"—those individuals with a net worth greater than $150 million and families with a net worth above $200 million—use their economic power is of concern to, among others, Lester Thurow who is concerned that they use their power to influence politics and remold society according to their own views.

Answers to the "For Thought" Questions

1. From what income shares do the "super-rich" get the greater part of their income? What indicates where their income comes from?

   They get most of their income from assets. Data shows that their income consists largely of capital gains, dividends, and interest, not wages and salaries.

2. Most American millionaires have at least some college education. How does this relate to the causes of unequal income distribution discussed above?

   The opportunity and motivation to attend college is unequally distributed among different groups in the population. The percentage of minorities that attend college is lower than the percentage of white Anglo Saxons. The lack of educational opportunity is related to the lack of financial assets in latter years.

3. Do you agree or disagree with Thurow that the concentration of economic power in America is dangerous and undesirable? Why?

   Open answer. Those who agree with Thurow might argue that in a democracy it is unhealthy for a small minority to have a great amount of political power based on wealth. Those who do not agree might argue that in a capitalist system wealth is the reward for success and that it is to be admired and not feared. Misuse of power is curbed by constitutional protections.

Who Is Poor in the United States?

This section describes how poverty is officially defined and examines the incidence of poverty among different groups of the population. Figure 4 on textbook page 220 shows a dramatic improvement in the incidence of poverty between 1959 and 1969 and a small improvement up to 1979. After that there was a deterioration of the poverty picture, with a rising percentage of the population falling below the poverty line. The biggest concentration of poverty today is in those families with female heads of households, highest among families with black female heads of households.

Study Question 6 brings out some of the reasons why there has been criticism of the way in which the poverty population has been calculated.

Case Application: Geronimo's Revenge

Sometimes differences of income are based on luck or fate, circumstances which cannot be analyzed. This application shows how the members of some Indian tribes have become quite wealthy, while the majority of Indians are still living in poverty. The wealth of these Indians has resulted from the chance that there are valuable mineral resources underneath the reservation lands on which their ancestors were forced by the government.

Answers to the "For Thought" Questions

1. In 1975 three-fourths of all American Indian families earned less than $3,000. How did this compare to the incidence of poverty among the rest of the population?

   The incidence of poverty among the Indians was much greater than that for the rest of the population. It can be interpolated from Figure 4 that less than 12% of the population as a whole had incomes less than the poverty line level of $5,500 that year.

2. What do American Indians have in common with other groups that have high rates of poverty?

   Like other groups that have high rates of poverty, the American Indians have had less education and fewer job opportunities than the majority of the population. Few of them are in skilled occupations or the professions which have high productivity.

3. Should the government pay reparations to the Indian tribes who had their lands forcibly taken from them in the last century? Why or why not?

   Open answer. Some feel the government owes a debt to the descendants of the Indians whose lands were taken away in the last century. They believe the lands were confiscated unjustly, if not unlawfully. Others believe that valid Indian claims for compensation can be pursued through the legal system. They believe that injustices committed by earlier generations under different conditions cannot be remedied today without undue hardship on present generations.

Can Poverty Be Eliminated?

Substantial gains were made in reducing the extent of poverty between 1960 and 1973. However, there are still a large number of people living below the poverty line, and there has been no progress—in fact, even a retrogression—since then. This section examines the various antipoverty programs and the proposed negative income tax.

Study Question 10 reinforces the student's understanding of the negative income tax.

Case Application: Down and Out in the U. S. of A.

The numbers of homeless and hungry people in the United States are greater than at any time since the depression of the 1930s. Some of these are "street people"—drug addicts and alcoholics. Others are mentally ill former patients of state asylums who were turned out to fend for themselves. Another component of the underclass consists of "new poor" who have lost jobs in heavy industry and agriculture or have never acquired a marketable skill and are unable to find employment. Federal and local assistance programs are not adequately meeting the immediate subsistence needs of these people, much less providing a long-term solution to the problem.

Answers to the "For Thought" Questions

1. What types of transfer payments can assist the urban poor?

   Rent subsidies, food stamps, and Aid to Dependent Children can assist the urban poor if they meet the requirements, including having a permanent address.

2. How has a lack of opportunity contributed to the problems of homelessness and hunger?

   Lack of educational and employment opportunity is a major cause of the problems faced by the "new poor."

3. Will workfare solve the problem of America's underclass? Why or why not?

   Open answer. The proponents of workfare maintain that it will give the hardcore unemployed work experience, in particular the experience of regularly reporting for a job. Opponents of workfare object that is at best make-work, which does not provide the jobless with any transferable skills, and at worst is a form of slavery.

Perspective: The Ideas of David Ricardo

Ricardo was an economist's economist. His logic was very clear, and he developed some powerful economic models. His model of the functional distribution of income is relevant today to the question of rent controls, as the Perspective points out. Many of today's economists might like to emulate Ricardo's ability to make money, but the truth was that he made his fortune before he learned anything about the science of economics.

Answers to Study Questions

1. In terms of economic shares (wages, rents, interest, profits) what type of income is "proprietor's income"?

   In terms of economic shares, "proprietor's income" is a mixture of factor returns which might include implicit wages for the owner's labor, implicit rent on property of the owner, implicit interest on capital put into the business by the owner, and profits.

2. If the proprietor of a dry cleaning establishment has $200,000 of his capital invested in the business, works an average of 60 hours a week running the firm, and has an average of $35,000 in proprietor's income a year, would you estimate his economic profits to be positive or negative? Why?

   His economic profits would be negative because the implicit interest on his capital invested, calculated at a modest 10%, would amount to $20,000 a year. Since his labor time is certainly worth more than $15,000 a year, his economic profits would be negative.

3. Are the high prices paid for admission to professional games the result of high players' salaries or the cause of high players' salaries? Or are these high salaries not related at all to high ticket prices? Why?

   The high salaries paid to professional sports players are the result of the high admission prices which can be charged by the teams. Because of the high prices that fans are willing to pay to see the games and the large fees that the television stations and their advertisers are willing to pay for broadcast rights to the games, and because the professional sports industry is monopolistic, large revenues are generated. These revenues are divided between the owners of the teams and the players according to their relative bargaining strength. Because the opportunity costs of alternative employments available to the players are generally much lower than their salaries, a reduction in salaries would not result in an appreciably smaller supply of players. Since the supply of players is inelastic, their salaries are determined more like a rent than like a wage.

   The height of the salaries depends entirely upon the demand, and therefore the high salaries are a result, not a cause, of high ticket prices.

4. All other things being equal, how would a rise in interest rates affect the amount of capital investment? Why?

   A rise in interest rates might or might not increase the amount of savings available for investment, but the higher interest rates would make borrowing capital more expensive. Hence, higher interest rates tend to discourage investments.

5. Has the relative income of the middle fifth of income receivers improved or worsened compared to other income receivers since 1960? What explanations might be found for the change in the relative income of middle income earners?

The relative income of the middle fifth of income receivers has declined since 1960. According to the table on page 213 of the text, their share of total income decreased from 17.8% in 1960 to 17% in 1984. There was an even larger decline experienced by the second fifth of income receivers. The explanations for this may be attributable to the declines in relatively well paid blue-collar jobs in heavy industry and to the incidence of government taxes.

6. What are the reasons why the official figures on the number of families below the poverty line may exaggerate the actual number of poor people?

The official figures on the number of families below the poverty line may exaggerate the actual number of poor people because nonmoney subsidies such as food stamps, free medical care, and subsidized housing are not included in the income calculation. Also, there is an alleged tendency for people to underreport their income.

7. Why do workers who work with large amounts of capital equipment generally earn more than workers who do not use large amounts of capital equipment?

Those who work with large amounts of capital equipment generally earn more than workers who do not use large amounts of capital equipment because their productivity is increased by the use of such equipment, and productivity is one of the principal determinants of earnings.

8. Why do workers in shared monopoly industries generally earn more than workers in more competitive industries?

Workers in shared monopoly industries generally earn more than workers in more competitive industries because shared monopoly industries make above normal profits and collective bargaining enables workers to share in the monopolistic profits.

9. What is "asset ownership," and what role does asset ownership play in income distribution?

Asset ownership refers to the individual's holdings of earning capital. The earnings on capital assets constitute the major source of income for the highest income earners.

10. How does the negative income tax proposal redistribute income?

The negative income tax proposal would redistribute income by providing transfer payments to those with incomes below a specified level. The lower the income, the larger would be the transfer payment.

Integrating *Economics U$A* Programs

(For information on Economics U$A *see the introduction, p. v.)*

Program 23 on "Profits and Interest: How Do You Get the Best Return?" contains material on the determination of interest and profits, but may be less relevant than some of the other programs. The first two applications show the effects interest rates have on housing sales and capital investments by business. Perhaps the most relevant part of the program is Gill's discussion of the role of profits in a market economy following the third application.

More directly pertinent to the content of the chapter is program 24, "Reducing Poverty: What Have We Done?" As with most of the programs in the series, it gives the historical background to the policy issues and the government's responses. The first application presents the establishment of the Social Security System as a response to the poverty of the elderly in the Great Depression. (Social Security is treated extensively in a text application in chapter 15, pages 386-87.) The second application describes a negative income tax proposal during the Nixon administration (the Family Assistance Plan) as an answer to "welfare bureaucracy," covering the pros and cons of the negative income tax. The third application deals with the establishment of the Job Corps training program, the predecessor of CETA, and the controversy during the Reagan years whether or not job training is a cost effective program.

Case Applications in Student Workbook

(Answers are supplied to students in the workbook.)

How Is Income Distributed?

Case Application: How Much Is a Nose Tackle Worth?

This application uses the salaries of professional football players and the 1982 players' strike as a basis for examining what determines factor incomes under conditions of monopolistic markets. A discussion of this application would be good preparation for answering Study Question 3 at the end of the chapter.

Answers to the "For Thought" Questions

1. The supply of National Football League games is best represented by which of the supply curves in Figure 2 on page 211 of the textbook?

The supply of National Football League games is best represented by supply curve Sl in Figure 2 on page 211 of the textbook. The number of games is perfectly inelastic, at least in the short run, and does not vary with the price for which tickets can be sold.

2. Why is the salary earned by Joe Montana, star quarterback of the San Francisco Forty Niners, more like a rent payment than a wage payment?

The salary earned by Joe Montana is more like a rent payment than a wage payment because its level is determined entirely by demand and not at all by supply. Joe Montana would be willing to work as a quarterback at only a fraction of the salary he receives if the demand for his services were lower. The high salary of gifted quarterbacks does not result in an increase in the number of such quarterbacks in the labor market, as would be the case with labor in general. The salary is therefore more like a rent on a resource in limited supply.

3. One of the contract demands of the Player's Association was the institution of a wage scale which would more nearly equalize the incomes of players at different positions. Was this demand justified? Why or why not?

Open answer. It seems only fair for players who do their jobs equally well and contribute equally to the success of the team, whatever position they are playing, to receive the same wage. However, it is the market that determines prices, and in the entertainment business those who have the most popular appeal receive the largest incomes. In the theater and movies, for example, character actors frequently have more acting ability than the stars but are paid much less.

What Causes Unequal Distribution of Income?

Case Application: The New Poor

The growing recession in 1982 cut deep into the ranks of workers who had previously been unaffected by less serious recessions. The application examines how increasing unemployment affects income distribution.

Answers to the "For Thought" Questions

1. What are the differences in the causes of poverty between the "old poor" and the "new poor"?

The "old poor" were poverty stricken because of such handicaps as lack of education, physical or mental disability, or exclusion from the work force. The "new poor" are poverty stricken because of structural dislocations in a number of industries, putting many experienced workers out of a job; and because of a

persisting high level of unemployment in general that makes it difficult for the unemployed to find new jobs.

2. Which group is likely to move out of poverty first when economic conditions improve, the "old poor" or the "new poor"? Why?

The "new poor" will move out of poverty first when economic conditions improve because the rising number of job openings will be available to them, whereas the "old poor" are likely to still be excluded.

3. Should private welfare agencies divert part of their resources away from aiding the "old poor" in order to provide assistance to the "new poor"? Why or why not?

Open answer. Private welfare agencies should aid everyone in need of help regardless of the reason for their conditions. On the other hand, it could be argued that the "old poor" are more in need of assistance than the "new poor" because they have been in poverty longer, have fewer resources to fall back upon, and will continue to be in poverty after the "new poor" have found jobs.

Who Is Poor in the United States?

Case Application: How Poor Is Poor?

This application delves into the allegation discussed on page 220 of the textbook that the official figures on poverty overstate the number of people that are poor. The application examines how this might affect the justification for spending on antipoverty programs. The case prepares students to answer Study Question 6 at the end of the chapter.

Answers to the "For Thought" Questions

1. If Congress decides to include non-cash income in determining who is poor, what effect would this have on the poverty line?

If Congress decides to include non-cash income to determine who is poor, this would raise the poverty line. The existing poverty-level income is not sufficient for a family without supplementary non-cash income. Counting non-cash supplements as part of the family's income would make it necessary to raise the income level which is considered the poverty line.

2. If poverty is redefined by considering the non-cash income, the percentage of elderly people who are considered poor would be less than the percentage of people under 65 who are considered poor. Why would this be the case?

If poverty is redefined by considering non-cash income, the percentage of elderly people considered poor would be less than the percentage of people under 65 who are considered poor because the elderly receive larger amounts of non-cash income, especially health care.

3. Should poverty be redefined to include non-cash income? Why or why not?

Open answer. Redefining poverty to include non-cash income would give a truer picture of the extent of poverty after taking into account government anti-poverty programs. However, it would then not show the extent of poverty before including government assistance and, therefore, would not show the extent of need for such programs.

Can Poverty Be Eliminated?

Case Application: Increased Opportunities for the Handicapped

This application examines the progress that has been made in opening job opportunities to the handicapped, a group that was previously excluded from the job market to a large extent. It discusses what problems of job discrimination against the handicapped still remain.

Answers to the "For Thought" Questions

1. How has the number of handicapped poor been reduced since 1973?

The number of handicapped poor has been reduced since 1973 by the enactment of federal and state legislation prohibiting employer discrimination against the handicapped.

2. Why are affirmative action programs to employ the handicapped needed?

Affirmative action programs to employ the handicapped are needed because there is a prejudice against hiring them. They frequently can be valuable employees, but fears on the part of employers about possible consequences prevent their being considered for jobs in the absence of affirmative action programs.

3. Should the government subsidize firms to hire the handicapped? Why or why not?

Open answer. Yes, the government should subsidize firms who hire the handicapped because they can make a contribution to output, and income they've earned reduces the need for government welfare payments and other assistance. No, the government should not subsidize firms to hire the handicapped because it could result in less efficiency in the production process, and the market should determine resource allocation without government intervention.

Chapter 10

Money

Chapter Overview

This is the first of six macroeconomic chapters which study the factors determining total output and incomes, employment, the overall price level, and the financing of government programs, as well as how to achieve the goals of stability and economic growth. This first chapter of the unit deals with how our monetary system works—generally one of the important revelations to students of introductory economics. The introductory article concerns the early forms of money and serves to demonstrate how money evolved to meet the changing needs of society.

The first section of the chapter identifies the different measurements of the money supply and near money. The case application discusses the function of credit cards.

The second section examines the functions of money as a medium of exchange, unit of measurement, and store of value. The case application is a favorite standard in economic literature about the development of a market system in prisoner of war camps during World War II, where cigarettes were used as money.

The next section explains how money is created in our contemporary economy. It shows that most money results from the extension of credit. The case application offers the student an actual example of how a loan adds to the money supply.

The last section deals with the Federal Reserve System and the methods it uses to control the amount of money in our economy. The case application discusses the Federal Reserve quandary over whether to aim its monetary control efforts at interest rates or the money supply itself.

Suggested Answers to the Learning Objectives

The knowledge acquired in this chapter should enable the students to:

1. Discuss the history of money.

   Dating from pre-Christian times, a variety of useful and useless items were employed as money. Metal coins were first used in the seventh century B.C. in Lydia. Paper money originated with the goldsmiths in seventh century London. In the United States, private commercial banks issued their own currency up to 1913

   when the federal government established a monopoly over currency issue.

2. Define the M1 money supply and describe its components.

   M1 is the narrowest measure of the money supply. It consists of currency in circulation, demand deposit accounts, NOW and ATS accounts, traveler's checks, and checkable money market accounts.

3. Explain how "near money" differs from money and discuss how near money relates to the broader definitions of M2, M3, and L.

   "Near money" consists of financial assets which are less liquid than those classified as money. The financial assets which constitute near money are ranged according to their liquidity into the broader categories of M2, M3, and L.

4. List the three functions of money and explain the characteristics money must have in order to be functional.

   Money serves as a medium of exchange, a unit of measurement, and a store of value. To adequately serve these functions, the medium should be universally recognized, have an adequate but limited supply, not be easily reproduced, be easily portable, and be durable. A unit of measurement should itself be stable in value. A store of value should be liquid, in the financial sense, as well as durable.

5. Discuss how currency is affected by public demand and explain money creation.

   More currency is put into circulation in response to demand from the public and businesses to have more of their money in that form rather than in demand deposits. Increases in the money supply result from borrowing by individuals, businesses, and government.

6. Describe the Federal Reserve Banking System.

   The Federal Reserve is the central bank of the United States, a government institution that acts as a "banker's bank," serves the monetary needs of the federal government, and controls the monetary system. There are 12 regional Federal Reserve banks under the overall authority of the Board of Governors in Washington, D.C.

7. List the means by which the Federal Reserve controls the money supply.

The Federal Reserve System controls the money supply by making it easier and cheaper—or harder and more expensive—for banks to extend loans. It does this through its control over bank reserve requirements, the discount rate, and its purchases and sales of Federal government securities in open market operations.

What Is Money?

Before reading this section, most students would probably define money as currency. It is important for them to learn that most of our money is not currency, but demand deposits. With the rapid changes in the banking system which have occurred in the last few years, it has become increasingly difficult to distinguish money from near monies. However, the exact defining of the supply of money is not as important as the student's understanding that highly liquid assets other than currency serve the same functions as money. This understanding is reinforced by Study Questions 1 and 2.

Case Application: Dealing the Cards

The widespread use of credit cards to make purchases complicates our understanding of what constitutes money. Credit cards might seem to serve in the place of money, but in actuality they only affect the timing of payment for transactions and are not themselves payment. Therefore, they are not money. Their use, however, can result in an increase in the money supply, as shown in the second "For Thought" question for this application.

Answers to the "For Thought" Questions

1. Is "plastic money" included in the money supply measured by Ml? Why or why not?

   "Plastic money" is not included in the money supply measured by Ml. The use of a credit card to "pay" for a purchase does not actually transfer any payment. The payment is not transferred until the seller sends the transaction slip to the credit card company and receives a check in payment. The credit card holder subsequently reimburses the company for its advance to cover the transaction.

2. If credit cards are not money, can their use lead to an increase in the money supply? How?

   The use of credit cards has led to an increase in the money supply by increasing the amount of loans

outstanding, since credit card balances are, by definition, outstanding loans.

3. Should the government tighten restrictions on credit card companies? What kinds of restrictions might be imposed?

   Open answer. There are two concerns about the rapid growth of credit card use. One concern is that some people may accumulate more debt than they can handle and end up declaring bankruptcy. The other is that the credit card issuers charge exorbitant interest rates, not justified by present circumstances in the financial markets. Both of these concerns could be met by setting limits on the interest rates they charge, which would force them to be more selective in their extension of credit. Opposition to such controls is based on the belief that government interference in the financial market will have harmful effects, such as a shortage of credit, and that if given a chance, competition between credit card issuers will bring interest rates into line.

What Does Money Do?

The most obvious function of money is to purchase goods and services, that is, to serve as a medium of exchange. Students may not have considered its other two functions— as a unit of measurement and a store of value. The demonstration in Figure 3 on textbook page 244, demonstrating the declining purchasing power of the dollar, shows that money's usefulness as a store of value declines over time. This anticipates the discussion in the next chapter on the problems of inflation.

Study Questions 3 and 4 reinforce the student's understanding of what is meant by the different functions of money.

Case Application: POW Money

During World War II, Allied internees in prisoner of war camps developed a surprisingly sophisticated market system under the adverse conditions. Because their "economy" was reduced to basics, it provides a clear demonstration of some of the fundamental market forces.

Answers to the "For Thought" Questions

1. Which functions of money did cigarettes perform in the POW camp?

   Cigarettes served all three functions of money in the POW camp. They served as a medium of exchange, a unit of measurement, and a store of value (at least for the nonsmokers).

2. Heavy air raids in the vicinity of the camp increased the consumption of cigarettes. What effect did this have on the prices of things?

The increased consumption of cigarettes reduced the money supply, thereby causing a deflation, lowering prices of the items bought and sold with cigarettes.

3. Sometimes the successful POW capitalists who profited from buying and selling things were resented by other prisoners. Was the hostility directed toward them justified? Were they providing a useful service or were they merely leeches on the POW society?

Open answer. In the movie "Stalag 17," William Holden played the part of such a POW capitalist. The film showed the extent of hostility directed toward him by the other prisoners. However, such individuals were performing a useful market function as middlemen. They performed as a clearinghouse and helped improve the efficiency of the market by disseminating information on the equilibrium prices which balance demand and supply.

How Is Money Created?

There is a general belief that the money supply is increased because the government prints more money to pay its bills. Generally, this is not true. It can happen that the money supply increases as a result of the government's "monetizing" the debt, but it is generally the businesses and the public that determine how much money the government will print, while the government only responds to their demands. The greatest increases in the money supply are not from printing currency but from increases in demand deposits, which are the result of borrowing by individuals, businesses, and different levels of government, mainly the federal government.

Study Questions 5, 6, and 7 enhance the student's understanding of how the money supply increases by the expansion of credit.

Case Application: How to Create Money

The application shows how an increase in the money supply can result from the actions of an individual and a bank. It lays a basis for understanding the banking system's multiple expansion of the money supply through credit.

Answers to the "For Thought" Questions

1. If you borrowed the $700 in cash rather than having it credited to your checking account, would the effect on the money supply be the same? Why or why not?

The effect on the money supply would be the same if the $700 were borrowed in cash rather than having it credited to a checking account. Since currency held by banks is not counted as part of the money supply, when the $700 was put into circulation it would increase the money supply by that amount.

2. When you pay off your bank loan, what happens to the money supply? Is the effect on the money supply any different whether you pay the bank by check or with currency?

When a check is written by a borrower to pay off a bank loan, it reduces the borrower's deposit account without being transferred to any other account and therefore reduces the money supply. It would similarly reduce the money supply if the loan were repaid by cash because the currency would be taken out of circulation.

3. There is an old adage that bankers are only willing to loan money to people who don't need it. Those who have plenty of financial assets that can readily be turned into cash have little trouble getting a loan, whereas those who have no assets have a great deal of difficulty. Should bankers make loans only to those who have enough assets to guarantee repayment of the loan? What are the consequences of making loans to people who are not good credit risks?

Open answer. The question of money lending and usury is an ancient moral dilemma. People should have access to credit when they need it, but people without an established credit history frequently have difficulty obtaining loans. This has been a problem particularly for young people and women. But if bankers only lent money to people who didn't need it, they would not do much business, since people are not inclined to pay bankers interest on money they don't need. However, it is not a good idea from the standpoint of the lender—or, in many cases, for the welfare of the borrower—to extend loans to those who do not have the capacity to repay them. This results in excessive interest charges and can bring on bankruptcy for the borrower. If it has too many defaulted loans, the lending institution can also go bankrupt.

How Is the Supply of Money Controlled?

This section explains why the Federal Reserve System was established and what its present functions are. It explains the instruments available to the Fed for controlling the money supply. This explanation prepares the student to understand the use of monetary policies to stabilize the economy, which is covered in the section of chapter 13 beginning on textbook page 333.

Study Questions 8 and 9 enhance the student's understanding of how the Federal Reserve monetary control instruments affect the money supply. Study Question 10 encourages the student to examine the reasoning behind the way in which the Federal Reserve is organized and governed.

Case Application: **Target Practice at the Fed**

In 1979 the Federal Reserve Board made a controversial change in the objectives of its monetary policy. Instead of concentrating on the management of interest rates to control the monetary system, it switched to managing the supply of money itself. The Fed has been criticised for this change because the erratic fluctuations of interest rates is said to create undue uncertainty in the business and financial communities, and, with respect to short-run changes, it has not been very successful in meeting its money supply objectives.

Answers to the "For Thought" Questions

1. What initial target is the Fed aiming at when it attempts to affect the Federal Funds rate?

   When it attempts to affect the Federal Funds rate, the Fed is initially aiming at the interest rate target.

2. One of the explanations given for the Fed's inability to hit its money supply target is the time lags involved in the response of the economy to changes in Fed policies. Why don't the tools of monetary policy immediately affect the money supply?

   The Federal Reserve tools of monetary policy do not directly affect the money supply, but rather create inducements for depository institutions to increase or decrease credit, thereby affecting the money supply. There is a lag first in the Fed being able to determine that certain policy actions are called for. It then takes time for the depository institutions to respond to the inducements created by the Fed. Finally, the borrowing public and business community must then respond to the changed availability of credit.

3. Do you think that the Federal Reserve ought to be made more directly responsible to the president and Congress? What would be the advantages and disadvantages of this?

   Open answer. As indicated in the case application, there have been proposals to change the length of tenure of the Federal Reserve Board members in order to make the Fed more directly responsible to the president. The advantages would be that the Federal Reserve Board policy and actions could be made consistent with other national economic policies and actions. Also, there would be more immediate accountability through the political process. The disadvantages would lie in the politicizing of the Fed. The Federal Reserve was intentionally made an independent agency when it was

established, and the governors were given 14-year appointments in order to provide freedom from political interference and allow the Fed to carry out its mandate. Removing its independence would subject it to manipulation for short-term political gains.

Perspective: **The Big Bank Controversy**

This Perspective shows the ambivalence that the United States has had historically toward the power of a central bank. It was a major political issue in the early years of the republic and continued to recur down through our history. In comparison to the major battles fought over the First and Second Banks of the United States, the present controversy surrounding the Federal Reserve System is very mild.

Answers to Study Questions

1. Have you ever transformed near money into money? How?

   Open answer. Students may very likely have transformed near money into money by making cash withdrawals from a savings account.

2. Are there any barter transactions that take place in today's economy? Why would anyone prefer barter to money transactions?

   Open answer. Barter transactions are sometimes used to evade income and sales taxes. Barter transactions may also be used in legal ways, such as trading services, with the payment of appropriate taxes. Organizations have been established to act as clearinghouses for such transactions. One motivation for these direct trades is to reduce marketing costs.

3. Using the criteria by which money is judged, how well would each of the following serve as a medium of exchange? 1) empty beer cans, 2) four-leaf clovers, 3) IOUs written on cards with the name and address of the writer, 4) fresh fish.

   1) Empty beer cans have deficiencies as a medium of exchange because they are not easily portable in large numbers and their supply is not sufficiently limited. 2) Four-leaf clovers are not sufficiently durable to serve as a medium of exchange. 3) IOUs written on cards with the name and address of the writer are not acceptable as a medium of exchange because the writer is not known to everyone, and the promise to pay is not universally recognized. 4) Considering what happens to fresh fish without refrigeration, they would not be easily portable or sufficiently durable to serve as a medium of exchange.

4. Which of the above items could serve one or both of the other two functions of money, even if it isn't a good medium of exchange?

Empty beer cans, like any durable commodity, could serve as a store of value. Empty beer cans and four leaf clovers could conceivably serve as a unit of measurement, as could fresh fish of a given size or variety.

5. Because many people take vacations in the summer, there is an increased demand for currency. How is this additional demand satisfied? Does it increase the money supply? Why or why not?

   In the summer the Federal Reserve supplies more currency to the banks who, in turn, provide it to their customers. Because the customers pay for the currency by writing checks on their accounts, the increase in currency in circulation is offset by the decrease in demand deposits, and there is no increase in the money supply.

6. Suppose that in one week the First National Bank made loans of $217,000. During that same week, repayment on earlier loans amounted to $220,000. What happened to the money supply as a result?

   There was a decrease in the money supply of $3,000.

7. Which would have a more expansionary effect on the money supply, the Treasury's sale of securities to the banks or to the general public? Why?

   Treasury sale of securities to the banks would have a more expansionary effect on the money supply because the banks would create new deposits to pay for the securities. When the government sells securities to the general public, the securities are likely to be paid for by the transfer of existing balances rather than the creation of new balances.

8. If banks have no excess reserves, what happens when the Fed raises the required reserve ratio?

   If banks have no excess reserves and the Fed raises the required reserve ratio, the banks must either reduce their deposit liabilities or add to their reserves by selling some of the securities they hold or borrowing from the Fed.

9. Since bank interest rates are always higher than the Fed discount rate, why does a rise in the discount rate discourage banks from making new loans?

   A rise in the discount rate discourages banks from making new loans because, in order to maintain the margin between their cost of borrowing and their returns from lending, they must increase their interest rates and become more selective in the borrowers that they are willing to lend to.

10. Why does appointing members of the Federal Reserve Board of Governors for terms of 14 years make the Board independent? Why was this provision put in when the Federal Reserve System was established?

    Appointing members of the Federal Reserve Board of Governors for terms of 14 years makes the board

independent because the terms of appointment span more than three presidential terms and many congressional elections. Since the board members are not directly responsible to whomsoever happens to be in power at the moment and their actions are not subject to political review, they can make their decisions relatively free of political pressures. This provision was put in when the Federal Reserve System was established because, with the history of politicizing of the First and Second Banks of the United States, Congress wanted the Fed to pursue its mandate without short-term political considerations.

Integrating *Economics U$A* Programs

(For information on Economics U$A *see the introduction, p. v.)*

There are two programs which are relevant for this chapter, one on how the banks operate and how they get in trouble and the other on the Federal Reserve System. The first is program 8, "The Banking System: Why Must It Be Protected?" The application on the failure of the Knickerbocker Trust in the Panic of 1907 discusses how banks make profits on loans and investments, sometimes taking greater risks for more profits. The next application deals with the collapse of the banking system in the 1930s and shows the process of multiple credit contraction during the depression. It discusses the establishment of the FDIC to prevent a recurrence of runs on banks. The last application covers the experience of the collapse of the Penn Square Bank which was overextended in oil loans when petroleum prices fell. Gill uses bank balance sheets, like Table 1 in the text on page 251 but much more simplified, to explain fractional reserve banking and how it effects the money supply. He shows how a bank deposit provides the basis for additional lending and how the fractional reserve system results in a multiple expansion of the money supply.

The other program for the chapter is 9, "The Federal Reserve: Does Money Matter?" The first application shows how the Panic of 1907 led to the Federal Reserve Act establishing the Fed in 1913. It also discusses how the Fed's inappropriate changes in the discount rate after the collapse of 1929 "pushed the country deeper into the recession." Gill analyses the effect of Fed actions on the money supply and how it impacts the economy. The second application describes the origin of open market operations by the Banking Act of 1935, how the Fed assisted the Treasury in financing World War II, and the post-war struggle over conflicting Fed-Treasury objectives, culminating in the 1951 accord freeing the Fed to use open market operations to combat inflation. Gill shows how bond sales by the Treasury are inflationary. The final application discusses how the Vietnam War and the Great Society program combined to sow the seeds of the stagflation of the 1970s. After viewing the program, it might be useful to ask the class what tools of Fed policy were brought out in the applications.

Case Applications in Student Workbook

(Answers are supplied to students in the workbook.)

What Is Money?

Case Application: What Isn't Money?

With deregulation of the banking system, many innovations have been introduced. New types of bank accounts have been developed, and it is difficult to distinguish whether they are deposit accounts or savings accounts. As a result, the delineation between what is included in the money supply and what is near money has become even more difficult. The application discusses these developments and the problems they pose.

Answers to the "For Thought" Questions

1. The expansion of money market mutual funds represented an increase in what type of money?

   The expansion of money market mutual funds represented an increase in near money.

2. Why are money market mutual funds more like money than certificates of deposit?

   Money market mutual funds are more like money than certificates of deposit because they are more liquid. Investments in money market mutual funds can be withdrawn immediately with no penalty, usually simply by writing a check. Investments in certificates of deposit, on the other hand, cannot be withdrawn by check and cannot be withdrawn before maturity without a penalty being imposed.

3. Is the deregulation of financial institutions a good idea? Why or why not?

   Open answer. The advantages of deregulating financial institutions are that it increases competition in the financial services market and allows different types of financial institutions to compete on an equal basis. Disadvantages are that some financial institutions may not be able to survive and some types of loans, such as those for home mortgages, may be more difficult and costly to obtain because other types of lending are more profitable.

What Does Money Do?

Case Application: Primitive Money

The introductory article for chapter 10 discussed the many different items that were used as money in early times. This application discusses the debate among anthropologists as to whether those various forms of money were used in the same way that we use money today. In some cases there is evidence that they were special forms of money which served cultural as well as economic functions.

Answers to the "For Thought" Questions

1. When the price of slaves was quoted in cows and brass rods in Nigeria, which function of money were they performing?

   When the price of slaves was quoted in cows and brass rods, those items were performing the function of a unit of account.

2. Why should the lack of conversion of denominations of one class of shells into another class among the Russell Islanders indicate the shells do not serve the same function as money does in the U.S.?

   The lack of conversion of denominations of one class of shells into another class among the Russell Islanders indicates the shells do not serve the same function as money does in the U.S., because money must be convertible into different denominations (e.g., five $1 bills for a $5 bill) in order to serve as a universal means of exchange.

3. Are there ways in which money in our society performs social functions as well as economic functions? For example?

   Open answer. Some possible ways in which it could be said that money performs social as well as economic functions in our society include lighting a cigar with a $100 bill to display affluence, leaving a small tip for a rude waiter to show dissatisfaction, or leaving a quarter under the pillow of a child from the "tooth fairy."

How Is Money Created?

Case Application: How the Government Creates Money

This application takes the student step by step through the creation of money by the sale of government securities. It provides the student with the answer to Study Question 7 at the end of this chapter in the text.

Answers to the "For Thought" Questions

1. If the U. S. Treasury prints a $10,000 bond and you borrow $10,000 from your bank to purchase the bond, by how much is the money supply increased? Who is directly responsible for the expansion of the money supply, you or the government?

   If the U.S. Treasury prints a $10,000 bond and you borrow the $10,000 from your bank to purchase the bond, the money supply is increased by $10,000. You are directly responsible for the expansion of money because it was your loan from the bank that increased the supply of money, not the printing of the bond by the Treasury.

2. If the government paid its bills by printing currency rather than by selling government securities, would this increase the money supply more, less, or the same amount? Why?

    If the government paid its bills by printing currency rather than by selling government securities, the result would be a greater increase in the money supply because some of the money paid for government securities represents a reduction in the privately held money stock.

3. The only government securities issued in the smaller denominations everyone can afford are savings bonds, which pay lower interest rates than other types of government securities. Is this fair? Why or why not?

    Open answer. The lower interest rates paid on savings bonds can be called unfair to small investors because they do not have sufficient funds to purchase higher denomination government securities. On the other hand, it could be argued that those who purchase U.S. savings bonds have the freedom to choose between those and other types of investments, and purchasing savings bonds may be considered patriotic.

How Is the Supply of Money Controlled?

Case Application: Who's in Charge Around Here?

This application concerns the divided authority over the nation's banking system between the Fed, the Comptroller of the Currency, and the FDIC. It discusses the proposal to delineate responsibilities more narrowly and the Fed's objections to the plan.

Answers to the "For Thought" Questions

1. The task force recommendation would reduce the authority of the Fed. What legislation expanded its authority in 1980?

    The Depository Institutions Deregulation and Monetary Control Act of 1980 (the Monetary Control Act) expanded the authority of the Fed by making non-member banks and other depository institutions subject to the same Fed regulations as those banks which are members of the system and providing them with the Fed's services, for which they must pay a fee.

2. What regulatory powers does the Fed need in order to implement monetary policy?

    The principal regulatory power that the Fed needs in order to implement monetary policy is mandating the required reserve ratio which the banks must maintain.

3. Should jurisdiction over the different areas of banking system control be assigned to specific agencies or should the present system of divided authority be retained? Why?

    Open answer. The overlapping authority of the three bank regulatory agencies may result in duplication of activities and responsibilities. Especially in these times of widespread bank failures due to unsound lending practices, there should be clear regulatory responsibility by a single agency over a specific banking activity. On the other hand, the Federal Reserve has the primary responsibility for implementing a sound monetary policy and should have broad regulatory authority rather than being confined to a service and policy-making role.

Chapter 11

Unemployment and Inflation

Chapter Overview

Two of the four primary economic goals outlined in chapter 1 were price stability and full employment. This chapter deals with the problems that arise when we have not satisfactorily achieved those goals. The main objectives of macroeconomic policy are to alleviate unemployment and stop inflation. The introductory article examines the troubling situation that, in spite of the third longest sustained economic recovery since World War II, the unemployment rate is still almost 7%. It looks at the reasons for this persistent high unemployment level.

The first section of the chapter examines the three different types of unemployment and the fact that some of the unemployed are not included in the statistics. The case application points out the areas of the country where job prospects are best and where they are worst.

The second section describes how we measure inflation and discusses different causes for it. The case application shows an example of how price indexes are constructed, using data on the changing costs of courting.

The next section examines the relationship between unemployment and inflation. It shows how the problem of stagflation developed in the 1970s. The case application uses the analogy of a roller coaster ride to illustrate the different phases of the business cycle.

The final section discusses the effects of unemployment and inflation on the economy and on people. In the case application extreme examples of inflation in other countries are reviewed, led by the German hyperinflation in the 1920s which provides a dramatic illustration of what can happen if inflation gets out of control.

Suggested Answers to the Learning Objectives

The knowledge acquired from this chapter should enable the students to:

1. Describe the three major causes of unemployment.

   The major causes of unemployment are: frictional unemployment, when people are temporarily between jobs; structural unemployment, when whole sectors of jobs have been eliminated in particular industries or particular geographic locations; and inadequate total demand, when workers are laid off because of falling sales in virtually all sectors of the economy.

2. Explain why some unemployment is hidden.

   Some of the unemployed are not included in the statistics because, after being out of work for a long period of time and unsuccessfully searching for a job, they become discouraged and give up looking. Since only those who are actively seeking a job are counted in the unemployment statistics, the discouraged workers are not included.

3. Define inflation and the C.P.I.

   Inflation is a continuously rising general price level. The C.P.I. is a statistical measure of changes in the prices of a representative sample of urban family purchases relative to a previous period.

4. Describe three causes of inflation and explain the usage of the quantity equation.

   Demand-pull inflation occurs when total demand for goods and services exceeds the productive capacity of the economy at or near full employment. Cost-push inflation is caused by a rise in the prices of one or more of the factor inputs in production. Monetary inflation is the result of an increase in the money supply which exceeds the increase in output of goods and services. The quantity equation $(M \times V = T \times P)$ shows the relationship between the money supply and the velocity of money circulation on one hand and the total of economic transactions and their average prices on the other. It is used to examine how changes in one of the variables might effect the others.

5. Explain the relationship between unemployment and inflation and use the Phillips curve to show this relationship.

   There is a trade-off between unemployment and inflation—the higher one is, the lower the other is. The Phillips curve shows the percentage of inflation compared to the percentage of unemployment, as diagrammed in Figure 8 on page 276 of the text.

6. Define stagflation and relate the price level to output and employment levels by use of the aggregate supply and aggregate demand curves.

   Stagflation describes a situation in which economic stagnation with high unemployment and inflation occur simultaneously. The price level rises as output approaches the full employment level. Depending on whether aggregate supply is constrained only at full employment or whether shortages appear well before the economy reaches full employment as shown by the rise in the AS curve, the trade-off between unemployment and inflation will be at a relatively low level or at high levels of both—stagflation.

7. Explain the consequences of unemployment and inflation.

   Unemployment results in a loss of purchasing power for families of the unemployed, which reduces their standard of living. Their loss of purchasing power reduces the income of many who are still employed. Unemployment reduces the aggregate output and growth rate of the economy, resulting in a smaller amount of goods and services for the population. The personal stresses resulting from unemployment cause a number of social problems such as family disintegration, suicide, and crime. Inflation reduces people's purchasing power and lowers their standards of living if their incomes do not rise as fast as the price level. It has an effect upon real output by distorting resource allocations, reducing productivity, and slowing the rate of growth.

What Causes Unemployment?

The seriousness of the unemployment problem depends upon what type of unemployment exists. There is always frictional unemployment of people who are between jobs. There is also usually some structural unemployment as particular industries or regions are contracting. Structural unemployment is a serious problem for those affected, but it is unavoidable in a dynamic market economy. The type of unemployment that public policy is most concerned with is unemployment due to inadequate total aggregate demand, sometimes called cyclical unemployment. Figure 3 on page 267 of the text is the first step in developing the GNP Tank national income model, which is important in the next two chapters.

It should be noted that the unemployment figures that are regularly reported in the news media tend to understate the seriousness of the problem. Many workers who are out of work for a long period of time become discouraged and are not reported as unemployed because they have given up looking for a job. Many other workers who are reported as employed have been put on short hours, so they are actually partially unemployed. Study Question 1 examines who is included and excluded in the unemployment statistics. Study Question 3 reinforces the classification of types of unemployment.

Case Application: "Go Northeast, Young Man, Go Northeast"

This application points up the location disparity between where job openings exist and where the unemployed are and the skills disparity between the training needed for high-tech

job openings and the lack of appropriate skills among the unemployed. Employment opportunities are expanding most in the suburbs, while the unemployment is concentrated in the central cities.

Answers to the "For Thought" Questions

1. If there are job openings in the suburbs but the jobless blue-collar workers in the cities don't have the necessary skills to fill them, what type of unemployment is this?

   This is structural unemployment.

2. Explain how the situation in this case application is illustrated by Figure 3B. What changes would bring about conditions such as those illustrated by Figure 3A?

   Figure 3B shows that the economy is underemployed. In most parts of the country, with the exception of the Northeast and a few states elsewhere, there are not enough jobs for all of those that want employment. An increase in aggregate demand to the full employment level would create enough new jobs to bring the unemployment level in the rest of the country down to that in the Northeast.

3. What can be done to solve the problem of the mismatch between where the jobs are and where the unemployed workers are? Does government have a responsibility in the solution of this problem or should it be left strictly to industry and the unemployed individuals to solve on their own? Why?

   Open answer. Providing information to the unemployed concerning job openings in other areas would help, as would improved public transportation facilities or employer-sponsored transportation pools. Elimination of discrimination in housing would also increase the possibility of matching suburban jobs with the urban unemployed. Those who favor government intervention might argue that unemployment is not just a personal problem for those out of work, but a macroeconomic and social problem for the whole country which only the government has the power and resources to cope with. Those who oppose government intervention might do so on the basis that the private sector, operating through the factor markets, can most efficiently match workers to jobs and that government bureaucracy is inefficient and wasteful.

What Causes Inflation?

The section begins with a discussion of the Consumer Price Index as a measure of inflation. It then explains three types of inflation: demand-pull, cost-push, and monetary. There is not universal agreement among economists that monetary inflation is a separate type of inflation. It could be argued that an increase in the money supply increases purchasing power and aggregate demand and therefore the inflation is a demand-pull inflation. However, its underlying cause—and hence, solution—are different than a demand-pull inflation that results from an increase in real demand, such as during a wartime period. The difference is apparent when you consider the case of the hyperinflation in Germany discussed in the case application on textbook page 288.

A useful class exercise to help the students understand the meaning of the quantity equation is to show a change in one of the variables and ask what they would expect to happen to the other variables under different circumstances. For example, assume an increase in the money supply (M) at full employment.

$$M \uparrow \times V = T \times P$$

What other variable or variables would you expect to change in which direction? The likely expectation is that prices (P) would increase.

$$M \uparrow \times V = T \times P \uparrow$$

Under what circumstances would you expect a different outcome? If there were a large amount of unemployment and excess capacity, output (T) might rise rather than prices.

$$M \uparrow \times V = T \uparrow \times P$$

Under what circumstances might the velocity of circulation decline instead?

$$M \uparrow \times V \downarrow = T \times P$$

If people feared a worse recession was coming, they might not increase purchases but hold more idle money balances in reserve for hard times.

Study Question 2 exercises the student's understanding of the causes of inflation. Study Question 4 reinforces his or her understanding of the quantity equation. Study Question 6 is a preparation for understanding supply-side economics in the next chapter.

Case Application: The High Cost of Loving

This application illustrates the way in which indexes such as the Consumer Price Index are constructed. It takes the prices of goods and services typically involved in dating and marriage and shows how an index of their prices measures changes in the cost of courting.

Answers to the "For Thought" Questions

1. The most inflationary item in the COL was the increase in diamond prices. The price of diamonds shot up in the 1970s because people were buying them as a hedge against inflation, and for speculation. Would you call the inflation of diamond prices a demand-pull or a cost-push type of inflation? Why?

   The inflation of diamond prices was a demand-pull inflation because of the increase in the demand for diamonds as a speculative investment.

2. Which index is a better measure of our purchasing power, the CPI or the COL? Why?

The CPI is a better measure of our purchasing power because it includes more of the types of goods and services which people typically spend most of their budget on.

3. Do you think that the high cost of loving has actually affected dating practices? How? Do price changes affect our buying habits in general? What implication does this have for the validity of the CPI?

Open answer. Students who are familiar with dating practices in earlier decades will probably respond that dating practices have changed, at least partly because of higher costs. There may be more mixed group activities in which everyone pays their own way. Also, whereas dating used to occur mainly in the teenage years, it now often extends well into the twenties or beyond.

Price changes do affect our buying habits, as shown in chapter 4. The implication of this is that the CPI is not as good a measurement of our cost of living during times of rapidly changing prices, since the sample of goods and services on which it is based is not representative of current purchasing patterns.

Is There a Trade-Off Between Unemployment and Inflation?

This section first examines the historic trade-off between unemployment and inflation using the Phillips curve diagram. It discusses the stagflation of the 1970s as an upward shift of the Phillips curve. It then explains the changed relationship between inflation and unemployment with the use of AD/AS diagrams. Finally, it examines the actual events that took place in the economy which explain the changes in the behavior of aggregate supply.

A transparency of Figure 11 on page 279 can be used to compare the relationship between output and prices with different assumptions about aggregate supply. Figure 11A shows aggregate supply behaving in a simplistic way so that there is no rise in prices until output reaches the full employment level. (This is comparable to the inflationary overflow of production capacity shown in Figure 7A on page 272.) Figure 11B shows an aggregate supply curve based on more realistic assumptions, with shortages of certain resources and types of labor, combined with speculation, causing prices to rise before full employment is reached. Figure 11C shows the aggregate supply curve after inflationary expectations have taken hold, resulting in stagflation.

Study Question 5 reinforces the student's understanding of phases of the business cycle by examining the current economic situation. Study Question 7 examines one effect of inflationary expectations on economic conditions.

Case Application: The Roller Coaster Ride

This application draws an analogy between the classic business cycle and a roller coaster ride. The analogy dramatizes the economic content in order to help the students learn and remember it.

Answers to the "For Thought" Questions

1. At what phase of the business cycle would you expect conditions to be at the upper left end of the Phillips curve? At the lower right end?

   You would expect conditions to be at the upper left end of the Phillips curve during the peak phase of the business cycle. You would expect conditions to be at the lower right end of the Phillips curve during the trough of the business cycle.

2. How does stagflation differ from the traditional business cycle?

   Stagflation differs from the traditional business cycle because prices correspond to the peak phase simultaneously with output and employment corresponding to the trough phase.

3. Which do you think is worse, stagflation or the traditional business cycle? Why?

   Open answer. The traditional business cycle could be said to be worse than stagflation because at the depths of a serious recession or depression there is such a large amount of unemployment that personal hardship is widespread and severe. On the other hand, in the traditional business cycle bad times are normally followed by a period of prosperity and relatively stable prices. With stagflation, on the other hand, conditions may not improve. If anything, they may progressively deteriorate.

What Are the Consequences of Unemployment and Inflation?

People are very much aware of the effects of unemployment and inflation on their income and purchasing power, but from this section students may obtain a new understanding of the effects on aggregate output. Output per capita is a measure of our standard of living. Using this yardstick, inflation might be considered the lesser of the two evils. Unemployment directly reduces total output and, hence, our standard of living. The effects of inflation on total output are less predictable. Unless it results in economic collapse as it did in Germany in the 1920s, not everyone loses from inflation. If output remains constant, the inflationary losses to some become the inflationary gains to others. Study Questions 8, 9, and 10 examine the effects of inflation.

Case Application: Inflation—How High Is Up?

The case of Germany in the early 1920s was a classic example of "printing press inflation." In order to pay its bills, including reparation payments from World War I, the German government simply printed money, resulting in a monetary inflation. The case application describes the resulting effects. It points out some countries today that are flirting with hyperinflation.

Answers to the "For Thought" Questions

1. Which effects of inflation does the case of hyperinflation in Germany during the 1920s illustrate?

   The hyperinflation in Germany illustrates mainly the real output effects of inflation, since it does indicate there were changes in real income. (The daily wage payments were a way of avoiding a decline in purchasing power.) The case application shows how and why the inflation discouraged production.

2. The German government was unable to sell bonds, so it had to resort to "printing press" money. Why would no one buy German government bonds in the early 1920s?

   The German government could not sell bonds in the early 1920s because of the inflation. If someone bought a bond, by the time it could be redeemed it would be practically worthless.

3. Do you think that hyperinflation could happen in this country? Why do you think it might, or what do you think would prevent it?

   Open answer. Short of a catastrophe—such as a nuclear war—hyperinflation is unlikely in this country. The U.S. government is committed to a reasonable level of price stability and would not follow in the path of 1920s Germany, except under the most extreme circumstances.

Perspective: Black Thursday and the Great Crash

The Perspective describes the day of the crash on Wall Street in 1929. It points out that, while this event signaled the beginning of the depression of the 1930s, the Wall Street crash was not the cause of the Great Depression. It shows how economic problems that were building in the 1920s led to the depression of the 1930s. It sets the stage for a discussion of the "Keynesian Revolution," which is the Perspective of the next chapter.

Answers to Study Questions

1. Mr. Jones was disabled in an accident in 1981 and has not been able to work since. Is he included in the unemployment statistics? Why or why not?

   He is not included in the unemployment statistics because he is not actively seeking a job.

2. If the average propensity to consume (chapter 4) increased, how might the price level be affected? Under what circumstances would such an increase be inflationary? Under what circumstances would it not necessarily be inflationary?

   If the average propensity to consume increased, the price level might rise. The increase in consumption would be inflationary if the economy was already at or near full employment. It would not necessarily be inflationary if there was substantial unemployment and production overcapacity.

3. A reduction in space exploration programs has resulted in a loss of jobs in the aerospace industry. This situation is an example of what type of unemployment?

   This situation is an example of structural unemployment.

4. Judging from the quantity equation, could the money supply go down and prices go up at the same time? What would have to happen for this to come about?

   The money supply could go down and prices go up at the same time if there were a large decrease in total output and/or the velocity of circulation of money increased substantially.

5. The economy is currently in what phase of business conditions—recovery, boom, peak, bust, contraction, recession, trough, or stagflation? How can you tell?

   Open answer. In early 1987 the economy was in a prolonged recovery phase. Students can tell the current phase from recent figures on changes in output, unemployment, and prices.

6. How can the production capacity of the economy expand from the amount shown in Figure 7A to the amount shown in Figure 7B on page 272?

   Production capacity expands as a result of investment in new plants and equipment.

7. If an anticipation of price inflation leads business firms to build up inventories of raw materials and semi-finished goods, what effect does this have on economic conditions? Why?

   If an anticipation of price inflation leads business firms to build up inventories of raw materials and semi-finished goods, there will be an increase in aggregate demand and the likelihood of shortages. As a result, the anticipation of price inflation will be a self-fulfilling prophecy because prices will rise.

8. Assuming an inflation rate of 10% per year for the next five years, what would be the effect on the purchasing power of the dollar at the end of that time?

   The purchasing power of the dollar would fall to approximately 62 cents. What originally cost $1 would cost $1.61 (an increase of 10% compounded for five years). Dividing $1 by $1.61 makes the purchasing power of $1 equal to $.621 five years later.

9. If Mrs. Sawyer were living on a fixed pension of $500 per month, how would she fare if inflation occurred at the rate indicated in Question 8?

   Her living standard would be substantially reduced. Her purchasing power would be only 62% of what it had been five years earlier.

10. Why did homeowners who bought houses in the early 1970s benefit from inflation?

    Homeowners who bought houses in the early 1970s benefitted from inflation because the rate of increase in the value of their house was greater than the average increase in prices of goods and services. As a result of the increased asset value of the capital investment in their house, they were wealthier than they would have been if prices had been stable.

Integrating *Economics U$A* Programs

(For information on Economics U$A *see the introduction, p. v.)*

There are two programs pertinent to this chapter. They are program 7, "Inflation: How Did the Spiral Begin?" and program 10, "Stagflation: Why Couldn't We Beat It?" The first combines a discussion of the effects of inflation with a discussion of policies, while the textbook considers them separately. The roots of inflation were in the policies followed in the administration of Lyndon Johnson in the latter 1960s. These policies were to pursue the war in Vietnam and a domestic war on poverty, with no tax increase. This formula produced inflation because aggregate demand exceeded the supply capacity of the economy. This is illustrated by Figure 7A on page 272. Economist Gill shows this "Keynesian-style" inflation with the use of an aggregate demand-supply model like that in Figure 11A on page 279.

The second part of the program examines who gains and who loses from inflation (text pp. 285-87). Gill reinforces the idea that every payment of a higher price is also a receipt of a larger income for someone. In analyzing the third case on Nixon's price and wage controls, Gill incorporates inflationary expectations into the AD/AS model. The result is like that in Figure 11C on page 279.

The other program on stagflation examines the difference between the normal demand-pull inflation and the cost-push inflation of the 1970s. The Phillips curve is explained, and Gill describes how the Phillips curve in the 1970s followed a zigzag path such as that shown in Figure 9 on page 277.

Case Applications in Student Workbook

(Answers are supplied to students in the workbook.)

What Causes Unemployment?

Case Application: Where the Jobs Went

This application surveys the country's job situation in the mid-1980s. It shows the types of jobs which had the highest levels of unemployment and discusses why unemployment was concentrated in those areas. It relates the unemployment to the structural changes that were taking place in the economy.

Answers to the "For Thought" Questions

1. The more than 100,000 jobs that were permanently lost in the automobile industry represented what type of unemployment?

   The more than 100,000 jobs permanently lost in the automobile industry represented structural unemployment. They were lost by an increase in the automation of automobile production methods and by an increase in the share of the U.S. automobile market accounted for by foreign car imports.

2. About one in every four women workers who were displaced from jobs that they had held for three years or more gave up looking for a new job. Were they counted as unemployed? What type of unemployment did they represent?

   Married women who lost their jobs because of the recession and did not try to find new jobs were not counted as unemployed because only those actively seeking jobs are considered unemployed. The housewives represented hidden unemployment.

3. What would you recommend to a 40-year-old steelworker, with a wife and four children to support, who lost his job when the steel mill shut down in Donora, Pennsylvania?

   Open answer. A 40-year-old steelworker, with a family, who lost his job would have difficult alternatives. One possibility would be to try and scrape by on unemployment compensation, as long as it lasted, and then on savings in hopes the steel mill would reopen. Another possibility would be to move his family to a state with a lower unemployment rate than Pennsylvania's in hopes of finding other work for which he was qualified. A third possibility would be for him to attempt to obtain retraining for a different type of work in an expanding industry. All of these choices involve difficulties and dangers for the economic security of his family.

What Causes Inflation?

Case Application: Talk About Inflation—

This application examines the reasons for some instances of really extreme inflation rates in other countries such as Bolivia, Argentina, and Israel.

Answers the the "For Thought" Questions

1. If dinner in a Bolivian restaurant cost 10 Bolivian dollars at the end of 1984, what would a restaurant patron have to pay for the same meal at the end of 1985?

   The restaurant dinner would have cost 340 Bolivian dollars in 1985. This is calculated by multiplying 10 Bolivian dollars by 3,400%. (Note that 3,400% of a number is 34 times the number, since the decimal point is moved two places to the right when expressing a percent.)

2. What types of inflation are described in this application?

   The types of inflation described in this application are demand-pull and monetary inflation.

3. Why do you think inflation was so much greater in those countries than in the United States?

   Open answer. Likely reasons why the inflation rates are so much greater in those countries than in the United States are: they have smaller economies than the U.S., so a monetary disturbance is not as easily absorbed as it is in the large U.S. economy; they have had more severe economic problems, such as the Arab-Israeli conflict and the Argentine war over the Faulkland Islands and the subsequent overthrow of the military government; and, probably the main difference, they do not have a monetary control as effective as the Fed in the U.S.

Is There a Trade-Off Between Unemployment and Inflation?

Case Application: Phillips Curve International

The application discusses the differences in attitudes of the United States and Western European countries with respect to the trade-off between inflation and unemployment. In the past, European countries have opted for lower rates of unemployment, along with higher rates of inflation. In the 1980s, however, the European countries were severely affected by stagflation and have been stuck with previously unacceptable unemployment levels.

Answers to the "For Thought" Questions

1. Prior to 1975, were the European countries operating more to the lower right or to the upper left on their Phillips curves, compared to the United States?

   Prior to 1975, the European countries were operating more to the upper left on their Phillips curves, with higher inflation rates and lower unemployment rates compared to the United States.

2. How did the rise in energy costs in the 1970s contribute to the upward shift in the Phillips curve in Western Europe?

   The rise in energy costs in the 1970s made European production costs higher which both raised the inflation rate and made their industries less competitive in the marketplace, thus slowing their economies and causing unemployment. The combination of higher prices and higher unemployment was represented by an upward shift in the Phillips curve.

3. In which direction on the Phillips curve do you think it is better for a country to be located, the lower right or the upper left? Why?

   Open answer. Answering this question is complicated and uncertain, depending on the assumptions and value judgements adopted. The upper left portion of the Phillips curve imposes the costs of inflation such as a burden on those with fixed incomes and possible declines in the efficiency and growth of the economy.

On the other hand, it minimizes the human, social, and output costs of unemployment. The lower right location on the Phillips curve increases those unemployment costs while minimizing the costs of inflation.

What Are the Consequences of Unemployment and Inflation?

Case Application: Disinflation Losers

The application discusses the consequences of the end of inflation for those who had benefitted from inflation and acted to protect themselves from its effects. It prepares the students to answer Study Question 10 at the end of the textbook chapter.

Answers to the "For Thought" Questions

1. Whose wealth and income were negatively affected by an end to inflation?

   The wealth and income of those who had purchased real assets such as houses, gold, precious gems, or commodities were negatively affected by an end to inflation. Debtors lose out when disinflation sets in, and the incomes of governments are also affected.

2. How would a decline in the price of gold and other commodities be likely to affect the output of those commodities? Why?

   A decline in the price of gold and other commodities would be likely to affect the output of those commodities because of the law of supply. Unless the supply is perfectly inelastic, a price decline will result in reductions in their output.

3. Is disinflation as bad as inflation? Why or why not?

   Open answer. A severe disinflation could be worse than inflation. A collapse of prices such as that occurring in the early 1930s would cause many business failures and high unemployment. A disinflation resulting in a stable price level, however, would be better than inflation because it would benefit equity, efficiency, and growth.

Chapter 12

The Economy's Output

Chapter Overview

This chapter deals with the measurement of total output and presents a model for analyzing what determines total output. The introductory article discusses the business of economic forecasting. It examines the fact that, despite advances in the technology and methods of forecasting, the science of economic predictions remains inexact.

The first section of the chapter explains Gross National Product and how it is measured. It also discusses the effect of inflation on the GNP figures. The case application provides an example of how an individual business contributes to GNP.

The second section presents a model for analyzing total output. It is the Keynesian macroeconomic equilibrium model presented in a way that is new but carrys forward the traditional circular flow model concept. The case application discusses the relationship of inventory changes to aggregate demand.

The last section of the chapter explains what is meant by supply-side economics. It examines the roots of supply-side economics in earlier economic thought and outlines the principal ideas in its current formulation. The case application shows how modern supply-side economics gained national attention and became a major force in economic policy.

Suggested Answers to the Learning Objectives

The knowledge acquired in this chapter should enable the students to:

1. Define the GNP and explain the two ways of measuring it and why they give the same result.

    GNP is the sum of the values of all goods and services produced during the year. The two ways of measuring GNP are the expenditures approach and the incomes approach. They give the same result because the expenditures on goods and services end up as incomes to factors of production.

2. List the four types of expenditures that make up the total demand for goods and services.

    The four types of expenditures are personal consumption expenditures, private domestic investments, government expenditures, and net exports.

3. Define National Income and discuss how it differs from GNP.

    National Income is the total of all incomes earned in producing the GNP. With the addition of capital consumption allowances and indirect taxes and other business transfers, it is equal to current dollar GNP.

4. Define constant dollar GNP and show how it relates to current dollar GNP.

    Constant dollar GNP is the value of GNP adjusted for changes in the price level in a base period. Current dollar GNP deflated by the price index gives constant dollar GNP.

5. Explain the Keynesian economic model and show under what conditions the output of the economy is at equilibrium.

    The Keynesian economic model shows that the level of total output is determined by the amount of purchasing power demand flowing into the economy from the consumption, investment, government, and foreign sectors.

    The income generated by economic activity flows out to four alternative allocations: consumption, savings, taxes, and imports. The income allocations to the consumption, financial, government, and foreign sectors provide purchasing power for the demand emanating from those four sectors. Except for the consumption sector, the purchasing power demand flowing from the sectors is not necessarily equal to the allocations of income to the sectors.

    If the amount of purchasing power injected into the economy from the four demand sectors is just equal to the allocation of income to the four sectors, the output level of the economy will be at equilibrium. If the injections of purchasing power into the economy are greater than the allocations of income from economic activity (the leakages), total output will increase. If the leakages are greater than the injections, total output will decline.

6. Define Say's Law

   Say's Law holds that when goods or services are produced, enough income is generated to purchase what is produced, thereby eliminating the problem of overproduction.

7. Explain how supply-side economics differs from demand-side economics.

   Supply-side economics differs from demand-side economics because it emphasizes the role of production incentives in determining the level of output and deemphasizes the role of the government.

How Much Does the Economy Produce?

This section begins by showing that there are two approaches to measuring total output—the expenditures approach and the incomes approach—and why they give the same results. This discussion of national income accounting does more than merely demonstrate what the terms Gross National Product and National Income mean. It shows the components of total demand (Table 1 textbook page 298), reviews the factor shares that compose total income, teaches the concept of value added, and shows the difference between current dollar and constant dollar measurements.

Study Questions 1, 2, 3, 4, and 5 provide the student with reinforcement of the concepts and measurements covered in this section.

Case Application: Harry's Sub Shop

This application relates a microeconomic case to the macroeconomic measurements of GNP. It provides a concrete illustration of the two ways of measuring output, the expenditures and income approaches, and allows the student to see why they give the same results.

Answers to the "For Thought" Questions

1. What was the value added to national output by Harry's Sub Shop in 1985?

   The value added to national output by Harry's Sub Shop in 1985 was $46,610. This was the value of the sandwiches which the store sold, less its purchases from other firms.

2. What happened to the firm's contribution to current dollar GNP in 1986 compared to 1985? What happened to its contribution to real or constant dollar GNP in that year compared with the previous year?

   If Harry raised the price of his subs only by the amount of the increase in the costs of the ingredients, the contribution of the firm to GNP in 1986 would be the same as in 1985 because the value added would be the same. Its contribution to real GNP was the same because it sold the same number of sandwiches.

3. While Harry was running his two businesses, his wife Margaret was taking care of their three children and the house. Since she didn't get paid for this, she was not contributing to GNP. Was she actually making no contribution to the nation's output? What might be the arguments for and against including housework in GNP?

   Open answer. It could be argued that it is illogical not to include housework in GNP because if it were done by maids rather than wives it would be included. It has been pointed out that if women paired off and did each other's housework, paying each other for the work, there would be an immense increase in GNP. Since housework is valuable, it can be argued that an estimate of its value should be made and included in GNP. The arguments against including the value of housework in GNP are that such an estimate would be very difficult to make. Since housework is a service not transacted (for the most part) in the market, it does not directly generate income and purchasing power; therefore, the new figures would not be comparable with earlier GNP data.

What Determines How Much the Economy Produces From the Demand-Side Point of View?

This section presents the Keynesian macroeconomic model in a way that students can understand more easily than the Keynesian cross diagram. It uses a diagram of a tank to show the output capacity of the economy, as introduced in the previous chapter. The GNP tank model shown in Figure 3 on page 303 is related to the circular flow model in chapter 2 on page 45, and reviewing it might be useful preparation for learning the GNP tank model in this chapter. The simple circular flow model includes only the consumption goods which are sold by the business sector to the household sector. This is the blue consumption flow in the GNP tank model.

In the Keynesian model there are three other sectors—investment, government, and the foreign sector. Total spending on goods and services flows into the economy from the four demand sectors through the pipes at the top of the tank marked X for exports, C for consumption, G for government spending, and I for investment spending. The income that is created by production activity then flows out of the tank through the pipes at the bottom and is allocated to purchase of domestically produced goods and services (C), imports (M), taxes (T), and savings (S). The allocation of income to domestic consumption, the blue pipe, flows directly back into the GNP tank as purchasing power. The other three income "leakages," however, do not go directly back into GNP. Instead, they flow into holding tanks representing the foreign sector, the financial sector, and the government sector. There the amounts are adjusted by the foreign trade balance, by the operation of the financial markets, and by government budgets before returning to the income stream. As a result of the adjustments in these sectors, the amounts of purchasing power flowing into GNP may be less than, equal to, or greater than the allocations of income flowing out of GNP. If the "injections" are greater than the "leakages," the level of total output represented by the purple area in the GNP tank will rise. If they are less, the level of output will fall and unemployment will increase. If they are the same (C + I + G + X = C + S + T + M) the level of output will be at equilibrium. The equilibrium GNP may be at any level, not necessarily at full employment.

The color transparency of Figure 3 from the transparency set can be used effectively to help the students understand the four sectors that make up aggregate demand and the relationship between the allocations of income to those sectors—the "leakages" from the bottom of the tank—and the purchasing power flowing into the top of the tank which determines aggregate demand. When the model is subsequently used to show how changes in one of the demand sectors affect GNP and employment, as in Figure 4 on page 307, the model is presented in schematic form to make it easier to work with. This schematic form of the model is especially helpful if you want to use the blackboard as well as, or instead of, the overhead projector. Study Questions 6, 7, 8, and 9 exercise the student's understanding of the macroeconomic model.

Case Application: The Inventory Paradox

This application explains the contradictory behavior of inventories during the business cycle. It also shows why the inventory paradox magnifies the extent of cyclical fluctuation.

Answers to the "For Thought" Questions

1. Which of the demand sectors incorporates the spending on inventories?

   The net change in inventories is one of the components of the investment sector.

2. Why does the inventory paradox tend to make business cycles worse?

   Because of the unintended investment in inventories when sales are falling, businesses cut back on new orders by a greater percentage than the decline in sales. This accelerates the decline in production and the increase in unemployment during the downswing. In similar fashion, there is overproduction during the

boom phase because of the multiplicity of new orders placed by firms in an attempt to restock depleted inventories.

3. Some economic fluctuations since the World War II have consisted almost exclusively of changes in inventory investment and are known as "inventory cycles." Under what conditions do you think an inventory cycle could touch off a major business cycle and under what conditions would it be unlikely to?

Open answer. As indicated in the previous question, the fluctuations in inventories can magnify the normal course of business cycles. However, if consumer spending, long-term investment spending, government spending, and net exports are stable and the only significant changes are in inventory spending, the economic fluctuations will be minor. An inventory cycle is most likely to touch off a major business cycle if the cycle phase is near its peak.

What Determines How Much the Economy Produces From the Supply-Side Point of View?

When President Reagan made supply-side economics the foundation of his economic program, there was no agreed-upon definition of what the term meant. It was not to be found in dictionaries of economic terms nor in glossaries or indexes of economics textbooks. Demand-side economics was called Keynesian economics, and what it meant had been explored in numerous volumes. Even now after much discussion of supply-side economics in recent years, its meaning is not very exact. However, supply-side economics is not entirely new, since it is related to earlier economic theories such as Say's Law of Markets. The main components of contemporary supply-side economics are: providing increased production incentives by reducing taxes and government regulations, cutting back government outlays on social services, and reducing government borrowing which "crowds out" private borrowing in the capital markets.

The transparency of Figures 5A and 5B shows the supply-side view of how the economy adjusts to a decline in investment spending. Comparisons between Keynesian and supply-side analysis in this and the next chapter can be clearly shown by use of the GNP tank model. Figure 7 dramatizes the "crowding out" of private investment by government deficit finance. The effect is exaggerated for illustrative purposes by eliminating the investment flow altogether. Study Question 10 has the student apply supply-side analysis.

Case Application: Supply-side Incubator

Modern supply-side economics appeared on the national scene with the Reagan presidential campaign of 1980, although its roots go back to early economists. Its structure was forged in the financial section of the *Wall Street Journal*, as described in this application.

Answers to the "For Thought" Questions

1. How would the increase in military spending advocated by the New Right affect the flows in the GNP tank model? Show on a diagram.

   An increase in military spending, all other things remaining the same (including the level of spending on other government programs), would increase government demand and stimulate output, increasing GNP. This would be shown on the GNP tank diagram by an increase in the "G" flow into the tank and a rise in the level in the tank.

2. If supply-side economists are correct about the results of a reduction in tax rates, how would lowering taxes affect equilibrium GNP? Show by means of diagrams.

   The Laffer curve is based on the assumption that lowering tax rates would increase investment and work incentives, resulting in increased economic activity and a rise in the equilibrium GNP. This would be shown on the diagram by an increase in the "I" flow and a rise in the level in the tank. According to the Laffer hypothesis, there would follow an increase in the "T" flow from the tank to government revenues.

3. Do you agree or disagree with the ideas of the New Right? Why?

   Open answer. Those who agree with the New Right generally believe in the superiority of unfettered capitalism over government intervention. They believe that market allocations of resources and production will provide the best economic outcome and any involvement by government, except for national military security, diminishes the effectiveness of the economic system. They believe that the standard of living is determined primarily by the profitability of investment and production. Those that do not agree with the New Right believe that the government has a necessary role to play in stabilizing the economy. They believe that the economy is not self-equilibrating and that total laissez-faire capitalism leads to alternating periods of severe recession/depression and inflationary booms. They think that maintaining an adequate level of aggregate demand is the most important thing in stabilizing the economy.

Perspective: The Keynesian Revolution

The macroeconomic model presented in this chapter is that of John Maynard Keynes, although he did not explain it in terms of a GNP tank. The Perspective deals with why his model was considered revolutionary. Today's supply-side economics might be looked upon as a counterrevolution. In economic policy there seems to be a search for a synthesis of Keynesian and supply-side economics that will provide a solution to the economic problems of the 1980s.

Answers to Study Questions

1. If you tutored a classmate for 10 hours at $4 an hour, what would be the effect on National Income?

   The effect would be to increase National Income by $40.

2. In the above case, if you had no expenses, what would be the effect on the nation's output as measured by GNP?

   The effect would be to increase the nation's GNP by $40.

3. Assuming in the above case that you had to spend $.50 for gas to drive to each 1-hour tutoring session, what would be the value added to GNP by your tutoring?

   The value added to GNP would be $35.

4. On January 1, 1986, a grocery store had on hand an inventory valued at $240,000. During 1986 the store had bought groceries worth $600,000. Sales for that year came to $800,000. How much did this firm contribute to the investment component of GNP for 1986?

   The store contributed (-)$200,000 to the investment component of GNP for 1986. Since sales for the year exceeded purchases by $200,000, the store had a net disinvestment in inventories of that amount.

5. If you had a $200,000 "dream house" built, what would be the effect on GNP? What component of aggregate demand would be affected?

   The effect would be to increase GNP by $200,000. This would be an increase in the investment component of aggregate demand.

6. You are working at a job with a take-home pay of $200 a week. You have been putting $15 into a savings account every week, but you want to build up your

savings faster, so you increase it to $25. What effect would this have on GNP?

If all other things remained the same, this would reduce GNP because of the increased leakage into savings.

7. Assuming the economy is at an equilibrium level of output, what are three examples of changes that would cause output to fall?

Open answer. Examples might include: an increase in the propensity to save (see preceding question), an increase in taxes, a decrease in investment, or a decrease in government spending.

8. If output were not at the full employment level, what are three examples of changes that would increase GNP?

Open answer. Examples might include: a decrease in taxes, an increase in government spending, a decrease in the propensity to save, or an increase in investment.

9. According to Keynesian economics, what would happen to output, employment, and income if government spending was reduced by 50% and taxes by 25%?

A simultaneous decrease in government spending by 50% and taxes by 25% would have a negative effect on GNP according to Keynesian economics. It would cause output, employment, and income to fall.

10. According to supply-side economics, what would happen to equilibrium GNP if government spending and taxes were both reduced by 50%?

According to supply-side economics, a reduction of 50% in both government spending and taxes would lead to an increase in equilibrium GNP because it would be an incentive to additional investment that would raise production, employment, and incomes.

Integrating *Economics U$A* Programs

(For information on Economics U$A *see the introduction, p. v.)*

The first of two programs that are appropriate for this chapter has a somewhat misleading title, "U.S. Economic Growth: What Is GNP?", which is the third program in the series. Most of the discussion deals with how much of our production capacity we were using at a particular time rather than with the growth of capacity. The first application recalls the depressed economic conditions in the 1930s and the need to know more about the actual level of output in order to devise appropriate policies. This need led to the creation of the national income accounting system measuring GNP. In his analysis segment, Gill shows the simple circular flow model. The second application concerns the mobilization of the economy for the war effort in the 1940s and how the national income accounts helped in the planning for mobilization. Gill elaborates the circular flow model by introducing the government sector. He makes an important

point in explaining why additional taxes were necessary during the war—to sop up purchasing power so that aggregate demand would not exceed production capacity. In terms of the GNP tank model, the taxes kept outflow equal to inflow so that the tank did not overflow with inflation.

The other program for this chapter is program 4, "Boom and Bust: Who Can Explain the Business Cycle?" You might prefer to show this program first because it is a logical continuation of the discussion in chapter 11 on the cyclical behavior of the economy. (See Figure 12 on page 280, the case application on page 281, and Figure 13 on pages 282-83.). The first application reveals that it was only in the early twentieth century that there was a gradual recognition by economists of the cyclical nature of the economy. Gill reviews the traditional economists' view of a self-correcting economy and explains Say's Law.

The second segment contrasts the views of Keynes and Joseph Schumpeter on how the economy worked, and Gill compares the Marxian view of free enterprise leading to poverty with Schumpeter's view that it produces a healthy "survival of the fittest." The last application concerns the crash of 1929 and the deepening depression which refused to correct itself, calling for a new explanation. That was supplied by Keynes. Gill shows how Keynes' explanation contradicted Say's Law by demonstrating that a fall in demand is not necessarily self-correcting.

Case Applications in Student Workbook

(Answers are supplied to students in the workbook.)

How Much Does the Economy Produce?

Case Application: Helen's Gift City, Inc.

This application compares a firm's normal income statement with a statement that would be drawn up to show the firm's contribution to Gross National Product. It illustrates specifically what would be included in value added to GNP.

Answers to the "For Thought" Questions

1. What was Helen's contribution to total output?

   Helen's contribution to total output was $110,000. This was the value added by the firm to the GNP, i.e., its sales revenue minus its purchases from other firms.

2. How much did the firm add to National Income? What accounts for the difference between its contribution to GNP and its contribution to NI?

   The firm added $86,000 to National Income. The difference between its contribution to GNP and its contribution to NI is accounted for by the firm's capital consumption allowance and business taxes.

3. Which provides the most useful information about Gift City, Inc., the business accounting statement or the national-income accounting statement? Why?

   Open answer. From the standpoint of the firm, the Account's Income Statement is the most useful organization of the information because it shows the total costs subtracted from sales to determine the firm's profit. The national-income accounting statement is the most useful for determining the contributions of the firm to GNP.

What Determines How Much the Economy Produces From the Demand-Side Point of View?

Case Application: Changes in Demand

This application shows the breakdown of GNP for the years 1981 to 1985 and how the various components changed from year to year. It demonstrates which of the components are the most unstable and cause cyclical fluctuations.

Answers to the "For Thought" Questions

1. In 1985, which GNP component was the weakest?

   In 1985, the weakest GNP component was net exports of goods and services, which fell 5% below the already depressed level of the year before.

2. What was the effect of federal government expenditures on GNP in 1985?

   The effect of federal government expenditures was to stimulate demand and raise GNP in 1985. The increased level of government spending from the year before helped to offset the decline in the foreign sector.

3. In the national-income accounts, consumption spending appears more stable than income. Is your spending more stable than your income? Why or why not?

   Open answer. Most people attempt to maintain their lifestyle in spite of fluctuations in their income. Some, however, may be cautious and reduce their spending sharply if their income falls in order to have a savings cushion in case their income falls further.

What Determines How Much the Economy Produces From the Supply-Side Point of View?

Case Application: Reducing Tax Burdens

The application presents the rationale of supply-side economic policies as explained in the 1982 Economic Report of the President. It discusses in particular the provisions and the reasons for the Economic Recovery Tax Act of 1981.

Answers to the "For Thought" Questions

1. What incentive provisions did President Reagan claim were in the Economic Recovery Tax Act of 1981?

   The incentive provisions President Reagan claimed were in the Economic Recovery Tax Act of 1981 were a reduction in marginal tax rates, making Individual Retirement Accounts available to all workers, cutting the top tax bracket from 70 to 50%, reducing the "marriage penalty," providing faster write-offs for capital investment, restructuring the investment tax credit, providing a new tax credit for research and development expenditures, and reducing the small business tax rate.

2. The 1981 tax law did not result in increasing the propensity of individuals to save rather than borrow and spend. If it had, what would have been the effect on the economy according to Keynesian *versus* supply-side theories?

   If the 1981 tax law had resulted in an increase in individuals' propensity to save, according to Keynesian theory this would have resulted in a decline in aggregate demand which would have reduced GNP and increased unemployment. According to supply-side theory, it would have made more capital available in the loanable funds market, causing an increase in investment spending which would increase production capacity and reduce unemployment.

3. Did the Economic Recovery Tax Act of 1981 achieve the objectives that the President claimed it would? What were the results?

   Open answer. The Economic Recovery Tax Act of 1981 achieved some of its short-run objectives. There was an increase in investment spending and economic growth in 1983 and 1984 and a decline in unemployment. On the other hand, it does not seem to have achieved some of its other goals in the long run. The propensity of individuals to save did not increase but actually fell to new lows. The increase in growth was not sustained and was not large enough to generate sufficient additional tax revenues to offset the reduction in tax rates. The unemployment rate leveled off at a rate higher than was previously considered normal and acceptable.

Chapter 13

Stabilizing the Economy

Chapter Overview

The problems of inflation and unemployment were described in chapter 11, and the model analyzing what determines total output, employment, and prices was covered in chapter 12. This chapter examines what measures are available to the government to reduce inflation and unemployment in order to achieve the goals of stable prices and full employment. The introductory article looks at the problems government policy makers have in getting the public and the economy to behave.

The first section describes what fiscal and monetary policies are. The case application deals with an example of a stabilization policy that worked better than expected—the "Kennedy" tax cut of 1964.

The second section explains how fiscal policy works, using the GNP tank model from chapter 12. It explains the multiplier effect and automatic stabilizers. The case application reports the results of giving large tax-cut breaks to businesses in 1981 to encourage investment. This is followed by a section explaining how monetary policy operates. The case application for this latter section deals with the real cost of borrowing, after adjustments for inflation and interest tax deductions.

The final section covers the skeptics' view of stabilization policies and the last-resort alternatives available if monetary and fiscal policies are not successful in stabilizing the economy. These alternatives range from the price controls that were instituted in the past in wartime situations to novel proposals called "gain-sharing" and the "Market Anti-inflation Plan." The case application shows how an individual business would operate under the Market Anti-inflation Plan.

Suggested Answers to the Learning Objectives

The knowledge acquired from this chapter should enable the students to:

1. Identify economic fluctuations over the past decade and the events which make economic stability difficult to achieve.

   Following the stagflation of the late 1970s, in the early 1980s the economy plunged into the worst slump since the Great Depression. External fluctuations in petroleum and other prices and the international value of the dollar have complicated the job of stabilizing the

economy, as has the unpredictable behavior of the public.

2. Identify the government's two major instruments of stabilization policy.

   The two principal instruments of stabilization policy are fiscal policy and monetary policy.

3. Differentiate between annually balanced budgets, cyclically balanced budgets, and functional finance.

   A policy of annually balanced budgets would prevent the government from spending more in any year than it took in that year from taxes and other receipts. A policy of cyclically balanced budgets would require that government deficits in some years be offset by budget surpluses in other years over a given period of time. A policy of functional finance calls for the government to utilize its fiscal activities to maintain full employment and stable prices regardless of the effects on the budget balance.

4. Explain how discretionary fiscal policy works from the Keynesian and supply-side viewpoints.

   During a recession Keynesian fiscal policy would call for tax cuts aimed at increasing consumption expenditures and for an increase in government spending. Supply-side fiscal policy would call for tax cuts aimed at increasing the amount of savings and investments and for a reduction in government spending and borrowing.

5. Describe the multiplier effect.

   The multiplier effect results when an initial increase in spending becomes income to the recipients of the spending, and they in turn increase their spending out of the new income. The process is repeated until all of the increments to income are absorbed in savings and taxes. The multiplier is the reciprocal of the sum of the savings and tax rates.

6. Define and give examples of automatic stabilizers.

   Automatic stabilizers are changes in government payments and tax receipts that automatically result from fluctuations in national income and act to offset those fluctuations. Examples include unemployment compensation and welfare payments such as Aid to Families With Dependent Children.

7. Explain how monetary policy is implemented.

Monetary policy is implemented by the Federal Reserve instruments of monetary control. The Fed can induce an expansion or contraction of credit in the financial markets by changing reserve requirements, changing the discount rate, or engaging in open market operations.

8. Discuss the "rational expectations" school of thought and describe three ways of preventing inflation other than monetary and fiscal policies.

The rational expectations school of thought holds that if the government attempts to implement a stabilization policy to change the economy, individuals will deduce what the consequences of the action will be for them personally and take measures to protect their own self interest, which will defeat the government's intention. Inflation can be prevented by direct price controls, by incomes policies which penalize price increases and/or reward price stability or decreases, by a system of "gain-sharing" which pays workers according to the profitability of the company, or by setting up a system of price credits which businesses must obtain in order to raise prices.

9. Define indexing.

Indexing is a system of adjusting incomes in line with inflation.

What Can the Government Do About Unemployment and Inflation?

This section describes the two principal stabilization policy instruments: fiscal policy and monetary policy. Contracyclical fiscal policy dates from the Keynesian revolution. Before that, the government's fiscal activities tended to reinforce cyclical swings. The objective of annually balancing the budget resulted in reductions in government spending and/or increase in taxes during periods of declining output. Contracyclical fiscal policy after World War II involved intentionally unbalancing the budget. Monetary policy is implemented by the Federal Reserve through its controls over the money creation process.

Study Question 1 brings out the point that fiscal stabilization policy became feasible only when the federal government reached a significant size.

Case Application: A Stabilization Policy Success Story

The success of the 1964 tax cut which restored the economy to relatively full employment is pointed to by both the Keynesians and the supply-siders as evidence that their policies work. Whether the success was due to Keynesian stimulus to demand or to supply-side investments (or to both), it did demonstrate that discretionary fiscal policy

works. But at that time there were no strong inflationary pressures that had to be dealt with simultaneously.

Answers to the "For Thought" Questions

1. Was the 1964 tax cut an application of fiscal policy or monetary policy? Why?

   The 1964 tax cut was an application of fiscal policy because fiscal policy includes the use of government taxing to influence general economic activity.

2. Did the passage of the Kennedy tax bill reflect an annually-balanced-budget philosophy or a functional-finance philosophy? How can you tell?

   The tax bill reflected a functional-finance philosophy because it cut taxes at a time when the federal budget was running a $5.9 billion deficit.

3. Do you think the success of a tax cut in stimulating output, employment, investment, and income can be attributed more to demand-side effects or to supply-side effects? Why?

   Open answer. Those who think that the level of demand is the main economic determinant would credit demand-side effects. Those who believe that the incentives to invest are the main determinant of the level of economic activity would credit supply-side effects.

How Does Fiscal Policy Help Stabilize the Economy?

In this section the operation of fiscal policy is explained with the assistance of the GNP tank diagram. Figure 2 on page 328 of the textbook shows a reduction in the tax leakage accompanied by an increase in government spending. With the resulting increase in purchasing power, consumption spending grows by a multiple of the fiscal policy stimulus. The result is an increase in production which raises the level of GNP toward full employment.

Supply-side fiscal policy is illustrated in Figure 3 on textbook page 329 in which both taxes and government spending are reduced, providing for an increase in savings and investment spending. The new investment increases output and employment, causing the GNP to rise toward full employment.

The multiplier effect can be illustrated with the GNP tank diagram by showing successive increases in the GNP level in the tank with each round of spending. You can use Table 1, page 330, alongside the GNP tank and draw arrows from each stage of the multiplier process in the table to a corresponding addition to the level in the tank.

Study Questions 2, 3, and 4 reinforce the understanding of how discretionary fiscal policy works. Study Question 5 reinforces the understanding of automatic stabilizers.

Case Application: Investment Incentives or Tax Loopholes?

The sizable investment tax credits given to businesses by the 1981 tax bill were intended to stimulate investment spending. The actual effects of the tax incentives are shown by two independent studies which are discussed in this application. One of the studies shows that the corporations that benefited most from the tax breaks spent less on investment than did an average company in the following few years while increasing dividends more, whereas the firms that received the least tax incentives increased investment spending by the largest amounts and raised dividends the least. The other study found that the types of investment which increased most after 1981 were investments that did not significantly benefit from tax credits, while those that did benefit increased only slightly.

The 1986 tax reform bill did away with the generous investment tax credits of the 1981 bill, leaving investment incentives to market forces—the sales of goods and services—where they apparently lay all along.

Answers to the "For Thought" Questions

1. Did the 1981 investment tax incentives for business represent Keynesian fiscal policy or supply-side fiscal policy. Show the intended effects with a GNP tank diagram.

    The 1981 investment tax incentives represented supply-side fiscal policy because they were aimed at raising profits and increasing production capacity rather than increasing consumer demand. The intended effects can be shown on a GNP tank diagram by indicating a reduction in the tax flow (T-) and an increase in the savings flow (S+) along with an increase in the flow of investment spending (I+). This results in an increase in the size of the GNP tank.

2. If, as a result of the 1986 tax reform, individuals' take-home pay increases $14 billion a year, what would be the potential multiplier effect on total spending with a savings rate of 5% and a tax rate of 20%?

    The multiplier would be 4 (1/.25) and the potential multiplier effect would be $56 billion (4 x $14 billion).

3. Do you think that the government should use the tax system to provide investment incentives? Why or why not? How about tax incentives to purchase a house (mortgage interest deductions) or save for retirement (IRAs)? How do you feel about government incentives for education (student assistance and student loans)?

    Open answer. Those who favor tax incentives for investment or housing or other purposes generally do so because they believe that the government has a legitimate function in actively encouraging certain types of business and consumer behavior. Those that are opposed to an activist role for the government believe

that such decisions are better left to the market and individual determination.

How Can Monetary Policy Help Stabilize the Economy?

The Federal Reserve System and the tools of monetary control were covered in chapter 10, textbook pages 249-53. This section explains how the Fed uses open market operations, the discount rate, and reserve requirements to implement monetary policy for stable prices and full employment. It compares the Federal Reserve objective prior to 1979 of controlling interest rates with the subsequent objective of controlling the money supply itself.

The GNP tank model can be used to show the effects of monetary policy on the economy as well as those of fiscal policy. Monetary policy effects operate through the financial sector, increasing investment demand (I+) which raises the level of GNP and reduces unemployment. When drawing the GNP tank model on the blackboard or an overhead transparency, it is of course not necessary to each time put in all four sectors, but only those sectors which are relevant to the discussion.

Study Questions 6 and 7 reinforce the student's understanding of material covered in this section.

Case Application: Cheap Money

The use of other people's money is less expensive in the United States than in any other major western country. This application explains how the "real" interest rate is lowered not only by inflation but also by the tax deductions permitted for interest paid. This, combined with the fact that interest earned is taxed as income, may explain in part the low savings rate in the United States compared with other countries. The 1986 tax reform reduced the incentives to borrow by eliminating tax deductions for interest paid except for mortgage interest. A house owner can get around this restriction by borrowing against a certain amount of equity in the home for other types of purchases.

Answers to the "For Thought" Questions

1. How do the Fed's efforts to control the money supply affect the nominal interest rate?

    When the Fed restricts the money supply it tends to raise interest rates, and loosening the money supply tends to lower interest rates.

2. Does the exceptionally low tax-adjusted real interest rate in this country have an influence on our money supply? How?

    The low tax-adjusted real interest rate expands the money supply because it encourages borrowing, which is one of the ways that money is created as shown on page 247.

3. Should the tax laws stop subsidizing all borrowing by individuals? By businesses? Why or why not? Should interest earnings on savings be exempt from taxation? What effect would this have on income distribution between the wealthy and the poor?

Open answer. It could be argued that tax subsidies for borrowing by individuals helps to keep the rate of savings artificially low in this country, and thus restricts the amount of loanable funds available for investment. It also boosts consumption and tends to cause imports to exceed exports. Tax subsidies for business borrowing helped to finance the corporate takeover frenzy (pp. 135-36), as well as financing real investment. On the other side, owning one's own home has been a fundamental goal in our society and few people would be able to do that if it were not for the tax subsidies on mortgage borrowing. Interest on business borrowing is simply another type of production cost which businesses need to deduct from their income before calculating taxes. Eliminating tax subsidies on business borrowing would hamper technological modernization and growth. The point of the proposal to exempt interest earnings on savings from taxation is to encourage a higher savings rate. However, this would principally benefit the wealthy, who obtain a greater part of their income from earnings on savings, throwing an increased burden of taxation on the poor.

What Can Be Done if Monetary and Fiscal Policies Don't Work?

The inability of fiscal and monetary policies to stabilize the economy in the 1970s and early 1980s led on the one hand to a skeptical view of the use of discretionary stabilization policies, as expressed by the rational expectations school of economists, and on the other hand to increased interest in alternative approaches to stabilization. These alternatives range from the familiar price and wage controls to some form of incomes policy as practiced in Europe to novel proposals such as gain-sharing or a Market Anti-inflation Plan. The section concludes with a discussion of accommodating inflation by indexing.

Study Questions 8, 9, and 10 bring out some of the merits and drawbacks of alternative stabilization measures.

Case Application: Running a Business Under MAP

This application examines how the Market Anti-inflation Plan would work in practice. It looks at the market for MAP credit from the standpoint of a firm and what the firm would have to gain. Whether or not MAP is ever seriously considered for implementation, an examination of how it

works provides some useful insights into the market mechanism.

Answers to the "For Thought" Questions

1. How does MAP differ from direct controls?

MAP differs from direct controls because it allows firms to make their own decisions about the pricing of their products. It provides a market method for limiting prices as compared to the bureaucratic method of direct controls.

2. MAP is supposed to eliminate inflationary expectations. Why would it do this?

Since the total amount of MAP credit is limited, the average level of prices cannot increase. As this becomes apparent to people, they will cease anticipating inflation.

3. If you were the owner of the designer jeans company, would you be in favor of MAP? If you were an employee of the firm, would you be in favor of MAP? Do you think Congress should enact MAP? Why do you think it should or should not?

Open answer. Those who look at MAP from the viewpoint of their own firm or their own job may oppose it because it limits their opportunity to obtain price or wage increases.

Also, those who are philosophically opposed to government intrusions into the economy may oppose MAP. On the other side, those who are concerned about the instability of the economy and do not believe that more traditional stabilization policies are effective may be in favor of MAP. Those who believe that the market is an efficient regulator of relative prices but that it is not an effective regulator of the overall price level may favor MAP as an optimum solution that combines the best features of market efficiency with stabilization controls.

Perspective: Monetarism—Does Money Matter?

This Perspective discusses Milton Friedman, one of the best known of contemporary economists, and the ideas with which he is most closely associated. It explains what constitutes the "Chicago School" of economic thought, the relation of monetarism to Keynesian economics, and the experience with monetarist policies.

Answers to Study Questions

1. If there had been such a thing at the time, would fiscal stabilization policy have been very effective in the early years of this century when the federal government was quite small? Why or why not?

Fiscal stabilization policies would not have been effective when the federal government was small because they depend for their effectiveness on changes in government spending and taxing impacting the economy as a whole. When government spending was an insignificant fraction of total spending, it could not have been an effective instrument of stabilization policy.

2. Why would annually balanced budgets make discretionary fiscal policy impossible?

Annually balanced budgets would largely eliminate discretionary fiscal policy because the effectiveness of fiscal policy depends upon changing the relationship between government injections of purchasing power into the economy and government withdrawals of purchasing power through taxation.

3. Why is government spending during an economic recession or depression like priming a pump?

Government spending during an economic recession or depression is like priming a pump because it generates additional income which is then spent on new goods and services, which in turn creates more income and expenditures. The multiplier effect is akin to the flow of water which is initiated by priming the pump.

4. What determines how much output will flow out of the economic "pump" after a given amount of priming?

The amount of outflow will depend upon the size of the multiplier, which is determined by the leakages into savings and taxes.

5. Why are the automatic stabilizers built into our economy in themselves insufficient to maintain full employment?

The automatic stabilizers are insufficient to maintain full employment because they are brought into play by changes in output and income. They serve to reduce the extent of the changes, but they do not reverse the direction of the change.

6. What explains the difference in the effectiveness of monetary policy at opposite ends of the business cycle?

Monetary policy can be effective in stopping inflation if the monetary controls are sufficiently restrictive. At the low point of the business cycle, however, an easy money policy may not be effective in stimulating increased economic activity because there may not be sufficient inducements to borrow, no matter how low the interest rate, due to the poor business prospects.

7. What might cause an increase in the velocity of circulation of money?

As can be seen from the quantity equation, the velocity of circulation of money might increase if people decided to increase their total spending with the money supply and price level held constant, if the price level went up with the money supply and total output held constant, or

if the money supply decreased with total output and the price level held constant.

8. Why would it be likely that the longer direct controls over prices and wages are kept in effect, the more difficult they become to enforce and the more they will result in economic inefficiencies?

The longer direct controls of prices and wages are kept in effect, the more difficult they become to enforce and the more they will result in economic inefficiencies because the demand and supply conditions in the product markets and in the markets for the factor inputs continually change. As demand and supply conditions change with no compensatory adjustments in prices and wages, the gap between the control price and the equilibrium price becomes larger and the temptation to evade the controls grows greater. Because the controls prevent a reallocation of resources to accommodate the changed demand-supply conditions, allocation inefficiency becomes more pronounced.

9. Why is an incomes policy such as TIP considered more efficient than direct controls?

Incomes stabilization policies are considered more efficient than direct controls because they allow for changes in relative prices, thereby permitting reallocations in response to changed demand-supply conditions. Although price increases are discouraged by the policies, the further the equilibrium price diverges from the existing price, the more likely it is the price will be changed. The price changes are linked directly to changes in the marketplace, and do not depend upon bureaucratic decision making as do price changes under direct controls.

10. Would it be possible to index all types of incomes to the cost of living so that literally no one would suffer from inflation? What types of income would present an indexing problem?

It would not be possible to index all types of income to the cost of living because not all incomes are set contractually. Those who sell personal services directly to the public and do not work for a contractual salary cannot have their income indexed. Those who derive their income from privately held assets would not be likely to have their income indexed. Private pensions, for example, could not be indexed unless they were subsidized by the government.

Integrating *Economics U$A* Programs

(For information on Economics U$A *see the introduction, p. v.)*

There are three programs that reinforce the concepts in this chapter. The first is program 6, "Fiscal Policy: Can We Control the Economy?" The first application in the program covers the commitment by Congress at the end of World War II to use the powers of government to promote full employment. In his analysis segment, economist Gill presents a rudimentary version of the Keynesian cross model, which is an alternative to the GNP tank model. The second section in the program discusses automatic stabilizers. The third section deals with the successful Kennedy tax cut of 1964 (text p. 327) and its validation of Keynesian economic policies.

Program 13 on "Monetary Policy: How Well Does It Work?" examines the monetary policies used to combat stagflation in the 1970s. At the end of the first section, Gill explains velocity and a model like the quantity equation covered in chapter 10 on page 274. Aside from using an alternative name—the "equation of exchange"—the difference between the two models is that the model presented by Gill has "Q" rather than "T" as the symbol for the quantity of goods and services transacted. But the difference between the two is more than simply using a different letter of the alphabet. Gill defines Q as representing only final outputs because he says P × Q is GNP. By comparison, T represents all transactions, including intermediate goods and goods produced in a previous year and resold, such as used cars. From an analytical standpoint, this broader interpretation is correct because total money payments (M × V) include all transactions, not just final products. The advantage of Gill's GNP interpretation of the right side of the equation is that it can be easily calculated from national income data that we have. Although it does not give an accurate measure of the absolute value of velocity, that is not important. What is important is how velocity changes, not its absolute value.

The last application in the program discusses the shift of the Federal Reserve policy target from interest rates to the money supply, the subject of a chapter 10 case application on page 254. It covers Milton Friedman and the monetarists, the subject of the Perspective on page 347.

The final program for this chapter is 14, "Stabilization Policy: Are We Still in Control?" At the end of the first segment Gill discusses the rational expectations theory covered in the text on page 338. The second section examines the relationship between the government budget deficit and the foreign trade deficit. The final section reviews the controversy over the use of discretionary fiscal policy to attempt to "fine tune" the economy.

Case Applications in Student Workbook
(Answers are supplied to students in the workbook.)

What Can the Government Do About Unemployment and Inflation?

Case Application: The Balanced-Budget Amendment

This application gives the text of the constitutional amendment which was introduced to Congress to require an annually balanced budget. There was, however, an escape clause which would permit a fiscal policy deficit with the concurrence of three-fifths of both houses of Congress.

Answers to the "For Thought" Questions

1. Could Congress circumvent the requirement for a balanced budget? How?

   Congress could circumvent the requirement for a balanced budget by a vote of three-fifths of the whole number of both houses of Congress.

2. What would be the consequences for implementing fiscal policy if the Balanced-Budget Amendment were to pass?

   Passage of the Balanced-Budget Amendment would virtually eliminate expansionary fiscal policy. If the government could not incur deficits when demand in the private sector was insufficient for full employment, there would be little it could do to combat recession or depression, since monetary policy may be ineffective at the bottom of a business cycle.

3. Are you in favor of or opposed to the Balanced-Budget Amendment? Why?

   Open answer. Those in favor of the Balanced-Budget Amendment believe that most of the time Congress and the administration do not have enough self-discipline to avoid budget deficits. They contend the political temptations to overspend are too great and, therefore, a balanced-budget amendment to the Constitution is necessary. Those who oppose the Balanced-Budget

Amendment believe it would handcuff the federal government and prevent it from serving the needs of the country, including the need to stabilize the economy and achieve full employment, or, if the restrictions of the amendment proved too hampering, Congress would simply override them.

How Does Fiscal Policy Help Stabilize the Economy?

Case Application: What Happens to Tax-Cut Dollars?

This application considers how the tax savings from the Economic Recovery Tax Act of 1981 were allocated and the supply-side rationale. It reviews the research results on how people allocate their tax-cut dollars between consumption and savings.

Answers to the "For Thought" Questions

1. What discretionary fiscal policy measure is discussed in this application?

   The discretionary fiscal policy measure discussed in the application is the reduction of federal taxes in order to stimulate output, investment, income, and employment.

2. Does the multiplier effect work on tax-cut dollars as well as on government-expenditure dollars? How?

   The multiplier effect works on tax-cut dollars as well as on government-expenditure dollars. When taxpayers have additional after-tax income they spend most of it on goods and services. The amounts they spend become income to other people, who in turn spend most of their new income on goods and services. The result is a multiplier effect which increases the total income generated by some multiple of the initial amount of tax reduction.

3. Was the Economic Recovery Tax Act of 1981 a wise and effective fiscal policy measure? Why or why not?

   Open answer. The Economic Recovery Tax Act of 1981 was a wise and effective fiscal policy measure to the extent that it helped the economy recover from the recession. It was not wise and effective to the extent that it resulted in increased federal government deficits and a more unequal distribution of income.

How Can Monetary Policy Help Stabilize the Economy?

Case Application: The Interest Rate Yo-Yo

The restrictive monetary policy adopted by the Federal Reserve to curb inflation had unfortunate consequences for many small businesses. This application discusses the microeconomic fallout from antiinflationary macroeconomic monetary policy.

Answers to the "For Thought" Questions

1. One reason interest rates were so high was because of Federal Reserve open market operations. How would open market operations result in raising the interest rates paid by businesses?

   When the Federal Reserve sells government securities in the open market, it "sops up" excess bank reserves. This restricts the banks' ability to expand credit to borrowers, which causes interest rates to rise.

2. As a result of the 1979 change in Federal Reserve Board strategy from controlling interest rates to controlling the money supply, interest rates have fluctuated widely. What are the consequences of wide fluctuations in interest rates?

   The consequences of wide fluctuations in interest rates are to increase the amount of uncertainty for business firms, which may have formulated their plans on the basis of one interest rate and then find their plans defeated by large changes in the interest rates. This may lead to bankruptcy of the firm.

3. Do you think the objective of controlling the money supply justifies the wide swings in interest rates? Why or why not?

   Open answer. Those who say that controlling the money supply necessitates wide swings in interest rates base their reasoning on the overriding importance of macroeconomic stability. They believe that the money supply is the key to putting an end to inflation and that interest rates are a secondary consideration. Those who are opposed to this policy believe that price stabilization can be achieved without the extreme swings in interest rates and/or that the costs which the policy imposes on individuals and businesses are too high to justify it.

What Can Be Done If Monetary and Fiscal Policies Don't Work?

Case Application: The Indexing We Already Have

The application examines the extent to which incomes in the United States are indexed to the cost of living at the present time. It shows that the incomes of millions of people are legally or contractually indexed and that the incomes of many others are indexed in practice. In view of the fact that such a large proportion of the nation's income receivers are protected from inflation, it raises the question of whether equity requires that all incomes should be so protected.

Answers to the "For Thought" Questions

1. What effect does indexing have on inflation?

    Indexing increases the inflation rate because a rise in prices automatically results in other price and cost increases, causing a new round of inflation.

2. Is it possible for indexing to result in a decrease in incomes? How?

    Indexing could result in a decrease of incomes during a deflationary period. If the average price level fell, incomes indexed to the price level would also be reduced. Looked at another way, if indexing helped to create hyperinflation and a collapse of the economic system, that would result in a decrease in real income.

3. Are you in favor of, or opposed to, indexing all incomes to changes in the price level? Why?

    Open answer. Those who favor indexing all incomes to changes in the price level might do so because they believe it is unfair for some groups to benefit from inflation while other groups are injured by it. They might believe inflation is preferable to high unemployment and therefore we should permit the inflation while protecting individuals from being injured by it by indexing all incomes. Those who oppose indexing might do so because they believe it compounds the inflation problem and prevents the necessary reforms to solve the country's economic problems.

Chapter 14

Economic Growth

Chapter Overview

This chapter takes up the fourth of the primary economic goals listed in chapter 1, that of economic growth. The topic is introduced by an article which deals with the emerging high-technology production methods based on computerized controls. The Perspective for chapter 2 on textbook page 49 discussed the industrial revolution of the nineteenth century; this article suggests that a new industrial revolution may be beginning which will have similarly momentous effects on the economy and our way of life.

The first section of this chapter draws the distinction between growth that only increases total output and growth that raises standards of living. The case application brings up the question of whether there will be enough skilled workers to implement the high-tech production operations that are evolving.

The second section investigates the relationship of growth to investment and the other factors affecting the rate of growth. The case application raises an alternative possibility for increasing the rate of growth without resorting to extensive capital investment by making better use of existing factors, labor in particular.

The final section raises the question of whether or not growth is a good thing. It points out some of the costs as well as the benefits of growth. The case application outlines the antigrowth "small is beautiful" philosophy.

Suggested Answers to the Learning Objectives

The knowledge acquired from this chapter should enable the students to:

1. Distinguish between extensive growth and intensive growth, and explain what causes each and the effects of each upon economic growth.

    Extensive growth increases the economy's total output, while intensive growth increases output per capita. Extensive growth is caused by increases in the factor inputs, including labor. Intensive growth is caused by an increase in capital investment per worker, improved technology, advanced labor skills, and other sources of increased productivity. Extensive growth results in higher total output but not increased living standards, while intensive growth raises living standards.

2. Define investment/GNP ratio and explain its relationship to economic growth.

    The investment/GNP ratio is the proportion of GNP which is allocated to private investment. The larger the investment/GNP ratio, the greater will be the rate of economic growth because capital accumulation is a major cause of increased productivity.

3. Explain how the capital/output ratio is determined and how it affects the growth rate.

    The capital/output ratio is determined by dividing the cost of new machinery or other investment goods by the value of the annual output produced by those investment goods. The higher the output per dollar spent on investment goods (the lower the capital/output ratio), the greater will be the growth rate.

4. Discuss how labor-force participation rates affect economic growth.

    If a larger proportion of the population enters the labor force, economic growth will increase.

5. Explain the importance to economic growth of investment in human capital.

    To get the maximum productivity out of new technologies, it is necessary to have a labor force that is well educated and trained in the necessary skills and that is flexible. Investment in human capital increases economic growth.

6. Compare the social costs of economic growth to the benefits.

    The benefits of economic growth are an increase in per capita consumption, an increase in employment opportunities, and an improved possibility for easing social problems such as poverty. These benefits are countered by such costs of economic growth as increased crowding, increased pollution, and increasing scarcity of natural resources.

What Causes Economic Growth?

This section draws the distinction between extensive growth and intensive growth and examines the causes of each. A nation may seek extensive growth in order to increase its political power, as in periods of imperialistic expansion (see the Perspective at the end of the chapter). But it is intensive growth that is desirable from an economic standpoint because it raises living standards. Study Questions 1 and 2 examine the meaning and implications of extensive and intensive growth.

Case Application: Shortage of Skilled Labor

The application discusses the projected shortage of skilled blue-collar labor in the years ahead. It raises the question of whether or not the shortages will retard intensive growth of our economy.

Answers to the "For Thought" Questions

1. Did the entry of 20 million new workers into the labor force in the 1970s represent principally extensive growth or intensive growth? Why?

    The entry of the 20 million new workers into the labor force represented principally extensive growth because intensive growth is characterized by an increase in productivity, and in the 1970s productivity increases were small.

2. How do apprenticeship programs affect the nation's stock of human capital?

    Apprenticeship programs improve the stock of human capital because they are a type of investment that makes labor more productive, just as investments in capital equipment make labor more productive.

3. Who has the major responsibility for paying for the training of young people for skilled blue-collar occupations—the government, the firms that hire such workers, or the young people themselves?

    Open answer. It can be argued that the government has the main responsibility for training because in our society education is principally a governmental function. If the different levels of government have assumed the responsibility for educating our youth to enter white-collar jobs and the professions, why should they not also educate youth for blue-collar jobs? It could, on the other hand, be maintained that the firms that make use of skilled blue-collar workers should train them because they derive the benefits of the worker's skills in improving production and reducing costs. It also could be argued that the trainees themselves should pay the costs because their earnings will be enhanced as a result of acquiring the skills and, therefore, they should pay for the training.

How Can Economic Growth Be Increased?

This section concerns the relationship between intensive growth and investment, including investment in both capital equipment and human capital. It explains how growth is dependent on the capital/output and investment/GNP ratios and how these can be increased. It examines the effect of an increase in the labor-force participation rate on economic growth and the relationship of increased labor skills to productivity.

Transparencies of Figures 3A and 3B on pages 358-59 show the results of increasing the investment/GNP ratio with the use of the GNP tank model. Study Question 3 reinforces the concept of the investment/GNP ratio and Study Questions 4 and 5 reinforce the capital/output ratio concept. Study Question 6 examines the causes of increases in the labor-force participation rate. Study Question 7 inquires into capital-saving innovations for growth.

Case Application: Working Smarter

This application discusses an improvement in the effective utilization of our existing resources, especially labor, as an alternative to capital investment to raise productivity. It compares the use of labor in Japan with the way labor is used in the United States and examines some recent changes in labor-management relations in this country.

Answers to the "For Thought" Questions

1. Which of the growth factors shown in Table 2 would be affected by the changes discussed in this application?

    Relaxation of work rules permits the introduction of improved technology. Sometimes the work rule relaxation is a trade-off by the union in return for increased capital input by the firm.

2. How would "working smarter" affect the capital/output ratio? Would it increase it or decrease it? How would this affect the investment/GNP ratio? Why?

    Working smarter would decrease the capital/output ratio because each dollar invested would produce a larger amount of output as a result of improved labor utilization. This would tend to increase the investment/GNP ratio because it would make the returns to investment greater, thereby inducing more investment.

3. Unions claim that work rules are necessary for worker safety (for example, to prevent accidents with power equipment due to work speed-up). Do you think that those rules should be relaxed in order to increase productivity? Would you have any safety standards and rules at all? If so, how would you decide how many to have?

    Open answer. Some believe that work rules have become too restrictive and create inefficiencies unnecessarily. They also believe that in difficult economic times it is in the best interests of the workers as well as the owners and consumers to increase productivity by relaxing work rules, contending this would result in saving jobs that otherwise would be lost. Others believe that the safety of workers comes first and takes precedence over cost considerations. They believe that saving workers' health, limbs, and lives is more important than saving jobs. But they believe that jobs should be protected by work rules which regulate the rates of introduction of equipment that will displace veteran workers.

Is Economic Growth Desirable?

The final section of the chapter examines the antigrowth versus progrowth argument. It discusses the problems that have been created by economic growth and also discusses the problems that economic growth helps resolve.

Study Questions 8, 9, and 10 call for student inquiry into the growth vs. nongrowth considerations.

Case Application: Is Small Beautiful?

This case application presents the view of British economist E. F. Schumacher in his book, *Small Is Beautiful.* His philosophy is that the world should adopt "appropriate-technology"—rather than high-technology—production methods in order to conserve on resources and the environment.

Answers to the "For Thought" Questions

1. What growth problems would decentralization of production solve?

   Decentralization of production would solve the problems that accompany increasing population density and urbanization, such as pollution, crowding, and scarcity of public facilities.

2. The Schumacher concept can be seen in a growth of "cottage industry" types of jobs, with people doing work in their own homes rather than in factories or offices. In what ways can this arrangement conserve on scarce resources?

   This arrangement can conserve on scarce resources by reducing the energy costs of commuting, reducing the energy requirements of workplaces, and reducing the need for expanding highways, parking facilities, and public transportation.

3. Do you think Schumacher's approach will replace traditional U.S. business methods as a general rule? Why might corporations retain the mass production methods they currently employ?

   Open answer. Those who think that Schumacher's ideas will be adopted by corporations take indications, such as those mentioned in the application, of changed practices by some companies as marking a turning point in the behavior of big businesses. They believe that the growth problems described by Schumacher will force society as a whole to change the traditional way of doing business in order to give more regard to the

environment, working conditions, and resource limits. Those who do not believe that there will be a major revolution in business practices either are skeptical that corporations are sufficiently flexible to change that much or do not think that such changes are desirable. The traditional mass production methods of U.S. business provided the strongest economy and the highest standards of living ever seen in the world. Corporations may not be willing or able to abandon mass production economies of scale.

Perspective: Economic Imperialism

The Perspective reviews the period of economic imperialism at the end of the nineteenth century. It examines the motivations for economic imperialism as propounded by Hobson and Lenin. It concludes with a critique of the Marxist analysis of economic imperialism.

Answers to Study Questions

1. Is the area in which you live displaying signs of extensive growth? What are these signs? Is the area exhibiting any indications of intensive growth? What are these indications?

   Open answer. Signs of extensive growth would include the establishment of new stores or other businesses in the area, new shopping centers, or new housing developments. Signs of intensive growth might be the installation of electronic cash registers at supermarket checkout stands, automatic bank teller stations, the installation of word processors in offices, or modernization of a local factory.

2. If there is an increase in the birth rate, the population expands, but there is a lag before the new additions to the population enter the labor force. What happens to per capita output during this lag?

   When there is an increase in the birth rate the per capita output would tend to decline during the period before the new additions to the population entered the labor force.

3. The investment/GNP ratio is based only on private investment. What are some examples of government spending that might increase economic growth?

   Government spending on the economic infrastructure (highways, waterways, and public transportation) increases the growth rate because it facilitates private economic activity. Government investment in human capital through the public education system has the same effect.

4. Why does the capital/output ratio vary between different industries within a country? Which U.S. industries would you expect to have a high capital/output ratio?

Which ones would you expect to have a low capital/output ratio?

The capital/output ratio in an industry depends upon the technology available. Some industry operations lend themselves more to automation than others and therefore have a higher capital/output ratio. Those expected to have a high capital/output ratio would be manufacturing industries, especially heavy industries such as refineries, metal fabrication, and automobile production. Industries expected to have a low capital/output ratio would be personal services such as dentistry, beauty services, home maintenance, and some light industries.

5. How would a reduction in the capital/output ratio be illustrated in a GNP tank diagram? How would it differ from Figure 3 on page 358?

The effect of a change in the capital/output ratio is illustrated in the GNP tank diagram by the amount of increase in capacity resulting from an increase in investment spending. It would differ from Figure 3 in the difference between the size of the GNP tank in 3A and 3B.

6. Why has the U.S. labor-force participation rate increased? What could be done to increase it further? What events might cause it to decrease?

The U.S. labor-force participation rate has increased because a larger percentage of women in the population have entered the labor force. It could be increased further by a continued reduction of barriers to women entering male-dominated occupations and by increasing pay equality for women. Events that might cause it to decrease would be a rise in the birth rate or more prosperous economic conditions which relieved the pressure for two-worker households.

7. What are some examples of technological improvements that do not require investment in new capital equipment? Why are these more beneficial for accelerating growth than those that do require new capital equipment?

Technological improvements that do not require investment in new capital equipment would include reorganization of the workers into autonomous teams, instituting flextime work schedules, and dispensing with rigid work rules. These changes are more beneficial for accelerating economic growth than those that require new capital equipment because they conserve scarce capital.

8. What are some observable negative effects of economic growth in your area?

Open answer. Effects of growth that might be noted are increased traffic and parking congestion, increased air or noise pollution, and higher utility costs.

9. What would be the economic and social consequences of a stationary state?

The economic consequences of a stationary state would be to stop the growth of output in goods and services and reduce material living standards. The social consequences might include increased strains on the social fabric by intensifying the struggle among different groups over material rewards. Or society might adopt new attitudes which reduce the emphasis on high consumption and give more emphasis to the quality of life and personal relationships.

10. What are some of the examples of the application of E. F. Schumacher's concepts in your area?

Open answer. Examples might include city planning decisions to reduce the density of new construction development, an increase in the number of people commuting to school and work by bicycle, or an increase in the use of launderettes in place of laundries.

Integrating *Economics U$A* Programs

(For information on Economics U$A *see the introduction, p. v.)*

The first of two programs recommended for this chapter serves nicely as a bridge from the content of chapter 13 to chapter 14. It is program 11, "Productivity: Can We Get More for Less?" The first application examines the reasons for the decline in U.S. productivity in the 1970s. One of the economists interviewed is Edward Denison, whose study of the sources of growth is discussed on pages 362-63 and shown in Table 2. The second application raises the question of what the government can or should do to promote economic growth.

The final application is the one that relates the discussion of stabilization policies in chapter 13 to the consideration of economic growth. It reinforces the statement at the top of page 357 that supply-side policies have more relevance for long-term growth than for short-term stability. There is a good point, counterpoint debate over supply-side versus demand-side effects, and economist Gill summarizes the arguments over supply-side tax policy.

The other program for this chapter is 25, "Economic Growth: Can We Keep Up the Pace?" The first application concerns the early years of the automobile industry and the production of Henry Ford's Model "T." Increases in productivity are characterized as "the engine of growth." One way Ford got productivity increases was to provide each worker with more capital equipment. Gill explains economies of scale and how labor productivity is related to the capital/output ratio.

The second application deals with the revolution in communications technology. In showing the contribution of new technology to economic growth, Gill cites the results of a study by Edward Denison that was done prior to the study referred to on pages 362-63 and in Table 2.

The final application discusses the merits of a controversial study called *The Limits to Growth* which predicted famine, resource exhaustion, and environmental disaster for the world in the next century. Gill demonstrates a model of the market response to shortages that refutes the conclusions reached by the study.

Case Applications in Student Workbook

(Answers are supplied to students in the workbook.)

What Causes Economic Growth?

Case Application: Capital Investment and Productivity

This application presents a table which shows the relationship between the growth rate of physical capital per worker hour and the growth rate of output per worker hour for three different periods. In two of these periods there is a close correlation, but not in the third. The questions inquire into the causes for this circumstance.

Answers to the "For Thought" Questions

1. Does the table in this application refer to extensive growth or intensive growth? How can you tell?

   The table in this application refers to intensive growth because the measurements are per hour worked. Therefore, what is being measured is productivity rather than increases in the number of workers.

2. What factors could explain the discrepancy between the annual growth in real capital and changes in labor productivity between 1978 and 1980?

   The discrepancy between rates of annual growth in real capital and changes in labor productivity between 1978 and 1980 could be explained by the instability of the economy during that time or it could be explained by the entrance into the labor force of many inexperienced youth and women.

3. To the extent that increased labor productivity is due to capital investment, should all of the increased revenue resulting from the higher productivity go to the owners of the business in the form of higher profits? Explain your answer.

   Open answer. Productivity depends on the combination of all of the factor inputs: labor, capital, and land. Because they are jointly involved in producing the product, it is difficult to attribute the productivity of any one factor separately. In the labor market, the demand for labor will result in wages that are equal to the value of labor's net value in production. If the worker's net value in production increases because of using more capital equipment, wages will rise. Similarly, if workers become more productive because of better education and training, the profits on capital investment will rise. Furthermore, if all of the added revenue resulting from

capital investment were to go to the owners and none to the workers, there would probably be insufficient customers to purchase all of the goods which were produced.

How Can Economic Growth Be Increased?

Case Application: How to Grow

This continues the discussion in the previous application by examining the relationship between spending on research and development and changes in Gross National Product and the relationship of education to economic growth. The correlations among these factors support the findings in Table 2 on page 362 of the textbook concerning the factors responsible for economic growth.

Answers to the "For Thought" Questions

1. What are the three factors in this application that affected economic growth?

   The three factors in this application that affected economic growth are expenditures on research and development, the number of years of education completed, and investment spending on plants and equipment.

2. What happened to the investment/GNP ratio between the 1960s and the 1970s?

   The investment/GNP ratio fell between the 1960s and the 1970s. This can be deduced from the fact that the rate of growth of investments declined by more than the rate of growth of GNP.

3. Judging from the relationships shown in the data in this application, what measures do you think should be taken to increase the rate of growth in GNP?

   Open answer. Measures that might be taken to increase the rate of growth of GNP include encouraging research and development (for example, by government sponsored research and development programs and subsidies); encouraging youth to obtain more education (for example, by student loans); and stimulating increased investments, for example by tax credits for plant modernization.

Is Economic Growth Desirable?

Case Application: Does the Coin Have Another Side?

This application puts the growth/antigrowth arguments in a dialogue between two people. One person presents the arguments in favor of continuing and accelerating growth, while the other presents the problems and drawbacks of growth as seen by those who are opposed to it.

Answers to the "For Thought" Questions

1. What costs of economic growth are cited in the application?

   Costs of economic growth cited in the application include pollution of the ocean and shore environment from offshore drilling, industrial pollution, and the creation of "Gross National Garbage."

2. How did the allocation of the growth product enter the debate?

   The allocation of the growth product entered the debate in the last paragraph, when it was argued that, "without

some economic growth it will be even harder to find solutions."

3. Who do you agree with in the debate? Why?

   Open answer. Those who agree with Rita might do so because they believe growth often deteriorates the quality of life by damaging the environment. Those who agree with Billy might do so because they believe the environmental costs of growth are less important than the country's need to keep pace with economic growth abroad and because they believe the environmental damage caused by growth can be remedied by allocating part of the growth product to solving the problem.

Chapter 15

Public Finance

Chapter Overview

This chapter deals with the economics of government itself at the federal, state, and local levels. The introductory article discusses the major problems confronting the federal government of large budget deficits and a high national debt, how we got into this situation, what it portends, and how we are attempting to extricate ourselves from it.

The first section of the chapter shows a breakdown of the types of federal government spending as well as state and local government spending. The case application discusses privatization as a way of reducing government spending.

The second section investigates the revenue sources for the different levels of government. The case application deals with the Social Security system and its funding problems.

The last section of the chapter inquires into the distribution of the tax burden on different segments of the population. The case application for this section concerns the tax reform bill passed in 1986.

Suggested Answers to the Learning Objectives

The knowledge acquired from this chapter should enable the student to:

1. Describe the size of government debt and deficits.

   The national debt is over $2 trillion—equivalent to a stack of $1,000 bills 134 miles high. In the mid-1980s the annual federal deficit was running about $200 billion. According to the Gramm-Rudman legislation, the deficit was scheduled to be reduced during the latter 1980s and eliminated by 1991.

2. Discuss the relative size of government economic activity.

   The budgets of federal, state, and local governments total somewhat over one-third of all spending in the economy. However, because a large part of their outlays are for transfer payments, the three levels of government account for only 20% of the goods and services produced in this nation. The federal government purchases 9% of total output.

3. List the most important types of federal government spending.

   The largest single federal government outlay is for national defense. After defense spending, the next largest item is Social Security. Third is interest on the national debt. All transfer payments together make up over 60% of federal outlays. All direct spending other than defense accounts for less than 11%.

4. List the most important types of state and local government spending.

   The most important types of state and local government spending are for education, public welfare, health care and hospitals, highways, and police and corrections.

5. Identify the principal sources of revenue for the federal, state, and local governments respectively.

   The principal sources of revenue for the federal government are personal income taxes, payroll taxes, and corporate income taxes. The largest source of revenue for state governments is sales taxes, and for local governments it is property taxes. Federal transfers are important to both state and local governments.

6. Explain the criteria for equity in taxation.

   The criteria for equity in taxation are: (1) taxes should be levied to provide horizontal equity so that all persons with comparable incomes pay comparable taxes; and (2) the tax structure should provide vertical equity so that those with low incomes should bear a less-than-proportionate share of the tax burden and those with high incomes should bear a more-than-proportionate share of the tax burden.

7. Describe how "bad" taxes decrease economic efficiency.

   "Bad" taxes are those which unintentionally distort the use of resources so that a less-than-optimum mix of output is produced and/or total output is reduced.

8. Define what is meant by the incidence of a tax.

   The incidence of a tax is the amount of a tax ultimately paid by individuals, irrespective of who initially pays the tax.

On What Do Governments Spend Money?

This section examines the allocation of federal government spending (Figure 2 on textbook p. 377) and state and local government spending (Figure 3 on textbook p. 379). It begins with a discussion of the size of total government spending relative to the output of the economy. The discussion makes a distinction between total government spending, including transfer payments, and that part of government spending which purchases output and constitutes "G" in the GNP tank model.

Study Question 1 reinforces the distinction between different types of government spending. Study Question 2 reinforces the understanding of transfer payments. Study Question 3 examines the effects of current changes in government spending on the local area. Study Question 4 focuses on the relationship between increased government efficiency and tax savings.

Case Application: Privatization

Privatization refers to governments turning over the provision of public services to private contractors. A number of state and local governments have turned to privatization as a way of reducing government spending. The application describes some instances in which it has been successful and others in which it has not. The federal administration has proposed privatization in a number of areas, mostly involving the selling of government property.

Answers to the "For Thought" Questions

1. Does privatization affect mainly direct government spending or transfer payments? Explain.

   Privatization affects mainly direct government spending because transfer payments do not involve the provision of services.

2. Why is privatization more applicable at the state and local level than at the federal level?

   It is more applicable at the state and local level because a larger proportion of state and local expenditures are allocated to the provision of services, whereas the greater part of federal spending is either transfer payments or national defense.

3. Should the federal government sell off government assets to the private sector? Why or why not? If so what assets should it sell? What assets should it not sell?

   Open answer. Those who favor privatization by the federal government maintain that the private sector can provide services more efficiently than can the government. Those who oppose privatization believe that the private sector sacrifices quality of services for higher profits and that privatization is merely a cover for reducing the level of government services. The extreme antigovernment position is to sell all government assets except defense installations. Opponents of federal privatization think it makes no sense whatsoever for the government to dispose of properties that return a profit.

Where Do Governments Get the Money to Spend?

This section shows the sources of federal government revenues (Figure 4 on textbook p. 383) and state and local government revenues (Figure 5, p. 385). The greatest revenue producer for the federal government is personal income taxes, with payroll taxes the next largest source. For state and local governments, the largest single source of funds is sales taxes and the next largest is the federal government through grants-in-aid.

Study Question 5 reinforces the concept of excise taxes. Study Question 6 brings in the idea of user fees and their consequences. Study Question 7 inquires into the status and outlook for Social Security.

Case Application: Social Insecurity

This case application takes a close look at the structure of the Social Security system and its financing problems. It reviews alternative proposals for solving the long-run funding problems of the system.

Answers to the "For Thought" Questions

1. How does the financing of Social Security differ from the financing of other government programs?

   Whereas most government programs are financed out of general tax revenues, the Social Security program is financed out of separate taxes levied on employees and employers. These taxes are accrued in four separate funds out of which the retirement, disability, and medical benefits are paid.

2. It has been said that Medicare is not properly a part of the Social Security system and should be transferred to the U.S. Department of Health and Human Services. What would be the effects of such a change on the budget?

   Since the revenue and outlays of the trust funds are included in the consolidated federal budget, transferring Medicare to Health and Human Services would not affect the budget as long as outlays and payroll taxes remained the same.

3. What changes do you think should be made in the Social Security system and why?

   Open answer. Students and younger workers are likely to opt for changes in the system which would reduce current retirement benefits, for example by reducing cost of living adjustments and extending the normal retirement age. Older workers would likely favor increasing Social Security taxes or supplementing the Social Security system out of general tax revenues.

Who Pays for Government Spending?

The two main criteria for taxation are that taxes should be equitable and that they should be efficient. This section outlines the conditions that need to be fulfilled if taxes are to meet these criteria.

Study Questions 8 and 9 examine some effects of taxation. Study Question 10 asks the student to determine the effects of the 1986 tax bill.

Case Application: The Great Tax Reform of 1986

The 1986 overhaul of the federal tax system was the most extensive in recent history. Its objective was to simplify the tax code and let the market rather than taxes determine the allocation of resources. It was also supposed to put more fairness back into the tax system. Whether or not the tax code was actually simplified and made more equitable is a matter of debate, but it did succeed in eliminating obsolete and inefficient tax incentives and abolishing abusive tax shelters. The application discusses some of the major changes provided for in the bill, while projecting a wait-and-see attitude regarding its ultimate effect on income distribution.

Answers to the "For Thought" Questions

1. Why was the previous tax code not considered equitable? Why was it not considered economically efficient?

   The previous tax code was not considered equitable because it permitted individuals with high incomes and businesses with large earnings to escape paying taxes through loopholes. It was not considered economically efficient because it caused investment and other allocation decisions to be made on the basis of their tax consequences rather than on the basis of their effects on productivity and output.

2. If we switch more of our taxation from income taxes to sales taxes, how will this affect the incidence of the tax burden? Why?

   It will cause taxes to be more regressive because, compared to higher income individuals, those with lower incomes spend a larger percentage of their income on consumption of goods that are taxed. As a result, sales taxes are regressive. Income taxes, on the other hand, are progressive or, in the case of a flat tax, proportional.

3. Do you think that the 1986 tax reform accomplished its objectives? Why or why not?

Open answer. It might be judged that the 1986 tax reform bill accomplished its objectives by largely abolishing the maze of tax benefits, credits, and shelters and by reducing the steps in the tax schedule from 15 to 2. Doing away with most of the special interest tax benefits should make allocation decisions more economically efficient and taxation more equitable. The opposing view is that the 1986 tax code is actually more complicated than the one it replaced and will force people to rely even more heavily on professional tax preparers than they did previously. Because it has made the tax rates less progressive by having only two steps and a maximum marginal rate of 33%, the regressive nature of other taxes will no longer be offset by the federal income tax whose progressivity in the past made the overall tax structure reasonably proportional.

Perspective: The Growth of Big Government

The Perspective traces the changes in government spending since the 1920s. It examines the causes of the major surges in the size of government spending and the variations in the relative importance of federal, state, and local spending. It notes a shift in the composition of spending from purchases of goods and services to transfer payments.

Answers to Study Questions

1. What types of government spending are included in GNP? What types are most readily subject to cost-cutting?

   The government outlays included in GNP are purchases of goods and services. The types most subject to cost-cutting are expenditures not mandated by law or backed by influential lobbies.

2. How many people in your family and how many friends with whom you are acquainted are receiving transfer payments? What type of transfer payments are they receiving?

   Open answer. Most students will probably have grandparents or other relatives receiving Social Security and many will know someone receiving veterans' assistance or public aid.

3. Have there been any recent reductions in government services in your area? What were they? In which level of government did they occur?

   Open answer. Many areas have been affected by reductions in local funding. Such things as closing branch libraries or cutting the hours, reducing state funding for public works such as highways, or curtailing federal funding for such things as school lunch programs are just a few examples.

4. If a candidate for national office promised, if elected, to double the efficiency of federal government operations

and thereby reduce taxes by half, why might you question that promise? What promises might that candidate make about tax reduction that you would find feasible?

A promise to cut taxes in half by increasing the efficiency of government operations could not be fulfilled because the cost of government operations is a small fraction of total government spending. The answer to the second half of the question is open, but, economically speaking, major reductions in the federal budget must come from entitlement programs or defense spending.

5. Approximately how much have you paid in excise taxes (taxes other than on income) in the past three days? On what items?

   Open answer. The most likely excise tax students would have paid is a sales tax.

6. What revenues do state and local governments receive, other than taxes? What is the impact on various income groups of these revenue sources?

   State and local governments receive revenues from user fees of various sorts and from license fees. These include such things as fares on public transit, state university fees, and drivers' license fees. Collecting revenue from user fees rather than from taxes shifts the cost of government to the groups that have the greatest need for those services.

7. What is the current outlook for the Social Security system? Do you believe that you will benefit from it in the future?

   Open answer. As of the date of publication, the Social Security system appeared solvent through the second decade of the twenty-first century. Today's students, however, face concerns about how much they will have to pay to fund the system and whether it will provide adequately for their retirement needs.

8. Why is it assumed that wealthier people have a smaller marginal utility for money than people with lower incomes?

   It is assumed that wealthier people have a smaller marginal utility for money than people with lower incomes because people allocate their incomes first to their most pressing needs. When their most pressing needs are satisfied they allocate remaining income to discretionary purchases of successively less important luxury consumption, or to savings. (Refer to the principle of diminishing marginal utility on p. 90 of the text.)

9. What are three things, other than cigarettes and liquor, the production of which is affected by a tax. What is the effect of the tax? What is the incidence of the tax?

   Open answer. Things affected by specific excise taxes include gasoline, airline tickets, and imported goods. However, the production of all goods is affected in some

fashion by taxes. The effect of taxes is to increase the cost and thereby reduce production. The incidence of the tax, at whatever stage it is collected, generally falls mainly on the ultimate buyer.

10. What have been the effects of the 1986 tax reform legislation?

    Open answer. There are likely to be two sorts of effects of the 1986 tax bill that will emerge. One type of effect will be to change the allocation of investment and production among different goods and services. The other type of effect will be on income distribution.

Integrating *Economics U$A* Programs

(For information on Economics U$A *see the introduction, p. v.)*

The relevant program for this chapter is program 12, "Federal Deficits: Can We Live With Them?" The first application deals with the financing of World War II. It makes the point that government borrowing during the war served two purposes: financing government spending and sopping up excess purchasing power to compensate for the lack of consumer goods on which to spend it. Gill points out that the economic costs of war are not passed on to the next generation by the debt in any direct sense—the same point made in the introductory article on page 374. But future generations do suffer from the wartime diversion of resources out of real investment for growth of civilian production capacity.

The second application on economic policy at the end of the Eisenhower administration provides a good review of contra-cyclical fiscal policy. In the final application, the fiscal situation of the mid-1980s is explored—how we got the twin horrors of giant deficits and a monstrous debt—and how they impact the economy.

Case Applications in Student Workbook

(Answers are supplied to students in the workbook.)

On What Do Governments Spend Money?

Case Application: Renovating America

This application deals with the deterioration of public facilities in the United States and the costs of restoration. As this problem has come to the forefront of public discussion, the term "infrastructure" has been used to refer to our basic public investments on which private economic activity is dependent. The parts of the infrastructure of particular concern are the roads, bridges, and sewage systems, but the term infrastructure could also include education, public health, and housing.

Answers to the "For Thought" Questions

1. Federal spending on renewal of the nation's public facilities would increase the size of which of the pie slices in Figure 2 on page 377 of the textbook?

   Federal spending on the renewal of the nation's public facilities would increase the pie slice in Figure 2 on page 377 of the textbook labeled "Other direct." That slice shows federal spending on non-defense goods and services.

2. What state and local government spending in Figure 3 on page 379 of the textbook will be affected by the need to renovate the infrastructure?

   The state and local government spending in Figure 3 on page 379 of the textbook that will be affected by the need to renovate the infrastructure is spending on highways and spending on other facilities such as municipal water and sewage systems (included in "All other").

3. What priority would you give to renewing America's infrastructure in relationship to other types of government spending? Why?

   Open answer. It could be argued that renewing America's infrastructure should have one of the highest priorities in government spending because continued deterioration of the nation's transportation system and other public facilities would lead to a decrease in economic efficiency and a slowdown of GNP growth, not to mention the dangers and inconveniences to the public. Those who oppose massive spending on the infrastructure might argue that we cannot afford the high cost it would entail because of more pressing needs such as an adequate national defense and/or adequate human services such as education, food programs for malnourished children, and medical care.

Where Do Governments Get the Money to Spend?

Case Application: Should the U.S. Have a Value-Added Tax?

The value-added tax has been proposed as a source of revenue for the United States government, similar to the important role it serves for financing European governments. This application explains how the value-added tax works and what its effects might be.

Answers to the "For Thought" Questions

1. If a value-added tax was imposed in the United States as a substitute for the existing Social Security taxes, approximately what percentage of federal government revenues would have to be collected by the VAT?

   If a value-added tax was imposed in the United States as a substitute for the existing Social Security taxes, approximately 36% of federal government revenues would have to be collected by the VAT. This can be seen from Figure 4 on page 383 of the textbook which shows the percentage of federal government revenues collected from payroll taxes.

2. What is the basis for the allegation that income taxes, payroll taxes, and corporate profit taxes reduce efficiency, investment, and work incentives?

   Income taxes, payroll taxes, and corporate profit taxes are said to discourage people and businesses from maximizing the amount of work and capital that they put into production because of the reduction in net returns after taxes. Those taxes are alleged to discourage risk taking because they cannot be passed on, while value-added taxes can be passed on in the form of higher prices.

3. Is a value-added tax for the U.S. a good idea or not? If it were used as a substitute for existing taxes, which taxes should be reduced? Why?

   Open answer. Those who favor a value-added tax claim it is superior because it does not reduce incentives as other taxes do, is easy to collect and difficult to evade, and would help our international trade situation. Those who oppose VAT do so largely because it is a regressive tax and because it would have a direct inflationary effect on the prices of goods and services. The taxes which are most often proposed for elimination in favor of VAT are the payroll tax, which is itself a highly regressive tax, or a portion of income taxes because they are alleged to reduce incentives and to be difficult and costly to collect.

Who Pays for Government Spending?

Case Application: A Look at the Flat-Rate Tax

This application discusses the advantages claimed for a flat-rate income tax. It also discusses the objections that have been raised to such a change in the tax system.

Answers to the "For Thought" Questions

1. What is the effect of the flat-rate income tax on the vertical equity of our tax system?

   A flat-rate income tax would eliminate the progressivity of the income tax structure and thereby change the vertical equity so that larger income earners would not pay higher percentages of their income in taxes.

2. How might the flat-rate tax increase the efficiency of the tax system?

A flat-rate tax could increase the efficiency of the tax system by eliminating the great complexity of income tax laws and regulations, thereby saving the enormous funds spent in the private sector to avoid taxes and the government expenditures on enforcing their collection. It might also reduce the degree to which the existing income tax laws distort the pattern of capital and other resource allocations.

3. Are you in favor of a pure flat-rate tax, the semi-flat tax passed in 1986, or the previous progressive income tax system? Why?

Open answer. Whether you favor a pure flat-rate tax, the semi-flat tax, or the progressive income tax system depends on your attitudes toward vertical equity in the tax system and your beliefs concerning the degree to which the progressive income tax system is more or less fair and efficient than a pure flat-rate tax system or whether a compromise semi-flat system accomplishes the efficiency and equity objectives better.

Chapter 16

International Trade

Chapter Overview

This first chapter in the unit on world economics deals with the basis and effects of foreign trade and payments. The introductory article is an Alice in Wonderland parody on our contradictory attitudes toward foreign trade and exchange rates. It is intended to both highlight the contradictions and incite the students to want to know what the "truth" of the matter is.

The first section outlines how absolute and comparative advantages form the basis for trade. It discusses specialization of production and why specialization is not complete. The case application discusses the return to barter as a way of conducting international trade.

The second section discusses who benefits and who is hurt by foreign trade. The application examines the change in attitude of the U.S. steel industry toward trade policy.

The third section of the chapter deals with international finance, including exchange rates and the balance of payments. The case application for the section deals with the emergence of the U.S. as the country with the largest foreign indebtedness of any in the world.

The next section covers the different types of trade restrictions. The application describes trade protection as practiced in Japan.

The final section of the chapter raises the question of whether or not we should restrict foreign trade. It discusses the various protectionist arguments. The case application is a satire on protectionism by an early French economist.

Suggested Answers to the Learning Objectives

The knowledge acquired from this chapter should enable the students to:

1. Explain absolute and comparative advantage and why specialization is normally limited.

   Absolute advantage exists when each of two countries can produce one of two products more efficiently than can the other country. Comparative advantage exists when one country can produce both products more efficiently than can the other country, but has a greater efficiency advantage in one of the products than in the other. Specialization is ordinarily limited because of increasing costs. Resources are not perfectly adaptable and not equally suited to different types of production. A country may have a certain amount of resources that

give it a comparative advantage in the production of a limited quantity of a good or service. Increasing production beyond that specified quantity entails using resources which are not well suited or efficient in that production, resulting in increasing costs of production.

2. Specify the effects of foreign trade upon economies and who benefits and who loses as a result of foreign trade.

   Foreign trade benefits countries that engage in it by raising living standards. However, its effects on different groups in a country vary. Consumers of imported products benefit from foreign trade because it increases their purchasing power and makes some goods available which could not be produced domestically. Producers and workers in export industries benefit from foreign trade because it expands their markets and increases their incomes. Producers and workers in industries which use imported raw materials benefit from foreign trade because it reduces the costs of production. On the other side, firms and workers in industries that produce goods and services which compete with imports lose as a result of foreign trade because it reduces the size of their markets and prevents them from obtaining the high prices or wages they could demand without foreign trade. Domestic customers who purchase products from firms that export part of their output lose from foreign trade because the larger market increases the price, unless the industry is a decreasing-cost industry.

3. Explain how foreign exchange rates are determined.

   The principal manner in which the foreign exchange rates are determined today is through the interaction of supply and demand for currencies in the foreign-exchange market. The market determines the equilibrium price (exchange rate) for currencies.

4. Distinguish between currency depreciation, appreciation, devaluation, and revaluation, and their causes.

   Currency depreciation results when the supply of a country's currency in the foreign-exchange market exceeds the demand for it, causing the exchange rate to fall. Currency appreciation results when the demand for a country's currency in the foreign-exchange market exceeds its supply, causing the exchange rate to rise. Devaluation occurs under a system of fixed exchange rates when a country officially lowers the exchange rate of its currency. Revaluation occurs under fixed exchange rates when a country officially raises the exchange rate of its currency.

5. Define balance of payments and identify the types of transactions that affect it.

   The balance of payments is an annual summary of all economic transactions between a country and the rest of the world during the year. The types of transactions that affect it are imports and exports of goods and services, short-term capital movements, long-term capital investments, and monetary gold transactions.

6. Compare the different types of restrictions imposed on foreign trade.

   Tariffs are import duties levied on foreign goods and services. Quotas are fixed limits on the maximum amount of a product that can be imported. Tariffs permit more flexibility in adjusting to changed demand-supply conditions than do quotas. Non-tariff barriers are administrative hindrances to imports. They are sometimes more difficult to identify and eliminate through negotiations than are tariffs and quotas. Export embargoes are restrictions on the export of certain products.

7. Discuss the different vehicles for trade negotiations and define "most-favored nation" treatment.

   The Reciprocal Trade Agreement Act of 1934 and its extensions allowed U.S. presidents to reduce trade restrictions through bilateral trade negotiations. The 1947 General Agreement on Tariffs and Trade set up a system of multilateral trade negotiations. Most-favored nation treatment extends any lower tariff concessions granted by one country to another to all other countries that are accorded most-favored nation status.

8. Evaluate the arguments in favor of trade restrictions.

   Protectionist arguments based on "unfair" competition from cheap foreign labor or designed to keep domestic purchasing power at home are fallacious because they do not take into account the benefits from specialization according to comparative advantage. The "infant industry" argument for trade protection has limited validity for developing countries. The terms of trade, neomercantilist, and balance of payments deficit, justifications for trade protection invite retaliation and are generally more costly than beneficial.

Why Do We Trade With Other Countries?

The concepts of specialization based on absolute and comparative advantage were introduced in chapter 2. You might want the class to review the discussion on pages 29–31 before covering this section, which shows how they form the basis for international trade. If you engaged in the dialogue with the class regarding the absolute and

comparative advantages of siblings that was suggested under the first section of chapter 2 in this guide, it would be helpful to remind the class of that discussion.

The section concludes with a discussion of specialization in international trade and the effect of increasing costs on limiting specialization. Study Questions 1, 2, and 3 reinforce the principles of absolute and comparative advantage.

Case Application: Barter Is Back

The application examines the fact that, although money has proved a very useful medium of exchange, in international trade the world recently has increasingly been turning to barter as a means of doing business. It examines the reasons for this use of barter and its drawbacks.

Answers to the "For Thought" Questions

1. Is barter appropriate for cases of absolute advantage but not for cases of comparative advantage? Why or why not?

   Barter is not the ideal mode of transaction for any case. However, it is more appropriate for cases of absolute advantage where the trade possibilities are more obvious than it is for comparative advantage where the trade possibilities are only made apparent by relative prices.

2. Would there be more specialization under a barter system or under a system of money transactions? Why?

   There would be more specialization under a system of money transactions because that type of system opens up more possibilities for expanding a country's markets through multilateral trade, allowing it to specialize in what it has a comparative advantage, compared to a barter system of bilateral transactions.

3. Would the U.S. be better off trading with the communist countries by barter, by money transactions, or not trading with them at all? Why? Who is likely to gain more from East-West trade, the communist countries or the western market economies? Why?

   Open answer. Someone who is distrustful of the motives of the communist countries might argue that we should only trade with them by barter or not trade with them at all in order to prevent them from obtaining dollars which they could then use to purchase high-tech goods from the West. Outside of such geopolitical considerations, the U.S. is better off trading with any countries by money transactions, because that provides for the most efficient and beneficial trade.

   The western market economies are likely to gain more from East-West trade than the communist countries because their market systems enable them to determine more accurately the true production costs of goods and services than can the communist countries with their arbitrary price systems.

Who Benefits and Who Is Hurt by Foreign Trade?

The vested interests that form the opposing camps in the dispute over free trade vs. protectionism are examined in this section. On one side are those in the import-competing industries that tend to lose from increased imports and on the other side are the export industries and the consuming public.

Study Question 4 enquires how the gains from trade could be distributed so that there are no losers.

Case Application: Steel Industry Does an About Face

The case of a vested interest that switched sides is illustrated in this application. When the U.S. steel industry had a comparative advantage and was a major supplier of steel to the rest of the world, it favored free trade. When it lost its comparative advantage, it switched to a protectionist position.

Answers to the "For Thought" Questions

1. Who will gain and who will lose as a result of the higher taxes on steel imports?

   The stockholders and employees in the steel industry will gain, while the industries using steel and the consumers of steel products will lose. If the higher taxes on steel imports result in retaliation abroad, U.S. export industries will also lose.

2. Why was the steel industry at one time in favor of free trade?

   The steel industry was in favor of free trade when it had a cost advantage in steel production. Because it could undersell foreign producers, the industry wanted to minimize world trade restrictions so it could have the largest possible markets.

3. Do you think that the steel industry should get more protection from imports? Why or why not?

   Open answer. Those who might answer in the affirmative may believe that the country should maintain job security for those who are employed in industries threatened by foreign competition. They might justify protection of the steel industry because it is historically one of the nation's basic industries, employs large numbers of people, is injured by subsidized imports from abroad, and has the ability to regain its competitive position. Those who oppose protection for the steel industry might do so because they think that the public should not subsidize an industry that is

inefficient, because they believe it is not unfair competition but the steel industry's failure to invest in modern plants and equipment that led to its decline, and because they fear that protecting the U.S. steel industry might initiate worldwide trade restrictions that would undermine the international economy.

How Do We Pay for Imports?

The first part of this section deals with the foreign-exchange market and how exchange rates are set under a freely-fluctuating exchange rate system and under a fixed exchange rate system. The second part of the section explains what constitutes a country's balance of payments, what is meant by a deficit in the balance of payments, and how a basic deficit is compensated in the residual accounts.

Study Questions 5, 6, and 7 reinforce the students' understanding of the exchange rate mechanism. Study Question 8 reinforces the understanding of the balance of payments.

Case Application: The World's Biggest Debtor

The United States has been transformed in the last few years from a net creditor nation to a net debtor nation, its indebtedness to the rest of the world exceeding $200 billion. This application discusses how the country got into this situation and what it means. It examines the efforts to lower the international value of the dollar and the consequences of doing so.

Answers to the "For Thought" Questions

1. How do foreign investments in the United States affect the U.S. balance of payments? If Table 2 (p. 417) was the balance-of-payments statement for the United States, in what account would the sales of Treasury securities to foreign buyers appear?

   Foreign investments in the United States are a credit item entry in the U.S. balance of payments. The sales of Treasury securities to foreign buyers would appear in the Capital Account as a new foreign investment.

2. How will the earnings of foreigners on their U.S. investments affect the exchange rate of the dollar in the future? Why?

   The earnings of foreigners on their U.S. investments will tend to lower the exchange rate of the dollar—to depreciate it. The transfer of those dollar earnings will increase the supply of dollars on the foreign exchange market, the increased supply causing its value to fall.

3. Should the U.S. restrict foreigners from acquiring assets in this country such as land, businesses, or financial securities? Why or why not?

Open answer. Some Americans are concerned about foreigners owning assets in this country such as land, businesses, and securities. They are concerned that the ownership of U.S. assets by foreigners could harm our country. Just as U.S. investments in foreign countries in earlier years mainly benefited them rather than hurting them, our fears concerning the dangers of foreign investments here are probably unfounded.

A valid concern is that extensive holdings of assets in this country by foreigners could generate such a large outflow of dollar earnings on those assets that it would be difficult for the U.S. to service its foreign debt—to earn enough money from its exports to pay the dividends and interest due to foreign investors. We might have to adopt an austerity program, as Mexico and some other debtor countries have had to do, in order to generate an export surplus to make the payments. Up to this point, however, the inflow of capital from foreign investors has enabled us to finance our import surplus and helped to finance our government deficits.

How Do We Restrict Foreign Trade?

This section explains the methods used to restrict trade. Tariffs are the most common trade restriction employed by the United States. Quotas and non-tariff administrative barriers are favored in other countries. Export embargoes are imposed infrequently.

Study Question 9 examines the difference in the way countries react to trade restrictions by small nations compared to large nations.

Case Application: Protection Japanese Style

The U.S. trade deficit with Japan has been a major issue recently. This application inquires into the reasons why it has been difficult for American producers to penetrate the Japanese market.

Answers to the "For Thought" Questions

1. What type of non-tariff barriers, other than quotas, restrict imports into Japan? Can you think of any similar barriers that restrict imports into the United States?

   Administrative requirements imposed on imported goods, such as additional documentation and testing, are examples of non-tariff barriers. There also exists in Japan an ethno-centric cultural barrier to foreign goods. The United States also has administrative barriers to imports, such as the requirement that

imported goods be marked with their country of origin, adding to the costs of the products. The "Buy American" campaigns in this country are a type of non-tariff barrier.

2. Would U.S. farmers and ranchers be able to export more to Japan if the Japanese applied tariffs rather than quotas to imports of agricultural products? What are the assumptions underlying your answer?

   U.S. farmers and ranchers would be able to export more to Japan with tariffs instead of quotas assuming that the U.S. has an increasing comparative advantage over Japan in agricultural production, thus widening the cost differential. This assumption is likely to be the case because of the limited amount of agricultural land available in Japan, the country's rising standard of living, and the shift in its consumption habits from fish to meat.

3. Do you think that more study of foreign languages should be required of American students? Why or why not?

   Open answer. After a number of years of decline in foreign language study, there has recently emerged a movement for increasing foreign languages in school curricula. The objective is to put the education received by Americans in foreign languages on a more equal footing with the education received by the students of other countries. One benefit of this would be to enable U.S. businesses to operate with more success in overseas markets.

   Those who are opposed to increasing the language requirements in schools believe that: mastery of foreign languages is not so important for Americans because the country only has one neighbor that speaks a different language; English has, to a large extent, become the world's universal language; and there would be a trade-off of sacrificed studies of other subjects or of students' leisure time if more language study were required.

Should Foreign Trade Be Restricted?

This section examines the various arguments for imposing restrictions on imports. Free trade is a policy upon which there is general agreement among economists. The one traditional protectionist argument which has logical validity under certain circumstances is the infant industry argument, but the circumstances do not apply in the United States.

Study Question 10 provides a useful exercise for the student in economic reasoning by finding the fallacy in an argument actually used concerning foreign trade.

Case Application: Bastiat's Petition

This application quotes a "petition" addressed by an early nineteenth century French economist, Frederic Bastiat, to the French Parliament. It cleverly satirizes the "unfair competition" argument for protection.

Answers to the "For Thought" Questions

1. What type of protectionist argument was Bastiat satirizing?

   He was satirizing the argument for protection as a result of unfair competition from cheap foreign labor.

2. If the French Parliament had adopted Bastiat's petition, what effect would this have had on the manufacturers of candles, wax-lights, lamps, and candlesticks? What would have been the effect on the French economy?

   If the French Parliament had adopted Bastiat's petition, it would certainly have greatly increased the market and the profitability of the illumination industries, which would no longer have the sun as a competitor. It would not, however, have been beneficial for the French economy which would have been burdened with greatly increased costs and reduced efficiency.

3. Do you think that the U.S. industries which are suffering from import competition should be accorded protection? Why or why not? Is there a difference between the argument for restricting the imports of textiles, steel, or Japanese automobiles and Bastiat's petition to restrict the competition from the sun?

   Open answer. Those who are convinced by the economic analysis which favors free trade would be opposed to import restrictions. They believe that the effects would be an increase in the cost of living for consumers, inefficient use of domestic resources, and the possibility of retaliation which might touch off a wave of additional trade restrictions. Those who favor import restrictions believe that American industries and workers have suffered too much from foreign competition, that Japan and other countries subsidize exports of their products, that the U.S. should retaliate for discrimination against our exports, and that American consumers should be willing to pay higher prices for U.S. built products out of patriotism.

   Bastiat's argument for protecting French lighting producers from the competition of the sun is the same as the reasons given by protectionists for protecting U.S. industries from "unfair foreign competition."

Perspective: Bring Back Gold?

The Perspective examines the workings of the gold standard in the context of current proposals for the country to adopt the gold standard again. It discusses why the gold standard was abandoned and the reasons given by those who want to see it revived.

Answers to Study Questions

1. If the United States has an absolute advantage in the production of rubber boots, does it necessarily follow that it will also have a comparative advantage in producing rubber boots? Explain.

   No. It is not the case that if a country has an absolute advantage in the production of a product it also has a comparative advantage in producing that product. A country has a comparative advantage in those products in which it has the largest absolute advantage (or the smallest absolute disadvantage) and a comparative disadvantage in those products in which it has a smaller absolute advantage (or a larger absolute disadvantage).

2. Why could a country have a comparative advantage in the production of a certain quantity of a good, but a comparative disadvantage in producing larger quantities of that same good?

   A country could have a comparative disadvantage in producing larger quantities of a good because the additional resources required to produce the larger amounts might not be as efficient as the resources used in previous production.

3. If all countries followed their comparative advantage and world output increased, who would get this increased output?

   The residents of both exporting and importing countries would benefit from the increased output resulting from specialization according to comparative advantage.

4. Since some people benefit from an increase in foreign trade while others lose, although the total benefits exceed the total losses, how could the benefits be redistributed so that everybody gains?

   Government assistance to businesses and workers injured by foreign imports to help them modernize or retrain and shift to other lines of production is one way of redistributing the gains from trade. A more direct way would be to use the proceeds from levies on imports and exports to compensate the import-competing businesses and workers for their losses.

5. Assuming that the price of the Swiss franc is 55 cents (U.S.), if there is a large increase in the demand for Swiss watches in this country, what would you expect to happen to the franc-dollar exchange rate under a system of freely-fluctuating exchange rates?

   An increase in U.S. imports from Switzerland, all other things remaining the same, would cause the Swiss franc to appreciate relative to the dollar so that it would be worth more than 55 cents.

6. Why does a rise in U.S. interest rates affect the foreign exchange rate of the dollar?

A rise in U.S. interest rates attracts capital from abroad for short-term investment in this country. The transfer of foreign capital to this country results in an increased demand for dollars in the foreign exchange market, causing the exchange rate of the dollar to appreciate.

7. Under the gold standard, if the U.S. dollar was valued at $35 per ounce of gold and the French franc was 700 francs per ounce of gold, what was the exchange rate between the dollar and the French franc?

The exchange rate was $1 = 20 francs.

8. Can a country have a surplus in its balance of trade and at the same time have a basic deficit in its balance of payments? How?

A country can have a surplus in its balance of trade and at the same time have a basic deficit in its balance of payments if its imports of services, long-term investments abroad, short-term capital exports, and other transfers such as economic and military assistance taken together have a net balance that is larger than its trade surplus.

9. Why are small countries not as likely to encounter retaliation when they increase trade restrictions as large countries are?

Small countries are not as likely as large countries to encounter retaliation when they increase trade restrictions because other countries orient their trade policies toward their major trading partners. Since large countries are more important markets for other countries' products, they are more likely to meet retaliation.

10. A U.S. Congressman favoring trade restrictions on textile imports released figures showing that foreign-made apparel cost 97% of the average retail price for U.S. made goods. Does this indicate that consumers would not be much affected by restrictions on imports of apparel? Explain.

Under free market conditions, there is naturally a close approximation of the prices charged for domestically produced goods and imports. If imports were restricted prices would rise for two reasons: there would be

higher monopolistic gains for producers and workers in the industries benefitting from the protection and costs would go up in those industries because of diminishing returns to the efficiency of resource usage.

Integrating *Economics U$A* Programs

(For information on Economics U$A *see the introduction, p. v.)*

There are two programs that are applicable to this chapter, one on the theory of international trade and protectionist policies and the other on exchange rates. The first is program 27, "International Trade: For Whose Benefit?" It begins with an examination of the potential for trade between the U.S. and China. Economist Gill illustrates the gains from trade based on comparative advantage with a numerical example. The second application describes how Japanese car imports generated pressures to protect the domestic auto industry which resulted in "voluntary" quotas. These quotas raised the prices of both Japanese and American cars. An estimate of the cost to consumers of protecting one American job is $100,000–$200,000 a year. In his discussion, Gill contrasts the short-run and long-run effects of free trade. The last part of the program discusses the problem of dumping—selling exports at less than their costs of production—with respect to the steel industry. (This is the situation that infuriated the Queen of Hearts concerning the foreign exporters of hats in the introductory article.) Gill discusses non-tariff barriers.

The other program is 28, "Exchange Rates: What In the World Is a Dollar Worth?" It discusses the international gold standard prior to the Great Depression, Hoover's attempt to keep the U.S. on the gold standard, and the effects on the economy—why it worsened the depression. Gill explains how the gold standard maintained equilibrium in the balance of payments. The next application shifts to the postwar international monetary mechanism set up at the Bretton Woods conference in 1944. It traces the reasons for changes in the U.S. balance of payments and exchange rates leading to the end of the Bretton Woods system of fixed exchange rates based on dollar convertibility to gold. Gill uses the familiar demand-supply model to show how exchange rates are determined. The final segment reviews the performance of the floating exchange rate system under the international financial stresses of the 1970s and the role it has played in the U.S. domestic economy.

Case Applications in Student Workbook

(Answers are supplied to students in the workbook.)

Why Do We Trade With Other Countries?

Case Application: U.S. Farmers Selling Less Overseas

Although U.S. exports of agricultural products have declined as a percentage of U.S. production and world consumption, the U.S. is still the major supplier of agricultural products internationally. The application contains a table giving U.S. exports as a percentage of world exports for a number of agricultural products. It also provides information on the destination of our exports to different parts of the world and changes in the allocation of our agricultural exports since 1970.

Answers to the "For Thought" Questions

1. Judging from the data on U.S. exports as a percentage of world exports, in what agricultural crop did the U.S. apparently have the largest efficiency advantage over the rest of the world?

   Judging from the data on U.S. exports as a percentage of world exports, the U.S. apparently had the largest efficiency advantage over the rest of the world in the production of corn, followed closely by soybeans. U.S. corn exports accounted for 77.8% of world exports of the crop, while U.S. soybean exports accounted for 77.4% of world exports.

2. Since the U.S. accounts for such a large percentage of world corn exports, it obviously has an advantage in corn production. Why, then, does it not completely specialize in corn production?

   The U.S. does not completely specialize in corn production because of increasing costs. If additional acreage were planted in corn which was not as productive or was located in areas of the country where the climate was not as suitable for growing corn, costs per bushel of corn produced would rise and the U.S. would not be as competitive in the world corn market.

3. Because exporting so much of our agricultural output tends to raise domestic food prices, some people say we should limit food exports in order to hold down the cost of living at home. What is your opinion about this proposal?

   Open answer. Adding world demand to the domestic demand for our agricultural output does tend to raise the prices for some food items at home. If holding down food prices is our only or main objective, restricting exports would be one way of doing that. On the other hand, policies in this country for some time have been aimed at supporting the prices of farm products, frequently by government subsidies. Restricting farm exports would hold down food prices at the expense of farmers' income and would hurt the sales of other industries to the farm communities. The cost of living might be lower, but so would people's incomes.

Who Benefits and Who Is Hurt by Foreign Trade?

Case Application: The Top U.S. Exporters

This application details the leading exporting firms in the United States. The table shows what products they produce and what percentage of their total production is exported.

Answers to the "For Thought" Questions

1. Among the top 10 exporters shown in Table 1 on page 410 in the text, what industry accounted for the largest amount of export sales? Did that industry also lead in total export sales of all U.S. industries as shown in Figure 3 on page 409 of the text? If not, what industry did?

   Among the top 10 exporters, the automobile industry accounted for the largest amount of export sales, with General Motors, Ford, and Chrysler exporting over $16 billion worth of vehicles and parts. In total exports, however, the major export industry is not automobiles— or aircraft or chemicals or food, although these are all important exports—but the largest export category is diverse types of machinery.

2. Are there other industries that do not export much or any of their production that benefit from international trade? If so, what types of industries are they and how do they benefit?

   A number of industries that do not export much or any of their production but nevertheless benefit from international trade are those that use imported raw materials or semi-finished products. They benefit because the production inputs might not be available domestically or, if available, would be more expensive.

3. What do you think is the explanation for the success of the leading exporters?

   Open answer. One explanation for the success of the U.S. car makers and other industries, both in domestic and foreign sales, is that they have economies of scale in production that enable them to mass produce at lower costs than most countries. Another advantage is the pool of skilled and trained labor available in this country. A third advantage is the large amount of capital available to develop and acquire advanced technological equipment.

How Do We Pay for Imports?

Case Application: The End of the World Credit Binge

This application discusses the international payments crisis touched off by the decline in the value of the Mexican peso in the latter part of 1982. It deals with the causes of the currency problems of the deficit countries and what the consequences might be.

Answers to the "For Thought" Questions

1. If the hypothetical balance-of-payments statement in Table 2 on page 417 of the textbook were for Mexico, in which column under which account would its loans from foreign banks appear? In which column under which account would the interest payments on those loans appear?

   In the balance-of-payments statement, Mexico's loans from foreign banks would appear in the left column as a credit item under the "Capital Account." Interest payments on those loans would appear in the right column as a debit entry under the "Current Account."

2. Was Mexico employing a freely-fluctuating exchange rate or a fixed-exchange-rate system? How can you tell?

   Mexico was employing a fixed-exchange-rate system. The peso was officially devalued to 70 pesos to the dollar by government action rather than depreciating to that level as the result of supply and demand in the foreign-exchange market.

3. The Mexican government resented the terms imposed by the IMF as a condition for extending it additional credit because Mexico felt that the demands infringed on its sovereignty. Do you think the IMF is justified in telling governments how to manage their internal affairs? Why or why not?]

   Open answer. The Mexican government believes it must pursue the domestic policies which maximize the welfare of its citizens. It is committed to a high-economic-growth rate in order to improve its low living standards. The IMF and its industrialized members, however, believe that since it is largely their funds and those of their private banking institutions that are at stake, the IMF must require Mexico to adopt austerity measures to insure that the loans can be repaid.

How Do We Restrict Foreign Trade?

Case Application: Made-in-America Japanese Cars?

This application covers the "local content" law proposed for foreign automobiles sold in the United States. It explains the effects of a local content law and how Mexico used a local content law for automobiles in the 1960s.

Answers to the "For Thought" Questions

1. Is a local content law more like a tariff, a quota, or a non-tariff barrier?

   A local content law is more like a quota because it limits the quantity of a commodity which can be imported, no matter how great the differential between foreign and domestic prices.

2. What would be the effect of a U.S. local content law on comparative advantage?

   The effect of a local content law would be to nullify comparative advantage. American resources would be used to produce automobile components even if they were relatively inefficient in that production. They would not shift to industries in which they were relatively more efficient.

3. What might be a useful trade policy for a developing country like Mexico might not be appropriate for an industrialized country such as the United States. Do you think that a local content law would have the same results in the two countries? Why or why not?

   Open answer. A local content law for the automobile industry would have the same results in Mexico and the United States in the sense that it would create more jobs and profits in the industry. It would have different effects because Mexico would benefit from developing new skills in its labor force and reducing industrial production costs, while for the United States a local content law would increase production costs and monopoly pricing in the industry.

Should Foreign Trade Be Restricted?

Case Application: Politics and Trade

This application discusses export embargoes, such as the one on equipment for Russia's gas pipeline to Western Europe, as a tool of foreign policy. It also discusses other political aspects of trade policies.

Answers to the "For Thought" Questions

1. How did the U.S. embargo on equipment for the Soviet gas pipeline resemble the neomercantilist position?

    The U.S. embargo on equipment for the Soviet gas pipeline resembled the neomercantilist position because it opposed the export of advanced technology and capital equipment.

2. Why is the infant-industry argument more justified for developing countries than for developed countries? What problem may result from restricting imports to foster infant industries in any country?

    The infant-industry argument is more justified for developing countries than for developed countries because small new industries in developing countries have high production costs due to low volume and cannot compete with the mass production efficiencies of the industries in developed countries. Developed countries have adequate capital and market size to support a large volume industry without restrictions on imports.

    In any country, however, the infant industry argument can be a smoke screen to protect inefficient producers, and the political influence of vested interests can be used to perpetuate protectionist tariffs and quotas indefinitely into the future, whether justified or not.

3. Do you believe in the use of trade sanctions as an instrument of foreign policy? Why or why not?

    Open answer. Foreign trade has often been used in the past as a weapon of diplomacy. It could be argued that a country has the right to control its trade in order to achieve its international political objectives. On the other hand, using trade sanctions as a diplomatic weapon is costly to the country imposing the sanctions as well as to the country against which they are directed, and may have an adverse effect on third parties as well. Furthermore, trade sanctions may not have their intended effects because of alternative sources of supply, evasion, or retaliation.

Chapter 17

Alternative Economic Systems

Chapter Overview

This chapter describes and compares the different types of economic systems in the world. The introductory article describes the problems and changes in the economic system of the Soviet Union as the leading example of a centrally-directed economy.

The first section defines the terms used to designate different types of economic systems and shows how a centrally-directed economy resolves the basic economic allocation decisions. The case application discusses the unique features of the Yugoslavian economy.

The second section examines the degree to which the centrally-directed Soviet economy meets the criteria for evaluating the performance of an economic system. The case application looks at the particular problems of running a production plant in the Soviet system.

The last section examines changes occurring in command economies and market economies and whether these changes are bringing the two types of systems into synthesis. The case application describes the elements of capitalism introduced in Hungary.

Suggested Answers to the Learning Objectives

The knowledge acquired from this chapter should enable the students to:

1. List the differences among capitalism, democratic socialism, and authoritarian socialism.

   Capitalism is a system in which the means of production are owned by private individuals and firms, with production and price decisions, including incomes, directed by market forces. Democratic socialism is a system in which the government owns basic industries but most production and pricing decisions are made by market forces. Income inequality is reduced by highly progressive tax systems, and the government is democratically elected. Authoritarian socialism is a system in which virtually all production is in the hands of government, with allocation and pricing decisions made by a central planning authority. Incomes are set by the government, which is self-perpetuating.

2. Explain how the Soviet Union answers the basic economic questions of what, how, and for whom to produce.

The Soviet Union determines what goods and services will be produced by a process in which Gosplan, on the basis of priorities established by the Soviet leadership, works out a set of control figures for major commodity groups. These control figures are sent to the economic ministries which in turn break them down into production targets for individual enterprises. The enterprises estimate the amount of factor inputs which they will need to produce their specified output. Their resource needs are communicated to the ministries, which forward the requests to Gosplan. Gosplan matches the resource requirements to the available supplies and formulates the final plan of what will be produced. Decisions about how to produce are made by the managers of industrial plants and agricultural collectives, but with control exerted by Gosbank over their use of capital equipment. Income determination is the result of government-set wages and bonuses to provide production incentives and allocate labor where it is needed.

3. Compare the performance of the U.S. and Soviet economies in terms of each of the following: static efficiency, dynamic efficiency, price stability, unemployment, growth, and economic security and freedom.

The economy of the Soviet Union ranks poorly in static efficiency. Although there are some sectors, such as public transit, where it performs better than the U.S., its per capita GNP trails far behind. In dynamic efficiency, it has done much better. Its growth rate was substantially higher than that of the U.S. from 1928 to the 1970s, but has slowed to about the same as the U.S. in recent years. Although prices are apparently more stable, there is a great deal of suppressed inflation in the Soviet Union, as evidenced by shortages. The U.S.S.R. maintains full employment better than the U.S. and has more economic security. On the other hand, there is not much economic freedom in the Soviet Union.

4. Define the "convergence hypothesis" and explain what evidence of convergence exists in modern command and market economies.

The convergence hypothesis contends that market economies and command economies are becoming like one another. The indications of convergence in command economies include: decentralization in planning and management; introduction of interest, rent, and profit; the use of price signals; increased importance of business administration; increased importance of consumption; increased importance of foreign trade; and a trend toward market socialism. Indications of convergence in market economies include: a growth of the public sector; extension of social-welfare measures; the use of planning and incomes policies; a toning-down of market forces; and an increased role for workers in production decisions and profits.

What Are the Major Differences Among Alternative Economic Systems?

In the table on textbook page 436 there is a summary of the characteristics of the three contemporary alternative economic systems: capitalism, democratic socialism, and authoritarian socialism (communism). This section examines how the Soviet Union resolves the "what," "how," and "for whom" questions.

Study Questions 1–5 examine different aspects of how the Soviet system resolves the basic economic questions and make comparisons with the way the U.S. economy resolves those questions.

Case Application: The Yugoslavian Way

Yugoslavia adopted a different economic system from that of the Soviet Union by giving workers in enterprises control of decision making and a share of the firm's profitability. The application describes the Yugoslav experience with a decentralized communist system.

Answers to the "For Thought" Questions

1. What is the principal difference between the Yugoslavian socialist system and that of the Soviet Union?

   The principal difference between the Yugoslavian and Soviet systems lies in the decentralization and worker control of enterprises in Yugoslavia.

2. Before it encountered economic problems in the late 1970s, Yugoslavia invested an extraordinarily high 28% of its Gross National Product each year. This was about twice the investment/GNP ratio of western countries. What was Yugoslavia's approximate ratio of investment to increased output (capital/output ratio)?

   Yugoslavia's capital/output ratio was approximately four to one. This is found by dividing the percentage of

Gross National Product allocated to investment by the annual growth rate in output. This assumes that population and other factors were constant.

3. Would you expect worker management of businesses to be efficient? Why or why not?

   Open answer. The success of American, Japanese, and German firms with involving the workers in decision making indicates that there are advantages in workers participating in management. On the other hand, workers' goals may tend to emphasize short-run rewards at the expense of long-run maximization of the firm's efficiency.

How Do We Evaluate the Performance of Alternative Economic Systems?

This section makes use of the framework of an economy's goals which was outlined in chapter 1 to evaluate the performance of the Soviet economy. According to these criteria, the Soviet economy has performed well in achieving some goals, such as economic growth, and poorly with respect to other goals, such as static efficiency.

Study Questions 6–9 examine various aspects of the Soviet performance in achieving economic goals.

Case Application: Problems of a Manager in the Soviet Union

This application brings out the difficulties of implementing Soviet plans by looking at production problems from the standpoint of an individual plant manager. It shows some of the devices adopted by plant managers to get around the problems that arise in an inflexible centrally-planned system.

Answers to the "For Thought" Questions

1. This application suggests that the Soviet system has problems achieving at least one of the major economic goals. Which one is that?

   The Soviet system has problems in achieving the goal of economic efficiency (static efficiency).

2. Does a plant supervisor in the U.S. encounter the problems faced by the plant manager in the U.S.S.R.? How does a market system make available enough of the proper bolts?

   A plant supervisor in the U.S. would probably not encounter the problems faced by the plant manager in the U.S.S.R. because a market system provides incentives for the needed bolts to be made available at the time and place required. If bolts are not available from the usual source, a plant supervisor can ordinarily obtain them elsewhere in the market.

3. The Soviet plant manager may have his income reduced and be reprimanded if the plant fails to meets its production target, but his plant probably will not be shut down, as plants are in this country for production losses. What do you think about the trade-offs of the two systems? Which makes a better disciplinarian, party leadership or the competitive market?

Open answer. The closure of plants and loss of jobs, which occur in a market economy as the result of demand fluctuations, management mistakes, or other operating losses, are costly in the short run. However, the flexibility and adaptability of a market system results in long-run efficiency of resource uses. Both central-planning authorities and competitive markets could be effective disciplinarians, but experience indicates that in practice competitive markets are more effective.

Are Socialistic and Capitalistic Systems Converging?

This section concludes the discussion of the comparison of the two main economic systems by discussing the ways in which they are becoming more similar. Both systems have been undergoing substantial changes in the last decades, and those changes appear to be reducing the extent of differences in the ways the systems operate.

However, the position of those who don't subscribe to the convergence hypothesis was strengthened in recent years by developments in the West. The "regulations revolt" in the United States, the election of the conservative Thatcher government in Britain, and the (temporary) ousting of the Social democrats in Sweden lent support to the argument that capitalistic institutions in the West will limit the movement toward central planning in western economies. Similarly, the crackdown on liberalization in Poland was evidence that the authoritarian socialist systems would not readily permit significant modification of their economies along the lines of a free market system. The acid test for the ability of the command economies to change may be found in success or failure of Gorbachev's "glasnost"—his attempt to open the Soviet economy to progressive change.

Study Question 10 reviews the indications of convergence.

Case Application: Goulash Communism

"If Karl Marx could see what the Hungarians have done to Communism, he might be shocked." This application describes the capitalistic alterations that Hungary has made in the Soviet model of a centrally-planned economy. Some of the reforms that worked well for Hungary are now being copied by Gorbachev in Russia.

Answers to the "For Thought" Questions

1. What indications do you find in the Hungarian economy that support the convergence hypothesis?

The Hungarian economy has become more like a capitalistic economy by allowing plant managers to determine their output mix and negotiate sales contracts, permitting firms to set their own prices and undertake investment projects out of retained profits, allowing small-scale free enterprise in business and professions, approving nonstate farm operations and off-shift private production in government plants, and decentralizing planning authority.

2. What are the economic advantages of having firms set their own prices?

The main advantage of firms setting their own prices is that they can match output to sales, avoiding the problem of surplus unsold goods accumulating on the one hand or shortages on the other. Another advantage is that it provides incentives to be more efficient.

3. Is convergence of command and market economies a good thing or a bad thing? Good or bad for whom? Why?

Open answer. Those who believe that convergence is a good thing might argue that it takes the best advantages of each system and combines them. They might believe that if the economic systems become more similar, it will reduce political tensions and the threat of war. If so, it could be good for the people in both systems.

There are others who believe that the introduction of command economy methods in our system will weaken the capitalistic economies, while the Communist countries will be strengthened by borrowing capitalistic methods from us. They maintain that the two systems are engaged in a life-or-death struggle for world domination, and our side will be weakened by convergence.

Perspective: Marx on Capitalism

The Perspective summarizes Marx's theory of dialectical materialism and how it applies to the evolution of capitalistic systems. It explains what he considered to be the central flaw of capitalism—the appropriation of surplus value by the capitalist class—which he said would result in depressions of increasing severity and, ultimately, in a workers' revolution.

Answers to Study Questions

1. How do the functions of Gosbank differ from those of the Federal Reserve System?

The functions of the Federal Reserve System are to manage the nation's money supply and provide central banking services to the private financial institutions. Gosbank participates more broadly and directly in economic activities by handling all financial transactions between firms, extending credit to firms, and auditing their plan fulfillment.

2. Is there a difference in the way pipeline workers in Siberia are convinced to endure harsh work compared to the way workers are induced to work in Alaska?

   The inducements to workers in the two cases are similar. They are attracted to work under harsh conditions by receiving a higher wage.

3. Since according to Marxian economics labor is the only factor input that should be paid and there is no justification for paying interest on the use of capital, why are Soviet firms now being charged interest on the capital they use, even though the interest payment comes from and ends up in Gosbank?

   Soviet firms are now being charged interest on the capital they use as a way of rationing the scarce capital to the most valuable uses. When firms have to pay for the use of capital they will economize on its use.

4. How would the economies of the Soviet Union and the United States handle each of the following problems? a) Determining the mix between the production of machinery and the building of houses. b) Setting the relative pay for doctors and plumbers. c) Fighting inflation. d) Keeping unemployment down.

   a) The Soviet Union determines the mix between the production of machinery and the building of houses by first establishing priorities and then developing a production plan which specifies the outputs of the machinery and construction sectors and allocates the resources to those sectors to produce the specified outputs. In the United States the output mix is determined by profit incentives which derive from market demand and cost relationships.

   b) In the Soviet Union the relative pay for doctors and plumbers is determined administratively to provide the required numbers of the different professions needed to fulfill the plan. In the United States the relative pay is determined by the market demand for their services, the cost of acquiring the skills, and the power of professional associations or unions in determining pay levels.

   c) The Soviet Union prevents inflationary price increases by administratively setting prices, resulting in suppressed inflation and shortages. The United States combats inflation by fiscal and monetary policies which reduce aggregate demand.

   d) The Soviet Union keeps unemployment down by creating production activity and by making it difficult for those who do not hold a job to get by. The United States keeps unemployment down by fiscal and monetary policies which generate increases in aggregate demand and occasionally by government work programs.

5. Why is it difficult for the Soviet Union to engage profitably in foreign trade based on comparative advantage?

   It is difficult for the Soviet Union to engage profitably in foreign trade based on comparative advantage because prices in the Soviet Union are administratively fixed and do not reflect the relative scarcity of resources and products. Since prices do not reflect the real cost of production, it is difficult for the Soviets to determine in which products they have a comparative advantage.

6. Why is a market system thought to be more efficient in allocating resources than a centrally planned system?

   A market system is an efficient mechanism for allocating resources because it automatically takes into account all of the demand and supply conditions affecting resource uses. The cost of acquiring and processing all of the information by a centrally planned system that a market system automatically makes use of, assuming that it were possible to do so, would be extremely high.

7. Why is the Soviet public's high rate of savings accumulation an indication of suppressed inflation?

   The high rate of savings accumulation in the Soviet Union is an indication of suppressed inflation because it provides evidence that goods which the public would like to buy are unavailable.

8. Why did the increased emphasis on providing more consumer goods and services slow down the Soviet growth rate?

   Producing more goods and services meant a reduction in the amount of resources allocated to the capital goods industries, which slowed the growth rate.

9. Since the paper mills around Lake Baikal are not owned by profit-minded capitalists, why do they pollute the lake by disposing of their waste in the streams that feed it?

   There is pressure on the managers of paper mills in the Soviet Union to minimize the costs allocated to their plants in producing paper. They can reduce their costs by disposing of their production wastes in the streams that feed Lake Baikal. This helps them to meet their production targets within the resource constraints which they have been given.

10. What are some recent developments in the Soviet or American economies that would support or refute the convergence hypothesis?

    Developments in the Soviet economy that would support the convergence hypothesis are: decentralization in planning and management; the introduction of interest, rent, and profits; the use of price signals; an increased importance of business administration; an increased importance of foreign trade; and a trend toward market socialism. Soviet developments that refute the convergence hypothesis are the opposition to liberalizing movements in the Soviet Eastern European satellite countries, such as the quashing of Solidarity in Poland. Developments in the American economy that support the convergence hypothesis are: the growth of the public sector; the extension of social-welfare measures; the consideration of planning and incomes policies; the toning-down of market forces; and the increased role of workers in production decisions and profits. Developments refuting the convergence hypothesis are the "regulations revolt" and the movement to reverse the expansion of social-welfare programs.

(There are no programs in the *Economics U$A* series that cover the content of this chapter.)

Case Applications in Student Workbook

(Answers are supplied to students in the workbook.)

What Are the Major Differences Among Alternative Economic Systems?

Case Application: Food Production in Russia

This application describes the structure of the Soviet agricultural system, how much the three different sectors of the system contribute to agricultural production, and how each operates. It compares production in Soviet farming with that in the United States. It discusses the reasons for the low productivity of Soviet agriculture.

Answers to the "For Thought" Questions

1. Which sector of Soviet agriculture is most typical of authoritarian-socialist production? Which sector is more similar to capitalist production?

   The sector of Soviet agriculture most typical of authoritarian-socialist production is the state farms (Sovkhozy). The state farms are directly controlled and administered through the planning system. The sector more similar to capitalist production is the private-plot sector.

2. What difficulties and deficiencies are there in the resolution of the "how to produce" food question in the Soviet Union?

   Difficulties and deficiencies in the resolution of the "how to produce" food question in the Soviet Union include the failure of the bureaucratic planning

hierarchy, the lack of an incentive system, and the lack of research facilities and organization.

3. If you were a member of the Council of Ministers of the Soviet Union, how would you recommend reorganizing the agricultural sector in order to meet the nation's food needs?

   Open answer. One solution to meeting Russia's food needs might be to increase the private plot sector, which is the most productive. Another solution might be to allow the collective farms to retain more of the value of their output and exchange it at more favorable prices. This would increase the incentives for the collective farmers, who constitute by far the largest segment of the farm population, while continuing to get maximum utilization of the scarce machinery and equipment.

How Do We Evaluate the Performance of Alternative Economic Systems?

Case Application: Business Cycle Hits Communist Countries

This application discusses the macroeconomic problems that have appeared in the Soviet Union and Eastern European countries in recent years. It shows how the stagflation of their economies is related to their external economic relations with the West.

Answers to the "For Thought" Questions

1. In the 1930s the Soviet Union achieved macroeconomic goals better than western countries did. Which two primary economic goals did it succeed at better than the West?

   The two primary economic goals which the Soviet Union succeeded in achieving much better than the West in the 1930s were full employment and economic growth.

2. Some western experts allege that an economic slump is worse for command economies than for market economies because their static efficiency is lower due to the rigidity of their systems. Why might an increase in petroleum prices create more problems for command economies than for market economies?

   An increase in petroleum prices might create more problems for command economies than for market economies because it is not as easy for command economies to adapt allocation and production to changed resource costs. In a command system, a change in one important variable, such as energy costs, requires conscious adjustment of countless allocation and production decisions throughout the system. In a market system, on the other hand, the changes automatically come about as a result of the operation of the price mechanism in marketplaces.

3. Do you think that Stalin was right in avoiding trade with the West for the economic well-being of the communist countries? Why or why not?

Open answer. It could be argued that if it were not for the increased trade relationships with the West, the communist bloc countries would not have suffered from the 1979 oil price shock and the slump of the early 1980s. On the other hand, without the imports of high-technology capital goods, food and industrial raw materials, and modern consumer products from the West, the communist bloc would likely have lower standards of living and a slower long-term growth rate.

Are Socialistic and Capitalistic Systems Converging?

Case Application: Centralization vs. Decentralization

The application is a simulation model comparing resource allocation under a system of scientific socialism with resource allocation under a market system. The optimum outcome under the two systems results in the same mix of outputs and the same total output.

Answers to the "For Thought" Questions

1. Which of the indications of convergence in command economies is best illustrated by the use of linear programming in scientific socialism?

The indication of convergence in command economies best illustrated by the use of linear programming in

scientific socialism is the increased importance of business administration. Linear programming was a business-management technique developed in the United States during World War II for scheduling defense production.

2. What are the differences and similarities between "scientific socialism" and "market socialism."

The similarities between "scientific socialism" and "market socialism" are that they both take into account the relative costs of inputs, the production techniques, and the relative values of final outputs. However, under market socialism these considerations are reflected in the market price mechanism, while with scientific socialism they must be determined by independent study and consciously incorporated into the planning process.

3. Do you think that a well-managed centrally-directed economy using the sophisticated methods of scientific socialism would be as efficient as a market economy? Why or why not?

Open answer. A well-managed centrally-directed economy using the sophisticated methods of scientific socialism might have the advantage in avoiding some of the wastes of a market economy such as business bankruptcies, time lost from strikes, misallocations due to monopolistic practices, the wastes of competitive advertising, and the social costs of unemployment and inflation. On the other hand, a centrally-directed economy based on scientific socialism would be very costly to administer because of the large amount of human resources required for gathering and processing data and developing, adjusting, and overseeing the planning. It is questionable whether or not, even with the use of sophisticated planning techniques such as linear programming and the availability of high-powered computers, it would be possible to efficiently take into consideration all of the myriad considerations and decisions that a modern economy must make, which are automatically accounted for in a market system.

Chapter 18

World Economic Development

Chapter Overview

This chapter deals with the less-developed countries (LDCs). The introductory article covers the swings in Chinese economic policy since the revolution, concentrating on the recent reforms.

The first section of the chapter examines the causes of the low standards of living in the Third World countries. The case application focuses on one of the major problems, that of population pressures, with respect to the Mexican economy.

The second section outlines four of the key decisions made by LDCs in formulating their development strategy. The case application examines the development program of India.

The final section looks at the major problems and the prospects for raising the Third World out of poverty. The case application discusses the role of the industrialized countries in assisting the LDCs to develop.

Suggested Answers to the Learning Objectives

The knowledge acquired from this chapter should enable the students to:

1. Discuss the Chinese Cultural Revolution and "second revolution" and their effects on China's economic development.

   The Chinese Cultural Revolution, instituted by Mao Tse-Tung to replace personal goals with social goals, disrupted the Chinese economy and set back its development. The "second revolution" was initiated by Deng Xiaoping in 1978 to bring about the modernization of agriculture, industry, science, and defense. It includes allowing private profit-making enterprises to operate along with the government businesses. This has created incentives which increase the rate of growth, but at the expense of a growth of corruption and inflation.

2. Describe the characteristics of less-developed countries and explain the World Bank's classification of countries.

   Less-developed countries have low per capita output and incomes, are primarily agricultural rather than industrial, have extensive underemployment and
   illiteracy, and have a low life expectancy of the population. The World Bank classifies countries as low-income, middle-income, upper middle-income, high-income oil exporters, industrial market, and East European non-market economies.

3. List four sets of alternate choices that affect development.

   The choices are: agriculture versus industry, basic industries versus consumer goods industries, centralized planning versus the market, and balanced versus unbalanced growth.

4. Explain the significance of the population growth rate in economic development.

   The population growth rate is significant for a less-developed country because it affects the amount of resources available to the country for capital accumulation and dictates the priorities for the use of a country's food and other resources.

5. List three factors that limit economic growth.

   Factors that limit economic growth include population pressures on resources, low capital accumulation, and high foreign debt that restricts government spending and imports.

What Makes Countries Poor?

The first part of this section provides definitions of a number of terms describing the less-developed world. There follows a discussion of the principal factors that have retarded growth in output and living standards in the LDCs. The table on page 467 of the text gives a number of basic indicators for different classifications of countries.

Study Questions 1–4 provide opportunities to further explore this question.

Case Application: Mexico's Burden

The Mexican economy has had more success than most other LDCs in generating economic growth. One of the things which is preventing it from breaking out of poverty is its high birth rate. The application discusses the implications of Mexico's rapid population growth.

Answers to the "For Thought" Questions

1. What is the rate of economic growth per capita in Mexico. How does it compare with that of the other largest LDCs?

   The average annual growth of GNP per capita in Mexico from 1965 to 1983 was 3.2%. This was higher than the growth rate in India, Bangladesh, and Pakistan, but lower than that in China, Indonesia, and Brazil (Table 1, textbook p. 467).

2. How could Mexico's large population of young people be turned into a human capital asset rather than a liability?

   Mexico's young people could be a human capital asset if they had education and training and if the economy provided them with jobs and capital equipment which enabled them to make use of their skills.

3. Should the Mexican government adopt the same strong measures to control population growth as China has? Why or why not?

   Open answer. To many people, this is more a philosophical, moral, or religious question than an economic question. But looking at it only in its economics context, the argument for vigorous population control measures is based on the desire to free the nation's resources from the necessity to provide subsistence for a rapidly expanding population in order to allocate more resources to capital development. An economic argument against population control might be based on the position that labor is a productive resource which can be used in the development of unpopulated geographic areas of the country. Based upon the logic of the answer to Question 2 above, in the best of all possible economic worlds a large population could be a productive asset.

What Economic Development Choices Do Less-Developed Countries Have to Make?

In working out a development strategy that will enable a country to break the bonds of poverty, there are some key decisions about which development path the country should follow. One of these decisions is the relative priority given to the agricultural sector versus the industrial sector. A second priority question is whether to develop basic heavy industries or light consumer goods industries. A third key decision is whether to depend upon the market or centralized planning for making the allocation decisions, and a fourth is whether to concentrate the scarce capital and other production inputs into one or a few leading industries or to spread them out over a broad range of industries.

Study Questions 5–7 deal with development strategies.

Case Application: The Indian Way

India has a larger population than any country in the world except China. Also, because it is strategically located between the eastern communist bloc and the western capitalist economies, what happens to Indian economic development may therefore be crucial. This case application looks at the Indian experience to date.

Answers to the "For Thought" Questions

1. What economic development choices has India made?

   India has chosen to give priority to basic industries over rural development and consumer goods industries. While basically a market economy, it has leaned in the direction of centralized planning.

2. What are the similarities and differences in development strategies between India and China?

   Indian and Chinese development strategies have both included the objective of self-sufficiency in basic industries. While China is basically a centrally-planned system and India basically a market system, there has been an effort in China to decentralize planning, while in India planning controls remain highly centralized. China has allocated more resources to agricultural development, while India continues to concentrate on the development of industry.

3. Which system do you think will be most successful in economic development, China or India? Why?

   Open answer. Those who conclude that China will be more successful in economic development than India may believe that the pragmatic policies adopted by the new regime in China in place of the dogmatism that previously hindered Chinese development will allow China to mobilize all of its resources for development more effectively than India. Those who contend that India will be the more successful of the two in the long run may believe in the superiority of a basically market system over a basically centrally-planned system.

What Are the Prospects for World Economic Development?

In the 1950s when the United States first began assisting what were then called the underdeveloped countries, it was assumed that the Marshall Plan assistance to those countries would achieve the same miracles that it had in the post-war recovery of Europe. The belief was that it would take one or two decades to develop self-sustaining economic growth in those countries. In retrospect three decades later, the obstacles to development were not sufficiently appreciated and the initial expectations were wildly overoptimistic. Some recent studies have raised questions about whether world economic development is even possible.

The Study Questions 8–10 look at the obstacles and prospects for development.

Case Application: Aid or Trade?

This application deals with the foreign aid program of the United States. It describes how the relative size of the U.S. aid program has diminished and reviews current policies concerning assistance to the LDCs.

Answers to the "For Thought" Questions

1. Much of the aid to underdeveloped countries is directed at increasing productivity in agriculture. Why should this sector be given priority by the World Bank and other lenders?

   Aid to agriculture is emphasized in the assistance programs of the World Bank and other lenders because food production is considered a key sector for development of the LDCs.

2. How can freer trade policies in the industrialized countries help to defuse the "debt bomb"?

   Freer trade can help developing countries by providing them with larger markets for the products in which they have a comparative advantage. If they are able to export more, they can earn the foreign exchange to pay the interest and principal on their debt and still import capital goods needed for development.

3. Do you think that the United States should increase, keep constant, or decrease its foreign aid? Why?

   Open answer. Those favoring an increase in U.S. foreign aid may believe that the United States has a responsibility as the world's leading economic power to assist the LDCs in rising out of poverty and/or that it is in the best interests of the United States' long-run welfare and security to do so. Those favoring a decrease in U.S. aid may believe that the country cannot afford to assist other nations because of its domestic economic problems and/or because foreign aid only makes the recipient countries dependent and does not promote development.

Perspective: The Malthusian Dilemma

The most important economic equation for the world is the food/population balance. The question of whether the world's population will outrun the food production capacity of the earth was one of the primary interests of Robert Malthus. The Perspective discusses Malthus' calculations and why his predictions have not materialized—yet.

Answers to Study Questions

1. Why is the development outlook better for China than for many of the Third World countries?

   The development outlook is better for China than for many of the Third World countries because China has a quantity of diverse resources and a large market to take advantage of economies of scale, has reduced her population growth rate, is not burdened by a large external debt, and has adopted a pragmatic approach to development strategies.

2. How can the LDCs increase the amount of capital available for investment in development projects which will increase their rate of economic growth?

   The LDCs can increase the amount of capital available for investment in development projects by increasing the savings rate and attracting savings into domestic investments. Aggregate savings can be increased by decreasing the population growth rate. Domestic or foreign investment capital can be attracted by political and economic stability, an adequate infrastructure, and broad-based income distribution.

3. Why are educational and health programs important to economic growth?

   Educational and health programs are important to economic growth because labor is the most important factor input, and improvements in the quality of human capital will increase productivity which will attract new capital investments.

4. What would it mean for a country if its population growth rate was higher than the growth rate of the GNP?

   If a country's growth rate was higher than the growth rate of its GNP, the GNP per capita would decline. This would lower living standards.

5. How does the existence of large amounts of unemployment and underemployment in LDCs affect their decisions about development strategies? What economic sectors might be stressed and what kind of technology might be used in those circumstances?

   When there is a labor surplus, intermediate technologies rather than state-of-the-art technologies should be used in order to make productive use of the surplus labor force. By concentrating on the sectors which can be competitive in world markets using intermediate technologies, such as textiles and clothing, a country can help to solve its unemployment problem and spread the distribution of purchasing power over a broad base.

6. Why do LDCs typically allocate a smaller fraction of GNP to basic industries rather than consumer goods industries than developed countries do?

LDCs allocate a smaller fraction of GNP to basic industries rather than consumer goods industries because basic industries require large concentrations of capital equipment and LDCs are short of capital. Consumer goods industries, on the other hand, can typically employ more labor-intensive production methods, thereby utilizing surplus labor.

7. Under what conditions should an LDC follow a balanced growth policy and under what conditions should it concentrate its resources in one type or only a few types of production?

   An LDC should follow a balanced growth policy if it is a large country with a diversity of resources, an extensive domestic market, and a broad base for capital accumulation. It should concentrate its resources in one or a few types of production if it is a small country with a limited variety of resources, a small domestic market, and a limited base of capital accumulation.

8. Why does a poor country typically have a much higher birth rate than a developed country? What causes the birth rate to fall as income levels rise?

   Poor countries have higher birth rates than developed countries because their social customs have a stronger hold, infant mortality rates are higher, they lack social security systems to provide income security for the elderly, and most of the population is confined to a subsistence standard of living.

   Birth rates fall as income levels rise because opportunities open up for raising the aspirations and living standards through educating a family's children, infant mortality rates fall, the development of social security programs reduces the importance of having surviving male heirs to support the elderly, and there is an increased acceptance of and accessibility to birth control methods.

9. Is it a good policy for the United States to tie its economic development aid to U.S. exports? What might be the disadvantages of such a policy?

   Open answer. The reason for tying United States economic development aid to U.S. exports is that it is a direct stimulus to American export industries. The disadvantage is that the recipient country cannot make the most productive use of the developmental assistance. Furthermore, in the long run U.S. exports are promoted as much by aid that is not directly tied as that which is.

10. Would a United States foreign policy of "trade, not aid" do more to benefit the Third World countries than previous assistance programs? Why or why not?

    Open answer. A U.S. policy of "trade, not aid" would benefit the Third World countries that have raw materials for export or competitive finished goods industries and could stimulate investment in their export industries. On the other hand, it would not benefit countries without exportable raw materials or low cost

industries. Even in those countries with exportable goods, expanded trade might benefit only a narrow segment of the population and not broaden the domestic income base, as was frequently the case under colonialism.

(There are no programs in the *Economics U$A* series that cover the content of this chapter.)

Case Applications in Student Workbook

(Answers are supplied to students in the workbook.)

What Makes Countries Poor?

Case Application: Report on Africa

This application is based on a 1982 World Bank report which shows the problems created for African countries by maintaining artificially low prices for their agricultural products. High population growth rates, combined with urbanization and falling per capita food output, have jeopardized successful economic development in even the most favored African nations.

Answers to the "For Thought" Questions

1. In the table on page 467 of the textbook showing the basic indicators for different types of economies, Nigeria is the only sub-Saharan country listed. Because of its large petroleum resources, it has a per capita GNP which classifies it as a middle-income country. What happened to its food production per capita between 1974-1976 and 1981-1983?

   As indicated by the average index of food production per capita of 98 for Nigeria, per capita food production declined by 2% between 1974-1976 and 1981-1983.

2. How does what happened to Nigeria's food production per capita between 1974-1976 and 1981-1983 bear out the point made in the case application about mismanagement of agricultural production in Africa? What implications does this have for the future of African economic development?

   Nigeria's reduced index of food production per capita indicates that the output of food was falling behind the increase in population. This substantiates the allegation of mismanagement of agricultural production in Africa. Because the relationship between food supplies and population is one of the crucial elements of economic development, the declining agricultural productivity is going to make African economic development more difficult. Instead of providing a surplus of earnings for investment in industry, agriculture is a drain on the economy. Food imports are crowding out the needed imports of capital equipment.

3. What policies do you think African governments should adopt with respect to agriculture and food prices?

   Open answer. African governments have adopted policies of keeping food prices low in order to hold down the cost of living for their urban populations. This policy is designed to help the poorer urban residents survive. However, it results in greater poverty in the agricultural areas, discourages farmers from increasing output, and deprives the agricultural sector of revenues for increasing capital investment and productivity.

What Economic Development Choices Do Less-Developed Countries Have to Make?

Case Application: Learning From Tachai: China's Self-reliance

A renowned case of self-reliant community development in China is described in this application. A small but highly motivated and committed village overcame geographic, climatic, and technological obstacles to achieve a dramatic improvement in the output and living standards of the village.

Answers to the "For Thought" Questions

1. How did land reform lead ultimately to the success of Tachai?

   The Communist Land Reform Program gave the landless peasants of Tachai control over the land they worked and provided incentives to increase its productivity.

2. How did the self-reliance of the Chinese peasants make unnecessary the difficult choices about how to use scarce capital resources in development?

   The Chinese peasants made the choices about how to use scarce capital resources unnecessary because they substituted their own labor to develop the land by terracing it instead of depending on capital investment in machinery, irrigation systems, or artificial fertilizer plants.

3. Do you think it would be possible to accomplish Tachai's achievements under a capitalistic system? If so, how? If not, why not?

   Open answer. In a sense, the achievements in Tachai were due to incentives similar to those of a private farmer in the capitalistic systems, although Tachai is a cooperative rather than a privately owned enterprise. After the land reform, each peasant had a stake in the improved productivity of the land. Under capitalism with private plots, however, it might not have been

possible to achieve the cooperation between all of the peasants in the village to accomplish the land reclamation project.

What Are the Prospects for World Economic Development?

Case Application: Growth Prospects for the LDCs

This application concerns World Bank projections of growth rates for the LDCs from 1985-1995. There is a table showing growth rates since 1960 of the industrialized countries, the LDCs as a whole, and the African countries separately, with 1985-1995 high and low projections. Even the most optimistic growth projections for the African countries show them losing ground in per capita output. This case application brings the discussion around full circle from the introductory story on the African famine in chapter 1 of the textbook.

Answers to the "For Thought" questions

1. Why are living standards expected to fall in the African countries between 1985 and 1995 even though their growth in total GDP will be comparable to that in other less-developed countries?

   Living standards are expected to fall in the African countries because their population growth rates will exceed the growth in GDP.

2. What will determine whether the LDCs achieve the high growth projections or the low growth projections for the period 1985-1995?

   The things that will determine whether the LDCs achieve the high or low growth projections include the success of their growth strategies; whether they are able to acquire the necessary economic surplus out of domestic production, foreign aid, or foreign trade to invest in increased output capacity and human capital development; and whether they avoid internal and external conflicts that waste resources.

3. Do you expect the gap in living standards between the industrial countries and the LDCs to get larger or diminish? Why?

   Open answer. If both the industrialized and the less-developed countries realize the high growth projections of the World Bank, the gap will widen. If both realize the low growth projections, the LDCs will narrow the gap slightly. If the LDCs achieve the high growth path, while the industrialized countries are on the low growth path, the LDCs will narrow the gap significantly. If it is the other way around, the gap will greatly increase. This would be a pessimistic outcome for the people in both sets of countries because of what it portends for world conflict—the possibility of wars of redistribution.

Understanding Charts and Graphs

Chapter Overview

Drawing on the adage, "a picture is worth a thousand words," economics makes extensive use of charts and graphs, both to present data and as a pedagogical tool. Of the various types of charts and graphs, line graphs are the most important and frequently used in teaching economics. They are particularly helpful in showing how changes in one variable are associated with changes in another—e.g., how changes in the unemployment rate are associated with changes in the rate of inflation—or how two variables determine a third—e.g., how demand and supply determine the price.

This appendix focuses on helping students, particularly those with little or no experience with graphs, to understand how graphs are constructed and how to use them. In order to allow the student to deal only with learning about graphs without having to be concerned about economic meanings, the examples of how line graphs are constructed and how they are read use a familiar non-economic situation that students can identify with, a car trip.

You can make a transparency of Figure 1A on page 493 from the master in the transparency booklet and, using a grease pencil or marking pen, take the class step-by-step through the creation of a graph, as shown in Figures 1B and 1C, and how to find information from the completed diagram, as shown in Figure 1D. You can show them how a change in the relationship between the two variables changes the curve, as in Figure 2.

For Figures 1A–1D and Figure 2 it may occur to the students that they can more easily find how long it will take to reach a certain spot on the trip by simple calculation without the use of a diagram. However, when you have a function that is not a constant, such as the travel curve that rises at an increasing rate in Figure 3, using the diagram to find the miles traveled at any given time is easier than calculating. (To show Figure 3, use the transparency for Figure 1A and draw the curve according to the information in the last paragraph on p. 495.) In any event, you might want to point out that diagrams in introductory economics are mostly used to help us see the relationships between variables, not to find specific information.

There are transparency masters for Figure 4, which shows a negative or inverse relationship between two variables, and Figure 5, which shows how the value of a variable can be negative.

As with most learning, students do not master diagrams until they do some themselves. There is a simple graphing exercise suggested at the end of the appendix which you might want to assign. Students will periodically have a chance to draw diagrams in answering the "For Thought" questions following the case applications and in the "Exercises in Analysis" at the ends of the chapters.

Schematic Outlines
From the Student Workbook

Chapter 1

Why Do We Have To Make Economic Choices?

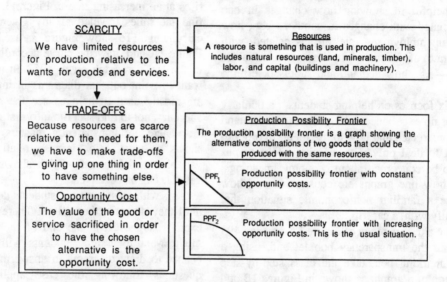

(This schematic outline covers the material in chapter 1, pp. 7-12, of the textbook.)

What Are Society's Economic Goals?

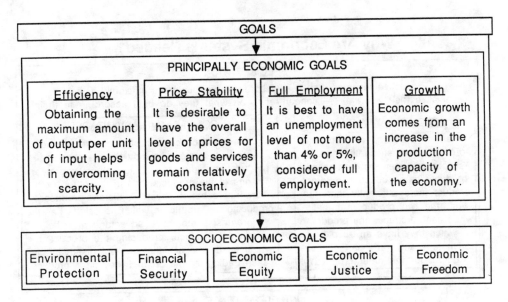

(This schematic outline covers the material in chapter 1, pp. 13-17, of the textbook.)

How Does the Study of Economics Help Us Make Choices?

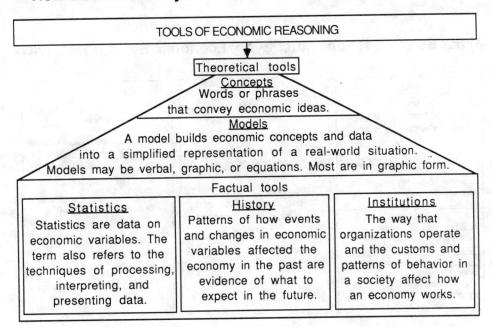

(This schematic outline covers the material in chapter 1, pp. 18-21, of the textbook.)

Chapter 2

Why Are Economic Systems Needed?

SPECIALIZATION

Productive resources, such as labor, can produce more efficiently if they specialize their activities — concentrating on what they do best according to their

ABSOLUTE ADVANTAGE		COMPARATIVE ADVANTAGE
When one producer can produce a product more efficiently than a second producer and the second producer can produce a different product more efficiently than the first, the two producers benefit when each produces the product in which they have an absolute advantage and trade part of their output for the other product.	or	When one producer can produce two or more products more efficiently than a second producer, but the ratio of advantage is greater in one of the products than in the other, both producers benefit by the efficient producer producing the product in which he or she has the greatest comparative advantage and the inefficient producer producing the product in which he or she has the smallest disadvantage, each trading for the product they don't produce.

INTERDEPENDENCE

Specialization according to absolute or comparative advantage results in interdependence, each producing unit depending on the other, necessitating an economic system to coordinate their activities.

(This schematic outline covers the material in chapter 2, pp. 29-32, of the textbook.)

What Basic Questions Must Every Economic System Resolve?

WHAT to produce	HOW to produce	FOR WHOM to produce
The economic system must decide what goods and services to produce with its land, labor, and capital.	The economic system must decide how to produce each good or service — determining what mix of land, labor, and capital to use in production and what production methods to employ.	The economic system must decide which members of society will receive how much of the goods and services produced — the process of allocating income.
Land All natural resources including fields, forests, mineral deposits, the sea, and other gifts of nature.		
Labor All human resources including manual, clerical, technical, professional, and managerial labor.		
Capital The physical means of production including factories, office buildings, tools and equipment. Alternatively : financial capital.		

(This schematic outline covers the material in chapter 2, pp. 33-36, of the textbook.)

What Are the Principal Types of Economic Systems?

MARKET ECONOMIES	CENTRALLY-DIRECTED ECONOMIES	TRADITIONAL ECONOMIES
are economic systems in which the basic questions of what, how, and for whom to produce are resolved primarily by buyers and sellers interacting in markets.	are economic systems in which the basic questions of what, how, and for whom to produce are resolved primarily by governmental authority.	are economic systems in which the basic questions of what, how, and for whom to produce are resolved primarily by custom and tradition.

MIXED ECONOMIES

are economic systems in which the basic questions of what, how, and for whom to produce are resolved by a mixture of market forces with government direction and/or custom and tradition.

(This schematic outline covers the material in chapter 2, pp. 37-42, of the textbook.)

How Does a Market System Resolve the Three Basic Economic Questions?

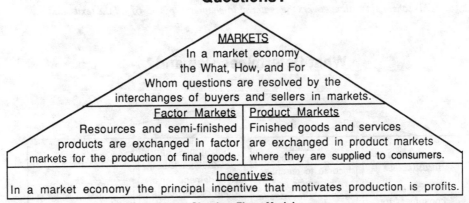

MARKETS

In a market economy the What, How, and For Whom questions are resolved by the interchanges of buyers and sellers in markets.

Factor Markets	Product Markets
Resources and semi-finished products are exchanged in factor markets for the production of final goods.	Finished goods and services are exchanged in product markets where they are supplied to consumers.

Incentives

In a market economy the principal incentive that motivates production is profits.

Circular Flow Model

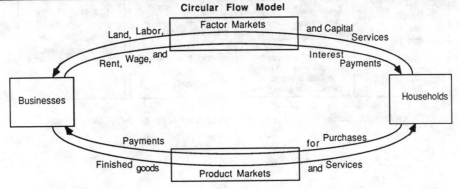

(This schematic outline covers the material in chapter 2, pp. 43-46, of the textbook.)

Chapter 3

What Forces Determine Prices in the Marketplace?

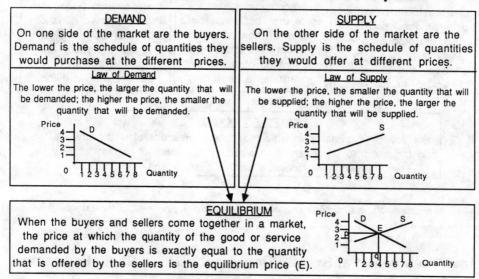

DEMAND	SUPPLY
On one side of the market are the buyers. Demand is the schedule of quantities they would purchase at the different prices.	On the other side of the market are the sellers. Supply is the schedule of quantities they would offer at different prices.

Law of Demand
The lower the price, the larger the quantity that will be demanded; the higher the price, the smaller the quantity that will be demanded.

Law of Supply
The lower the price, the smaller the quantity that will be supplied; the higher the price, the larger the quantity that will be supplied.

EQUILIBRIUM
When the buyers and sellers come together in a market, the price at which the quantity of the good or service demanded by the buyers is exactly equal to the quantity that is offered by the sellers is the equilibrium price (E).

(This schematic outline covers the material in chapter 3, pp. 55-61, of the textbook.)

What Determines Demand?

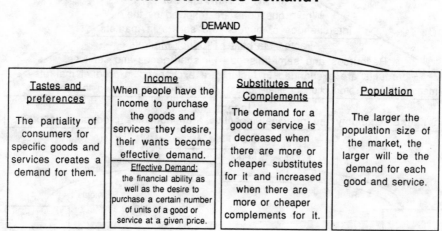

DEMAND

Tastes and preferences

The partiality of consumers for specific goods and services creates a demand for them.

Income
When people have the income to purchase the goods and services they desire, their wants become effective demand.

Effective Demand:
the financial ability as well as the desire to purchase a certain number of units of a good or service at a given price.

Substitutes and Complements

The demand for a good or service is decreased when there are more or cheaper substitutes for it and increased when there are more or cheaper complements for it.

Population

The larger the population size of the market, the larger will be the demand for each good and service.

(This schematic outline covers the material in chapter 3, pp. 62-64, of the textbook.)

What Determines Supply?

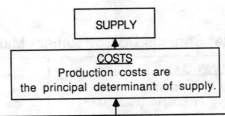

SUPPLY

COSTS
Production costs are
the principal determinant of supply.

Short Run
In the short run output can be increased or decreased by changing the amount of labor and materials used in production. The size of the plant and the amount of major equipment cannot be changed in the short run. Production costs depend on the relationship between the amounts of resources used and the amount of output.

Long Run
In the long run all factor inputs can be altered. Production capacity can be increased or decreased by adding to or reducing investment in plant and equipment. The amount of capital investment determines long-run supply.

(This schematic outline covers the material in chapter 3, pp. 65-66, of the textbook.)

Why Do Prices Change?

SHIFTS IN DEMAND
If there is a change in any of the four determinants of demand — tastes, incomes, prices and availability of substitutes and complements, population size — there will be a shift in the demand schedule. An decrease in demand means that at each and every price less would be purchased than previously.

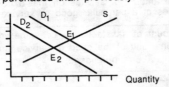

SHIFTS IN SUPPLY
A change in production costs results in a shift in the supply schedule. If production costs increase, less will be supplied at each and every price.

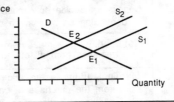

(This schematic outline covers the material in chapter 3, pp. 67-71, of the textbook.)

Chapter 4

What Choices Do Consumers Make?

SPENDING CHOICES
People continuously make spending decisions in order to satisfy their consumption needs and desires for necessities and luxuries.
Price Elasticity of Demand
The extent to which the quantity demanded of a good varies with small changes in its price is its elasticity of demand.
Measurement of elasticity

Elasticity Ratio = $\dfrac{\text{\% change in quantity}}{\text{\% change in price}}$

Consumer sovereignty
means that the spending decisions of consumers dictate what producers make and how resources are allocated.

SAVINGS CHOICES
The other alternative for consumers' after-tax Income is savings.
Average Propensity to Save
The amount we typically save out of a dollar of income is our average propensity to save. In this country it tends to be around 5%. The other 95 cents of each dollar we spend on goods and services. That is our average propensity to consume.

(This schematic outline covers the material in chapter 4, pp. 81-88, of the textbook.)

How Do Consumers Make Choices?

UTILITY
Consumers decide how much of their income to spend on different purchases depending on how much satisfaction or utility the item has for them.
Total utility is a measurement of the amount of satisfaction that a consumer receives from all of the purchases of a particular good or service.
Marginal utility is the additional amount of satisfaction a consumer receives from the purchase of one additional unit of the good or service (or the additional satisfaction from the last unit purchased).
Diminishing Marginal Utility
The more of a particular good or service that a consumer purchases, the less additional satisfaction an additional unit purchased will provide. Virtually everything has diminishing marginal utility.

CONSUMER EQUILIBRIUM

In order to get the maximum satisfaction from their income spending, consumers should allocate their purchases so that the last dollar spent on each good or service provides the same marginal utility as the last dollar spent on every other good or service purchased. When this is true, they are at consumer equilibrium — the allocation of their income that provides them with the maximum total utility possible.

(This schematic outline covers the material in chapter 4, pp. 89-92, of the textbook.)

How Can Consumers Make Better Choices?

<u>INFORMATION</u>

In order to allocate their incomes to obtain maximum utility, consumers need to have adequate and accurate information about the availability, characteristics, quality, sources, and prices of the goods and services that they might be interested in buying.

Limits on Information
Ideally, consumers should have as much information as possible about available products, but there are costs to acquiring, disseminating, and evaluating information.

<u>Advertising</u>

The most common source of information about products and services is advertising. Advertising is beneficial when it provides consumers with better information for making choices and when it reduces production costs by expanding the market for a product. But it is detrimental when it is false or misleading and when it adds to costs.

(This schematic outline covers the material in chapter 4, pp. 93-97, of the textbook.)

Chapter 5

What Are the Forms and Economic Functions of Business Firms?

FORMS OF BUSINESS ORGANIZATIONS

<u>Proprietorships</u>	<u>Partnerships</u>	<u>Corporations</u>	<u>Cooperatives</u>
are owned and operated by one individual or one family.	are the pooling of capital and/or business efforts of two or more people.	are owned by stockholders and managed by officers of the company.	are business associations of producers or consumers.

FUNCTIONS OF BUSINESS ORGANIZATIONS

<u>Identifying consumer wants</u>	<u>Organizing production</u>	<u>Allocating revenues</u>	<u>Real capital investment</u>
Business firms determine what to produce on the basis of consumer wants.	Firms decide what mix of the factors of production will best achieve the desired output.	Firms allocate their revenues to pay employees, suppliers, and investors.	Firms increase the stock of real capital by investing in plant and equipment.

(This schematic outline covers the material in chapter 5, pp. 106-113, of the textbook.)

What Determines a Firm's Profits?

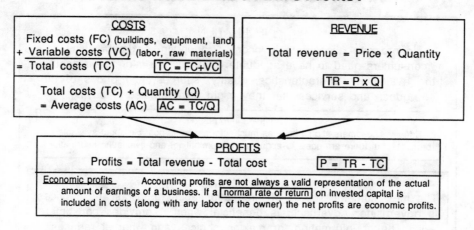

(This schematic outline covers the material in chapter 5, pp. 114-118, of the textbook.)

How Does Industry Market Structure Affect Price and Output Decisions?

PURE COMPETITION	PURE MONOPOLY	SHARED MONOPOLY	DIFFERENTIATED COMPETITION
An industry in which there are so many producers of a standardized product that no one firm can affect the market price.	An industry in which there is only one producer.	An industry in which there are a few producers of a standardized or a differentiated product.	An industry in which there are many producers of a differentiated product.
Diminishing returns When one factor input is fixed in supply, an increase in the other inputs results in output increasing at a diminishing rate.	**Maximum profit point** A monopolist will produce the output at which the revenue from the marginal unit produced just equals the cost of producing it. Marginal Revenue = Marginal Cost $MR=MC$	**Price leadership** When there only a few firms in an industry, each one is affected by the pricing policies of the other firms. A price cut by one firm to increase sales is likely to start a price war. Consequently, the firms stabilize prices in the industry by means of price leadership.	Firms in the industry attempt to gain customers by differentiating their product from those of their competitors. This frequently involves spending on advertising and packaging.
In the long run, economic profits in pure competition tend toward zero due to easy entry.	Monopolistic firms restrict output in order to keep the the price at the level which will maximize profits.		Ease of entry into the industry causes profits to tend toward zero.

(This schematic outline covers the material in chapter 5, pp. 119-128, of the textbook.)

Chapter 6

How Monopolistic Is American Industry?

MARKET CONCENTRATION

Market concentration refers to the number of firms in an industry that are competing for customers.

Concentration Ratio

The concentration ratio in an industry is measured by the amount of sales by the largest four firms in the industry as a percent of the total sales of the industry.

If the largest four firms sell less than 25% of the total industry sales, the industry is considered competitive. If they sell more than 50%, the industry is considered monopolistic. If they sell 25% — 50%, it is between competitive and monopolistic.

About one-third of the sales of U. S. industry are found in each of the three groups.

↓

AGGREGATE CONCENTRATION

Aggregate concentration refers to the percentage of the total sales of all industries together that is accounted for by the largest firms. There is no standard measurement for aggregate concentration, but it is increasing.

(This schematic outline covers the material in chapter 6, pp. 137-140, of the textbook.)

What Are the Causes of Concentration in Industry?

MERGERS	BARRIERS TO ENTRY	PREDATORY PRACTICES
A horizontal merger is one which joins two firms producing the same or very similar products. A vertical merger is a combination of firms at different stages of the production process. A conglomerate merger is a combination of firms producing and selling products in different industries.	Control of resources Patents and copyrights Excessive capital needs Economies of scale	Price discrimination Sales below cost Kickbacks Malicious interference

(This schematic outline covers the material in chapter 6, pp. 141-146 of the textbook.)

What Are the Consequences of Concentration in Industry?

MONOPOLISTIC PRICING

With only one or a few firms in an industry, barriers to entry of new firms, and a lack of close substitutes, monopolistic firms can charge prices substantially above production costs and make monopoly profits.

MISALLOCATION OF RESOURCES

By limiting output in order to keep prices high, monopolists restrict their use of labor, raw materials, and capital.

HIGHER COSTS

Monopolistic firms are not forced by market pressures to operate at or near their most efficient production levels as competitive firms are. In avoiding price competition, they engage in various forms of non-price competition that drive up costs such as product differentiation.

INSTABILITY

Monopolistic pricing policies contribute to inflationary pressures in booms and to unemployment in recessions.

(This schematic outline covers the material in chapter 6, pp. 147-149, of the textbook.)

Chapter 7

What Does the Government Do to Regulate Monopoly?

ANTITRUST LEGISLATION

Interstate Commerce Act (1887)
Established the Interstate Commerce Commission (ICC) to regulate the railroads; abolished rate discrimination.

Sherman Antitrust Act (1890)
The nation's basic antitrust legislation that prohibits monopoly and outlaws attempts to monopolize an industry.

Clayton Antitrust Act (1914)
Reinforced the Sherman Act by specifying specific illegal practices. Exempted unions.

Celler-Kefauver Antimerger Act (1950)
Prohibits mergers that would lessen competition. Reduced horizontal mergers.

PUBLIC UTILITY REGULATION

When an industry is a natural monopoly because it is more efficient for one firm to serve all of the customers in an area, the government regulates the firm through establishing a public utility commission.

DEREGULATION

In recent years there has been a move to deregulate industries to increase competition.

(This schematic outline covers the material in chapter 7, pp. 158-163, of the textbook.)

Why, in a Market Economy, Does the Government Produce Goods and Services?

COLLECTIVE GOODS

Some goods and services that are considered essential to society but are not adequately provided by the private sector are supplied by the government as collective goods (public goods).

> <u>External economies</u> One reason for providing collective goods is the existence of external economies, which arise when there are benefits from a good or service that accrue to the public that are in addition to the benefits to the consumer of the good or service. Something that raises the cultural level of society is a | merit good.|

> <u>Collective goods and equity</u> Another reason for the government to provide goods and services is to achieve the goal of greater equity in real income by providing essential services, such as housing and transportation, to those who cannot afford them.

(This schematic outline covers the material in chapter 7, pp. 164-168, of the textbook.)

What Is the Role of Government in Protecting Consumers, Workers, and the Environment?

<u>CONSUMER PROTECTION</u>	<u>WORKER PROTECTION</u>	<u>ENVIRONMENTAL PROTECTION</u>
Government agencies involved in protecting the consumer include: • Department of Transportation (DOT) • Food and Drug Administration (FDA) • Consumer Product Safety Commission (CPSC) • Federal Trade Commission (FTC) • Securities and Exchange Commission (SEC)	The principal government protection for workers is the | Occupational Safety and Health Act (OSHA).|	The principal agency is • The Environmental Protection Agency (EPA) <u>External costs</u> An economic justification for protecting the environment against pollution is the existence of |external costs|. Efficiency of resource allocation is improved when producers |internalize the external costs|

(This schematic outline covers the material in chapter 7, pp. 169-173, of the textbook.)

Chapter 8

What Determines Wages in a Market Economy?

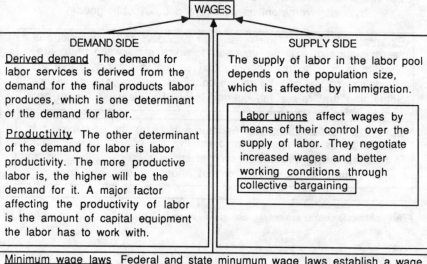

(This schematic outline covers the material in chapter 8, pp. 182-188, of the textbook.)

What Do Labor Unions Do?

COLLECTIVE BARGAINING
Passage of the National Labor Relations Act (Wagner Act) in 1935 requires management to bargain in good faith with labor unions. It established the National Labor Relations Board (NLRB) to enforce and administer the law.
Unions engage in collective bargaining with management over wages, working conditions, grievance procedures, fringe benefits, and hiring and firing practices. Collective bargaining agreements may contain a union shop provision that mandates all workers be required to join the union. Some states have passed right-to-work laws that outlaw such provisions.

Wage Demands	
Neoclassical theory Assumed that when there was unemployment, wages would fall until all workers who wanted to work would find jobs.	Modern theory Asssumes that wages are sticky because labor resists wage cuts. In recent years there have been give-backs in labor contracts.

Strikes — work refusals by labor unions to enforce contract or other demands.
Boycott — refusal to purchase or handle the products of a struck firm or industry (primary boycott) or one which does business with it (secondary boycott — illegal).
Jurisdictional dispute — conflict over which union represents workers.

(This schematic outline covers the material in chapter 8, pp. 189-195, of the textbook.)

What Do Workers Want?

MONETARY REWARDS	SECURITY AND WORKING CONDITIONS	PSYCHIC REWARDS
American industries tend be either high-wage or low-wage.	Workers in general put a higher priority on security in their jobs than on higher pay. Factory work that is characterized by unpleasant working conditions such as noise, confinement, and routine can result in the "blue-collar blues" and high absenteeism.	Workers are becoming more involved in making decisions regarding their work, thereby increasing their job satisfaction, by programs known as: • codetermination • quality circles • quality-of-worklife
High-wage industries include those in which both the union and the firms have a good deal of market power. **Low-wage industries** are those in competitive sectors. Workers earn about half as much in direct wages as those in high-wage industries.		
Only about 15% of the labor force is employed in high-wage industries.	A growing practice to improve working conditions is flexitime which permits workers to set their own hours.	

(This schematic outline covers the material in chapter 8, pp. 196-200, of the textbook.)

Chapter 9

How Is Income Distributed?

FUNCTIONAL INCOME DISTRIBUTION	PERSONAL INCOME DISTRIBUTION
The types of income according to their economic function are: • Wages and salaries (74% in 1985) Implicit wages A part of proprietors' income that is compensation to the owners for the time that they put into the business should also be included in wages and salaries. • Rents (.4% in 1985) Some other income behaves like rent when there is a fixed supply of the factor. In those cases the price is determined entirely by the demand level. • Interest (9% in 1985) Implicit interest Some profits are actually implicit interest on the owner's invested capital. • Profits (9.3% in 1985) This figure includes corporate profits only. To this should be added a portion of proprietors' income. • Proprietors' income (7.5% in 1985) The remainder of profits after subtracting the implicit interest and implicit rent are the rewards to entrepreneurs.	The proportion of total income received by different income groups represents personal income distribution. **Lorenz curve** A common way of describing how income is distributed is with the use of the Lorenz curve. 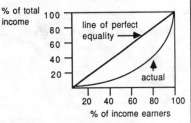 Income has been becoming more unequally distributed since 1970.

(This schematic outline covers the material in chapter 9, pp. 209-215, of the textbook.)

What Causes Unequal Distribution of Income?

DIFFERENCES IN PRODUCTIVITY	DIFFERENCES IN OPPORTUNITY	DIFFERENCES IN ASSET OWNERSHIP
Factors affecting the productivity of workers are: • Education • Training • Ability • Amount of capital equipment per worker	Incomes are affected by lack of educational and job opportunities. Civil Rights Act of 1964 prohibits employers from discriminating in the hiring, firing, promotion, job assignment, compensation, or training of workers. Equal Employment Opportunity Commission (EEOC) enforces the law.	The greatest differences in income are the result of differences in the amounts of assets owned by different groups in the population. Capital gains is the largest source of income for those with incomes of more than $1 mill. per year. Their second largest source of income is dividends.

(This schematic outline covers the material in chapter 9, pp. 216-218, of the textbook.)

Who Is Poor in the United States?

THE POVERTY LINE

The official designation of who is considered poor in the United States is defined by the poverty line, initially established in 1964. The poverty line is adjusted each year for changes in the cost of living.

Groups below the poverty line

• Women — Families headed by women constitute about one-half of the total number of families below the poverty line, although they make up only 15% of the population.
• Racial and ethnic minorities — Over one-third of the black population is classified as poor.
• Children — More than one-fifth of all children live in poverty. Among black and Hispanic children the ratio is nearly one in two.
• Southern states — The proportion of families in the southern states who are below the poverty level is nearly 50% greater than in the rest of the country.

(This schematic outline covers the material in chapter 9, pp. 219-222, of the textbook.)

Can Poverty Be Eliminated?

> ### INCREASED OPPORTUNITY
> One way to achieve more equitable income distribution is to remove obstacles to economic opportunity caused by racial, sexual, or age discrimination. Affirmative action programs are aimed at increasing educational, training, and employment opportunities for minorities and women.

> ### TRANSFER PAYMENTS
> - Money transfers — welfare, Social Security benefits, unemployment income.
> - Food stamps — food subsidies for low-income households.
> - Aid to Families With Dependent Children — an entitlement program for families below the poverty line with women heads of household.
> - Medicaid — federally financed health care for low-income families.
> - Housing — housing subsidies and public housing.
>
> > Negative income tax A proposal to change the federal income tax laws to provide a tax subsidy to those below the poverty level that is progressive the lower their income.
>
> Workfare requires welfare payment recipients to work for government or other non-profit agencies in order to receive transfer payments.

(This schematic outline covers the material in chapter 9, pp. 223-228, of the textbook.)

Chapter 10

What Is Money?

> ### CURRENCY
> Currency is that part of the money supply that consists of coins and bills.
> Currency constitutes about one-fourth of the money supply.
> The amount of currency in circulation depends on the demands by individuals and businesses for holding their financial assets in the form of currency.

> ### DEMAND DEPOSITS
> Demand deposits are liabilities of depository institutions that are payable on demand, such as checking accounts.
> Deposits payable on demand constitute nearly three-fourths of the money supply.

> M1 The most commonly used measurement of the money supply includes currency, traveler's checks, demand deposits, and other checkable deposits such as negotiable order of withdrawal (NOW) accounts.

> ### NEAR MONEY
> Near money is a type of financial asset which can, more or less, easily be turned into money. This includes savings deposits, certificates of deposit (CDs), and shares in money market mutual funds.

(This schematic outline covers the material in chapter 10, pp. 239-242, of the textbook.)

What Does Money Do?

MEDIUM OF EXCHANGE	UNIT OF MEASUREMENT	STORE OF VALUE
Money is used as an intermediary in the exchange of goods and services in place of direct barter because it simplifies making transactions. Attributes of a good medium of exchange: * Universally recognized * Adequate but limited supply * Not easily reproduced (forged) * Easily portable * Durable	The money unit serves as a common denominator in which the value of other things can be measured. Attribute of a good unit of measurement: * Should itself be stable in value	Money serves as a form in which wealth can be held. Attribute of a good store of value: * Should be liquid – readily converted without loss of value

(This schematic outline covers the material in chapter 10, pp. 243-245, of the textbook.)

How Is Money Created?

CURRENCY

The government prints paper money and mints coins in the amounts required by the public. The currency is disbursed to businesses and households through the banking system.

PRIVATE BORROWING

Borrowing from a bank increases the money supply by increasing the amount of demand deposits. Repayment of a loan decreases the money supply.

GOVERNMENT BORROWING

When the local, state, or federal governments sell bonds or Treasury bills acquired by banks, new demand deposits are created that increase the money supply just as in the case of private borrowing.

(This schematic outline covers the material in chapter 10, pp. 246-248, of the textbook.)

How Is the Supply of Money Controlled?

THE FEDERAL RESERVE SYSTEM (FED)

The Fed is the central bank of the United States, a government institution which serves as a "banker's bank," provides for the monetary needs of the federal government, and controls the money supply. Control of the money supply is the Fed's most important function, which it accomplishes by the following means:

RESERVE REQUIREMENTS	DISCOUNTING	OPEN MARKET OPERATIONS
The Federal Reserve specifies the amount of reserves that banks must have on deposit with the Fed as a % of their deposit liabilities. The magnitude of the required reserve ratio determines the money multiplier. By changing the reserve requirement ratio, the Fed can permit a larger or smaller money supply.	The Fed can reduce the amount of bank lending by raising the discount rate that it charges the banks on funds that they borrow from the Fed to supplement their reserves. Or it can encourage bank lending and increase the money supply by reducing the discount rate that it charges the banks.	The Fed can draw funds out of bank reserves by selling government securities on the open market, thus reducing the amount of money the banks can create. Or it can encourage bank lending by buying bonds and Treasury bills on the open market, thus adding to bank reserves.

(This schematic outline covers the material in chapter 10, pp. 249-254, of the textbook.)

Chapter 11

What Causes Unemployment?

FRICTIONAL UNEMPLOYMENT	STRUCTURAL UNEMPLOYMENT	CYCLICAL UNEMPLOYMENT
In a market economy there will always be people in between jobs. Those who are out of work for a short period of time while changing jobs constitute frictional unemployment in the economy. From the end of World War II to the 1970s, 3-4% frictional unemployment was considered normal.	When there are changes in market conditions that affect major industries or regions, this can cause structural unemployment. Causes of structural unemployment: * Decline in demand for a product * Increased foreign competition * Automation of production * Lack of labor mobility between occupations or between regions	When aggregate demand in the economy is not sufficient to provide jobs for all those who are seeking work, cyclical unemployment results. When the economy is operating at production capacity there is full employment aggregate demand.

Hidden Unemployment

In addition to those officially counted as unemployed, there are others who have become discouraged about the possibility of finding a job and have given up looking. Consequently, they are not counted as unemployed, constituting hidden unemployment. There are other workers who are involuntarily working only part-time. They are not counted among the unemployed, even though they are underemployed.

(This schematic outline covers the material in chapter 11, pp. 264-270, of the textbook.)

What Causes Inflation?

<u>Measuring inflation</u> — The most commonly used measure of average prices in the economy as a whole is the consumer price index (CPI).		
<u>DEMAND-PULL</u>	<u>COST-PUSH</u>	<u>MONETARY</u>
When the demand for goods and services exceeds the production capacity of the economy, the excess demand spills over into demand-pull inflation. Inflation is compounded when prices are rising due to shortages as goods and resources are bought and held off the market by speculators.	Inflation can arise from changes in the costs of production of goods and services. An increase in prices of raw materials, labor, or capital results in cost-push inflation. Cost-push inflation may reinforce demand-pull inflation through labor contracts containing cost of living adjustment (COLA) clauses.	Monetarists maintain that inflation is caused by excessive growth of the money supply. According to the quantity equation the money supply times the velocity at which it changes hands equals the number of transactions times the average level of prices $M \times V = T \times P$

(This schematic outline covers the material in chapter 11, pp. 271-275, of the textbook.)

Is There a Trade-Off Between Unemployment and Inflation?

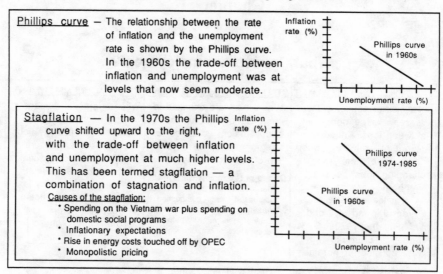

<u>Phillips curve</u> — The relationship between the rate of inflation and the unemployment rate is shown by the Phillips curve. In the 1960s the trade-off between inflation and unemployment was at levels that now seem moderate.

<u>Stagflation</u> — In the 1970s the Phillips curve shifted upward to the right, with the trade-off between inflation and unemployment at much higher levels. This has been termed stagflation — a combination of stagnation and inflation.

<u>Causes of the stagflation:</u>
* Spending on the Vietnam war plus spending on domestic social programs
* Inflationary expectations
* Rise in energy costs touched off by OPEC
* Monopolistic pricing

(This schematic outline covers the material in chapter 11, pp. 276-283, of the textbook.)

What Are the Consequences of Unemployment and Inflation?

UNEMPLOYMENT

Income effects
— Loss of income and fringe benefits (medical insurance) by unemployed
— Loss of income to others because of reduced purchasing power
— Reduced tax income and increased outlays for governments

Real output effects
— Each 1% of unemployment results in a reduction of $100 billion in output
— Lower real investment means less growth and reduced future output

Social effects
— Health problems (e.g., depression)
— Increased suicides
— Families break up
— Increased child abuse
— Increased crime

INFLATION

Income effects
— Reduced purchasing power of the $
— Reduced real income for fixed income receivers
— Reduced real wealth of savings
— Benefits those whose incomes rise faster than the inflation rate
— Benefits owners of real assets (e.g., precious metals, real estate)
— Benefits debtors

Real output effects
— Inflation initially stimulates output
— Near full employment, there arise bottlenecks in supplies
— Costs begin rising faster than prices
— Interest rates accelerate, discouraging new investment

(This schematic outline covers the material in chapter 11, pp. 284-288, of the textbook.)

Chapter 12

How Much Does the Economy Produce?

GROSS NATIONAL PRODUCT

The measure of the total amount of goods and services produced in the economy is the Gross National Product (GNP). There are two methods of measuring GNP:

Expenditure categories

C — personal consumption expenditures
I — gross private domestic investment (buildings, equipment, inventories)
G — government spending
X-M — net exports (exports minus imports)

$$GNP = C + I + G + (X-M)$$

Income categories

National Income (NI)
    Wages and salaries
    Proprietor's income
    Corporate profits
    Interest
    Rent
+ Capital Consumption Allowances
+ Indirect Taxes
= GNP

Value added — To avoid double counting in adding up the total amount of goods and services produced, only the value added at each stage of production is counted, excluding the cost of intermediate goods.

Current and constant dollar GNP — In order to measure real changes in GNP, eliminating the effect on the figures of inflation, the current dollar values are adjusted by a price index to give figures in the constant dollar value of an earlier base year.

(This schematic outline covers the material in chapter 12, pp. 297-302, of the textbook.)

What Determines How Much the Economy Produces From the Demand-Side Point of View?

KEYNESIAN ECONOMICS

One of the two principal interpretations of what determines total output is the demand-side analysis based on the writings of British economist John Maynard Keynes in the 1930s. The Keynesian model assumes four demand sectors:

Consumption	Investment	Government	Foreign
Consumption demand (C) is the largest flow of purchasing power into the economy. The size of C is basically determined by the amount of people's disposable income which they allocate to consumption (C).	Investment demand (I) consists of business spending for equipment, factories, offices, and inventories. It also includes new residences. The corresponding allocation of income is savings (S) which flows to money markets.	Government demand (G) is federal, state, and local government purchases of goods and services. The corresponding outflow is the taxes (T) paid by households and businesses.	Foreign demand (X) is the amount of domestic production which is exported. The corresponding leakage of purchasing power from the income stream is imports (M).

Equilibrium output — Total output is at the equilibrium level, with no tendency to increase or decrease, when the aggregate demand from the four demand sectors is just equal to the amounts allocated from income to the four sectors. The economy thus will not be rising or falling when $C + I + G + X = C + S + T + M$. Since the allocation of income to consumption expenditures is identical to consumption demand (C=C), the condition for equilibrium GNP can be stated as $I + G + X = S + T + M$

(This schematic outline covers the material in chapter 12, pp. 303-309, of the textbook.)

What Determines How Much the Economy Produces From the Supply-Side Point of View?

SUPPLY-SIDE ECONOMICS

The main alternative explanation of what determines the total output of the economy is supply-side economics, which was the foundation of "Reaganomics."

Say's Law — The roots of supply-side economics go back to the ideas of J. B. Say. According to Say's Law of Markets, "supply creates its own demand" so that production creates enough income to purchase what is produced and there will not be overproduction and unemployment.

Incentives — Modern supply-side economics emphasizes the importance of incentives in determining output. Increasing the returns to producers by reducing taxes and other costs provides an incentive for them to produce more, thereby creating jobs and income to purchase what is produced. Reducing taxes also is assumed to result in larger savings, which makes more funds available for investment.

Government deficits — Supply-side economics emphasizes the negative effects of government deficits on the availability and cost of capital to investors in the private sector, with government borrowing crowding out private investment borrowing in the money market.

(This schematic outline covers the material in chapter 12, pp. 310-315, of the textbook.)

Chapter 13

What Can the Government Do About Unemployment and Inflation?

FISCAL POLICY	MONETARY POLICY
One arm of government stabilization policies is fiscal policy — the use of federal spending, taxing, and debt management to influence general economic activity.	Monetary stabilization policies are under control of the Federal Reserve System. The Fed implements monetary policy through its powers to manage the money supply by changing the reserves of depository institutions, reducing them to tighten the money supply in order to combat inflation or expanding them to loosen the money supply in order to encourage business expansion in a recession.

Budget Philosophies

Annually balanced budget
An objective of balancing the federal budget each year rules out any discretionary fiscal policy by the government to counteract economic instability in the private sector.

Cyclically balanced budget
Balancing the federal budget over the course of the businesses cycle, with surpluses in boom years covering deficits during recessions, would make active government fiscal policy possible.

Functional finance
Pursuing fiscal stabilization policies without regard to budget balance is functional finance.

(This schematic outline covers the material in chapter 13, pp. 324-327, of the textbook.)

How Does Fiscal Policy Help Stabilize the Economy?

DISCRETIONARY FISCAL POLICY

Keynesian	Supply-side
Keynesians focus on the use of fiscal policy to compensate for inadequate or excessive demand in the private sector by increasing government spending and decreasing taxes in a recession or by reducing government spending and increasing taxes in a period of inflation.	Supply-side fiscal policy would reduce both taxes and government spending in a recession. The decreases in taxes would be directed toward savers rather than consumers.

Multiplier — The impact on the economy of a change in taxes or government spending is increased by the multiplier effect.

$$\text{Multiplier} = \frac{1}{\text{savings rate} + \text{tax rate}}$$

AUTOMATIC STABILIZERS
Besides discretionary fiscal policy, there are various automatic stabilizers in government spending and taxing that counteract recession and inflation.

(This schematic outline covers the material in chapter 13, pp. 328-332, of the textbook.)

How Can Monetary Policy Help Stabilize the Economy?

MONETARY POLICY TOOLS		
<u>Open Market Operations</u> Fed offers to buy or sell government securities on the open market. Buying increases bank reserves and encourages expansion of money supply, while selling decreases reserves and reduces money supply.	<u>Discount rate changes</u> Fed reduces discount rate on loans to banks in order to encourage increase in reserves and expand money supply, raises discount rate to discourage bank borrowing of reserves and reduce money supply.	<u>Required reserve ratio</u> Fed reduces the % of banks' liabilities that they must have on deposit in their reserves in the Federal Reserve Bank to permit increase in money supply, increases % to reduce money supply.
<u>Controlling interest rates</u> The target of Fed monetary policy prior to Oct. 1979 was the control of interest rates. Bringing about a decline in interest rates stimulated economic activity, while raising interest rates was deflationary.	<u>Control of the money supply</u> In 1979 the target of monetary policy was changed to control of the money supply. The Fed sets a target for growth of the money supply sufficient to finance economic expansion but restrictive enough to prevent inflation.	

(This schematic outline covers the material in chapter 13, pp. 333-337, of the textbook.)

What Can Be Done if Monetary and Fiscal Policies Don't Work?

<u>RATIONAL EXPECTATIONS</u>
A school of thought has emerged that maintains government stabilization policies are counterproductive because the public has learned to anticipate what measures the government will introduce in specific circumstances and people undertake actions in their own self-interest that negate the stabilization measures.

<u>ALTERNATIVE PROPOSALS</u>

<u>Direct controls</u> — Wage and price controls have been used in the past to hold down inflation, notably in wartime.

<u>Incomes policies</u> — Guidelines are set for maximum price and wage increases during the year. A Tax-based Incomes Policy (TIP) would discourage price and wage increases by imposing tax penalty.

<u>Gain-sharing</u> — A more recent proposal for encouraging full employment and spiking inflation would separate workers' wages into two parts; a constant wage base and a variable wage addition that would depend on the company's profitability.

<u>Market Anti-inflation Plan (MAP)</u> — Another novel system proposed for bringing about price stability would establish price credits which would be needed by firms to raise prices.

<u>Indexing</u> — A different approach to the inflation problem is to permit prices to rise and offset the effects on income distribution by automatically adjusting all incomes to keep up with the rate of inflation.

(This schematic outline covers the material in chapter 13, pp. 338-344, of the textbook.)

Chapter 14

What Causes Economic Growth?

EXTENSIVE GROWTH	INTENSIVE GROWTH
One cause of an expansion of production capacity over time is an increase in population and corresponding increases in other factors, resulting in extensive growth. Population growth provides additions to the labor supply, but it also requires more output to satisfy people's needs. Thus, extensive growth does not necessarily raise living standards.	The most important type of growth is intensive growth because it increases productivity as well as total production, thereby raising living standards. An increase in the use of capital equipment, automation, improved technology, and improvements in human capital through education, training, and better health care are sources of intensive growth.

(This schematic outline covers the material in chapter 14, pp. 353-356, of the textbook.)

How Can Economic Growth Be Increased?

INCREASING CAPITAL INVESTMENT — Economic growth can be increased by raising the proportion of the nation's output that goes into capital formation.
Investment/GNP ratio — The fraction of each year's GNP that is allocated to investment goods.

INCREASING CAPITAL EFFICIENCY — Increasing the quality of capital investment by substituting more technologically advanced equipment and production methods is a major source of economic growth.
Capital/output ratio — The ratio of the cost of new investment goods to the value of annual output produced by those goods.

INCREASING LABOR-FORCE PARTICIPATION RATE — Economic growth is increased when a larger % of the population is active in the labor force. The increased participation by women in the labor force in the last two decades has contributed significantly to U.S. economic growth.

INCREASING INVESTMENT IN HUMAN CAPITAL — The quality of the labor force is a determinant of the rate of economic growth. Investment in education and occupational and on-the-job training increases the growth rate.
Learning curve — In a new plant or when a new production process is introduced, the output per worker increases over time at a steeper rate the better the training and attitudes of the labor force.

(This schematic outline covers the material in chapter 14, pp. 357-364, of the textbook.)

Is Economic Growth Desirable?

POPULATION DENSITY

An increase in the population size relative to land area results in higher population density, with a reduction in the amount of open area.
A growing population stimulates investment and growth but contributes to scarcity of resources and the possibility of inflation.

URBANIZATION

Concentration of population in urban centers results in air, water, and noise pollution, traffic problems, and personal alienation.
On the positive side, large urban centers provide high-quality medical services, educational opportunities, cultural and artistic programs, and other conveniences and opportunities.

ALLOCATION OF GROWTH PRODUCT

The increase in output resulting from intensive growth can be used to help solve pollution problems and develop primary, capital, and human resources.

INCOME DISTRIBUTION

Intensive growth can facilitate relieving poverty by making it possible to allocate more output to the needy while at the same time maintaining or improving the living conditions of the rest of the population.

Stationary state — a condition in which no real growth is taking place.

(This schematic outline covers the material in chapter 14, pp. 365-367, of the textbook.)

Chapter 15

On What Do Governments Spend Money?

Size of government spending

— About 37% of all spending in the economy is channeled through governments.
— But governments account for only about 20% of purchases. The difference is transfer payments.

FEDERAL SPENDING	STATE AND LOCAL EXPENDITURES
— National defense is the largest item in the federal budget (27%) — Other direct expenditures (11%) — The balance of federal expenditures are transfer payments for • social security (20%) • interest on the national debt (14%) • Medicare and other health programs (11%) • grants-in-aid to state and local governments (10%)	— Education absorbs the largest part of state and local budgets (35%) — Other large expenditures include • public welfare (13%) • health and hospitals (10%) • highways (8%) • police and corrections (6%) — Interest costs on state and local government debt amount to only about 5% of their budgets

(This schematic outline covers the material in chapter 15, pp. 376-382, of the textbook.)

Where Do Governments Get the Money to Spend?

FEDERAL REVENUES	STATE AND LOCAL REVENUES
— The largest federal revenue source is individual income taxes (46%) — The second largest is payroll taxes and pension contributions (36%) — Corporate income taxes (8%) — Excise taxes (5%)	— Sales taxes (17%) — Property taxes (15%) — Federal transfers (15%) Fiscal federalism — the system by which the federal government collects revenues which it transfers to lower government levels to finance their activities

(This schematic outline covers the material in chapter 15, pp. 383-387, of the textbook.)

Who Pays for Government Spending?

EQUITY	EFFICIENCY
Horizontal equity — people who are equally able to pay bearing the same tax burden. Vertical equity — those with higher incomes paying a larger % of their income in taxes. Benefits principle — taxes levied on the users of government services in proportion to the amount of use.	Taxes should be levied in such a way as to minimize their interference with the allocation of resources and their discouragement of production. Sin taxes — an exception to the above rule in the case of goods (tobacco, alcohol) that public policy wishes to discourage.

INCIDENCE

Taxes are often shifted by those on whom they are levied to others.
The incidence of the tax is on those who ultimately pay it.
Income taxes cannot be shifted, but excise and property taxes are.
Corporate profits taxes and payroll taxes are likely shifted to consumers
in the form of higher prices and to workers in the form of lower wages.
Progressive taxes — a higher % of tax is levied on larger incomes.
Regressive taxes — lower income earners pay a larger % of their income in taxes than higher earners.
Proportional taxes — the same % of income is paid in taxes at different income levels.

(This schematic outline covers the material in chapter 15, pp. 388-393, of the textbook.)

Chapter 16

Why Do We Trade With Other Countries?

ABSOLUTE ADVANTAGE	COMPARATIVE ADVANTAGE
When a country has the resources that enable it to produce one good more cheaply than a second country and the second country has the resources to produce a another good more cheaply than the first, each country will benefit from producing the good in which it has an absolute advantage and trading part of its production for the good in which it has a disadvantage.	When one country has an absolute advantage over a second country in the production of two goods but has a greater advantage in the production of one of the two goods than the other, it will benefit both countries for each to produce the good in which it has a comparative advantage and trade with the other country for the good in which it has a comparative disadvantage.

SPECIALIZATION

Nations tend to specialize their production in accordance with their available resources. Those countries with an abundance of capital relative to labor specialize in high-technology industries, while countries that lack large capital resources specialize in labor-intensive industries.

> Increasing costs — For most products, specialization is not complete. Because the amounts of resources that are suited to the production of a particular good are limited, as more of the good is produced there are increasing production costs that prevent the country from producing all of the good that it consumes. The difference is imported.

(This schematic outline covers the material in chapter 16, pp. 403-406, of the textbook.)

Who Benefits and Who Is Hurt by Foreign Trade?

BENEFITS	LOSSES

CONSUMER BENEFITS	IMPORT-COMPETING FIRMS' AND WORKERS' LOSSES
Consumers benefit from foreign trade by being able to consume some products that would not be available without trade. More importantly, consumers benefit by being able to purchase many products at lower costs than if there were no foreign trade both because of the lower prices of imported goods and because competition from imports holds down the prices of domestic goods.	Competition from imports can be costly to domestic firms and their workers in lost sales and lower prices. These costs are similar to the costs of competition from new domestic producers or from new substitute products.
PRODUCER AND WORKER BENEFITS	Mobility of capital and labor — The costs of free trade to import-competing firms and workers can be minimized by mobility of capital and labor to alternative employments.
Domestic industries that use imported inputs benefit. More importantly, export industries, their workers, and their suppliers benefit from the sales to markets abroad.	**DOMESTIC CONSUMERS OF EXPORT INDUSTRIES** The export of part of the output of an industry tends to raise the price of the good to domestic consumers.

(This schematic outline covers the material in chapter 16, pp. 407-411, of the textbook.)

How Do We Pay for Imports?

<u>FOREIGN-EXCHANGE MARKET</u>
The conversion of one currency into another takes place in the foreign-exchange market, which is not a place but a set of banks and other institutions in the U.S. and other countries that deal in foreign currencies.

<u>Exchange Rates</u>

SYSTEM	CHANGES IN RATES
<u>Fixed exchange rates</u> — governments stipulate the rate at which their currencies will exchange for other currencies and support that rate.	<u>Devaluation</u> — the government lowers the value of its currency in exchange for other currencies. <u>Revaluation</u> — the government raises the value.
<u>Freely-fluctuating exchange rates</u> — exchange rates are allowed to float in response to demand and supply in the foreign-exchange market.	<u>Depreciation</u> — the value of a currency falls due to a change in its market demand-supply. <u>Appreciation</u> — the market exchange value rises.

<u>BALANCE OF PAYMENTS</u>
The annual accounting record of all transactions between a country's residents and residents of the rest of the world is the country's balance of payments.
<u>Current account</u> — records imports and exports of goods and services.
<u>Balance of trade</u> — the difference between merchandise imports and exports.
<u>Long-term capital account</u> — records the flow of public and private investment into and out of country.
<u>Short-term capital account</u> — records the flow of liquid funds such as bank deposits between countries.
<u>Residual accounts</u> — record-balancing short-term capital and gold movements to cover a basic deficit.

(This schematic outline covers the material in chapter 16, pp. 412-419, of the textbook.)

How Do We Restrict Foreign Trade?

<u>TARIFFS</u>
Taxes on imports are not imposed primarily for revenue but to shelter domestic firms from foreign competition. They may be based either on value or on quantity.
<u>Bilateral trade negotiations</u> — are engaged in to reduce trade restrictions between two countries.
Most-favored nation clauses in trade agreements extend the trade concessions to other countries.
<u>Multilateral trade negotiations</u> — reduce trade restrictions among many nations simultaneously.
General Agreement on Tariffs and Trade (GATT) provides for non-discrimination between nations.

<u>QUOTAS</u>
Restrictions imposed on the quantity of a good that may be imported may be set in terms of physical quantity or value and may be by country or in total.
<u>Tariff quota</u> — allows a given quantity or value of a commodity to enter duty-free or at a low tariff, with larger quantities or values entering at a higher rate of duty.

<u>NON-TARIFF BARRIERS</u>
Protectionist measures in addition to tariffs and quotas include label of origin requirements, additional tests and inspections, and slow customs clearance.

<u>EXPORT EMBARGOES</u>
Exports may be restricted to keep new technologies out of the hands of other countries or for political reasons or to hold down domestic prices.

(This schematic outline covers the material in chapter 16, pp. 420-422, of the textbook.)

Should Foreign Trade Be Restricted?

TRADITIONAL PROTECTIONIST ARGUMENTS

Cheap foreign labor

The argument for protecting American workers against competition from cheap foreign labor ignors the fact that workers' real income is determined by their productivity — low productivity means low wages but high real costs.

Increase aggregate demand

Restricting imports increases demand in the import-competing industries, but reduces demand and employment in export industries because of retaliation.

Infant industry

If there is a new industry which has the potential to be efficient and competitive, it may be justified to protect the industry from foreign competition while it matures. This is the only traditional protectionist argument that generally has recognized validity among economists.

TERMS OF TRADE ARGUMENT

Imposing trade protection to lower the average price of imports relative to exports can obtain more imports per unit of exports, but is subject to retaliation.

NEOMERCANTILIST ARGUMENT

Like the mercantilists of Queen Elizabeth's time, today's neomercantilists want to restrict trade in order to maintain the advantages of technological superiority.

BALANCE-OF-PAYMENTS ARGUMENT

Restricting imports to eliminate a basic deficit in the balance of payments would be subject to retaliation by the countries affected.

(This schematic outline covers the material in chapter 16, pp. 423-426, of the textbook.)

Chapter 17

What Are the Major Differences Among Alternative Economic Systems?

ALTERNATIVE ECONOMIC SYSTEMS

System		Commonly called
Market	→	Capitalism or free enterprise
Centrally-directed or command	→	Communism
Democratic socialist	→	Socialism or welfare state

OPERATION OF COMMAND SYSTEMS (SOVIET UNION)

WHAT TO PRODUCE

Gosplan — the central planning agency gathers information about the economy and leadership priorities (e.g., on the consumption-investment mix).

Control figures — for about 2,000 major commodity groups are sent to economic ministries which set production targets for each enterprise.

Priority sectors — are given preference in the allocation of resources. The USSR priorities have been investment for growth and the military.

HOW TO PRODUCE

Gosbank — the state bank handles all financial transactions among enterprises and through this monitors input use and production output.

Collectivization — farmers were forced to join collectives, and agricultural productivity has been low.

FOR WHOM TO PRODUCE

Income distribution in the USSR is based on wage incentives to allocate labor where it is needed. High officials receive large bonuses and non-wage benefits.

(This schematic outline covers the material in chapter 17, pp. 435-442, of the textbook.)

How Do We Evaluate the Performance of Alternative Economic Systems?

EFFICIENCY	PRICE STABILITY	FULL EMPLOYMENT	GROWTH
<u>Static efficiency</u> — measured at a given point in time, the level of productivity of labor and capital in the USSR are low. <u>Dynamic efficiency</u> — over a period of time, the growth of output in the USSR has demonstrated high dynamic efficiency.	Theoretically, the government can keep prices almost perfectly stable because they are established by state agencies. But now that the Soviets are more concerned about the rational allocation of scarce resources, they raise prices in response to shortages.	Officially, the USSR guarantees jobs for everyone and effectively has full employment. There are problems with the distribution of labor because there is a labor surplus in some areas and labor shortages elsewhere.	Soviet annual growth in real GNP has been exceptional, unmatched by any other country either in aggregate or per capita terms. However, exceptionally high growth in the USSR came to a halt in the 1970s, and its growth rate recently has been about the same as U.S.

SOCIOECONOMIC GOALS

<u>Environmental protection</u> — Because of planning failure to include environmental costs, the USSR has has pollution problems, the worst instance being the Chernobyl nuclear power plant explosion.
<u>Security</u> — There is a high degree of job and basic needs security in the Soviet Union.
<u>Equality</u> — Income is generally more evenly distributed than in the West, except for high officials.
<u>Freedom</u> — Economic freedom is limited by the absence of private ownership and by the requirements of planning. The Soviets trade off economic freedom for stability and security.

(This schematic outline covers the material in chapter 17, pp. 443-451, of the textbook.)

Are Socialistic and Capitalistic Systems Converging?

<u>CONVERGENCE HYPOTHESIS</u> — There is evidence that the market economies of the West and the command economies of the Soviet Union and its satellites are becoming more similar.

INDICATIONS OF CONVERGENCE

IN COMMAND ECONOMIES	IN MARKET ECONOMIES
<u>Decentralization in planning and management</u> — major decisions are still made at the top level, but decision-making powers on many matters have been delegated to lower levels. <u>Introduction of interest, rent, and profit</u> — Soviet-style economies have begun to employ these devices to help improve allocation. <u>Use of price signals</u> — use of prices to reflect scarcity or surplus is reforming the price system. <u>Increased importance of business administration</u> — Soviets are training new-type managers for dealing with the decision making needed for modernization of industrial methods. <u>Increased importance of consumption</u> <u>Increased importance of foreign trade</u> <u>Trend toward market socialism</u> — the market socialist model duplicates the rational allocation process of a market system.	<u>Growth of the public sector has been expanding</u> — growth of government participation in the economies of western nations through government ownership of the means of production, expenditures on public goods and services, and income transfer programs. <u>Extension of social welfare measures</u> — capitalist governments are spending more on health, education, and welfare. <u>Planning and incomes policies</u> — some market economies are adopting a national economic plan that indicates the direction of the economy and adopting incomes policies to control prices and wages. <u>Market forces toned down</u> — regulation and control to decrease market uncertainty, the formation of trading blocs, cartels, mergers, and multinational companies. <u>Increased role of workers in decisions and profits</u>

(This schematic outline covers the material in chapter 17, pp. 452-456, of the textbook.)

Chapter 18

What Makes Countries Poor?

POVERTY — Most of the world's population lives in the less-developed countries
(LDCs) of the Third World that have per capita incomes of only a few
hundred dollars a year. Reasons for their poverty include:

LACK OF TECHNOLOGY AND CAPITAL
In order to break out of the vicious circle of a subsistence economy, a country needs an economic surplus over and above consumption needs to allocate to investment in real capital and human capital for intensive growth.

OVERPOPULATION
The standard of living depends on the amount of goods and services available relative to the numbers of people. A large and rapidly growing population absorbs all of the economic surplus, trapping a country in the vicious circle.

EXPLOITATION
The legacy of external exploitation in their colonial past may have retarded economic development for the LDCs. A greater obstacle to development could be the internal exploitation of one class by another, with ownership of land usually concentrated in the hands of a wealthy elite class that controls the government.

(This schematic outline covers the material in chapter 18, pp. 466-473, of the textbook.)

What Economic Development Choices Do Less-Developed Countries Have to Make?

AGRICULTURE VS. INDUSTRY
LDCs are mainly agricultural. They must decide whether to devote resources to increasing the productivity of the agricultural sector or to promote rapid industrialization, or try to do some of each with their limited resources.

BASIC INDUSTRIES VS. CONSUMER GOODS INDUSTRIES
Concentrating available investment resources in such basic industries as steel, electric power, and capital equipment, as the Soviet model of growth, emphasizes investment in heavy industry, but has negative consequences for standards of living and lack of incentives to motivate labor to increase productivity.

CENTRALIZED PLANNING VS. THE MARKET
LDCs make their choices about whether to use a centrally planned economy for rapid development or depend on a relatively free market system. China and others are using central planning combined with more or less free enterprise in markets.

BALANCED VS. UNBALANCED GROWTH
A problem for the LDCs is whether they should continue to fulfill their historic colonial role as suppliers of raw materials and labor-intensive exports to the industrialized world or whether they should diversify into manufacturing by protecting their infant industries from foreign competition and develop a more balanced but, at least initially, high-cost manufacturing sector.

(This schematic outline covers the material in chapter 18, pp. 474-479, of the textbook.)

What Are the Prospects for World Economic Development?

THE POPULATION BOMB	THE DEBT BOMB
The high rate of population growth in the less-developed countries is a threat to their development prospects and to the ability of world agriculture to satisfy the food needs of future generations. The population pressures on food and other resources, on energy, and on the environment are potentially a bomb that could destroy living standards and create domestic and international conflicts.	Of immediate concern to the LDCs and to the creditor countries that lent them vast sums of money is the debt crisis triggered by the fall in oil prices and the prices of other primary products that were counted on to provide export income to service and repay the debts. Widespread defaults on the loans would create an international financial crisis, but the austerity imposed to avoid defaults has caused domestic unrest in the LDCs.

UTOPIA OR APOCALYPSE

Inability to cope with the population bomb, the debt bomb, and the other problems of the LDCs could result in a super inflation, a worldwide depression, World War III, or wars of redistribution. Or the problems may be overcome with technological and organizational tools, guided by Adam Smith's "invisible hand."

(This schematic outline covers the material in chapter 18, pp. 480-484, of the textbook.)

List of Master Transparencies
Contained in Booklet

Chapter 11

Chapter 12

Chapter 13

Chapter 14

Chapter 15

Understanding Charts and Graphs

All Schematic Outlines Contained in this Teacher's Guide

(continued from the inside front cover)

5. Describe predatory business practices. p. 144
6. Explain the four consequences of high concentration in industries. pp. 147–48

Chapter 7. Government and Business

1. Explain the purposes of the Interstate Commerce Act and the Sherman, Clayton, and Celler-Kefauver Acts. pp. 158–59
2. List the causes of natural monopoly and indicate what industries fall under that classification. pp. 159–60
3. Explain how public policy deals with natural monopolies. pp. 160–61
4. Discuss the positive and negative aspects of regulation. pp. 160–62
5. Explain the reasons for and the consequences of deregulation. pp. 161–62
6. Identify the kinds of goods and services that constitute collective goods, and explain why the government provides them. pp. 164–65
7. Describe the concepts of external economies and external costs. pp. 165–67, 172
8. Explain how external economies and external costs are dealt with through government actions and internalization. pp. 169–72

Chapter 8.

1. Explain what determines the demand for and supply of labor and how demand and supply influence wages. pp. 182–84
2. Describe the effects of minimum wage laws. pp. 184–85
3. Discuss how mechanization affects labor demand and wages. pp. 185–86
4. Explain what labor unions do and describe the laws that affect union activities. pp. 189–90
5. Explain what "sticky" wages are and discuss their impacts in labor markets. pp. 190–91
6. List the differences between the different types of strikes and boycotts. pp. 192–93
7. Explain what jurisdictional disputes are and why they are becoming increasingly important to unions. p. 193
8. Describe the principal concerns of workers regarding their jobs. pp. 196–99

Chapter 9. Income Distribution

1. Define the different income sources that make up the functional distribution of income. p. 209
2. Identify the unique characteristics of the determination of rent compared to the determination of other sources of income. pp. 209–11
3. Describe how the personal distribution of income is measured, how it has changed over time, and how the distribution is shown on a Lorenz Curve. pp. 212–14
4. List the causes of unequal distribution of personal income. pp. 216–17

5. Explain how poverty is defined and list those socioeconomic groups that have a high incidence of poverty. pp. 219–21
6. Distinguish between programs which try to reduce poverty by increasing economic opportunities and those which try to reduce poverty by supplementing real income. pp. 223–26
7. Explain how negative income tax works. pp. 225–26

Chapter 10 Money

1. Discuss the history of money. pp. 237–38
2. Define the M1 money supply and describe its components. pp. 239–41
3. Explain how near money differs from money and discuss how near money relates to the broader money definitions of M2, M3, and L. p. 241
4. List the three functions of money and explain the characteristics money must have in order to be functional. pp. 243–44
5. Discuss how currency is affected by public demand and explain money creation. pp. 246–47
6. Describe the Federal Reserve banking system. pp. 249–53
7. List the means by which the Federal Reserve controls the money supply. pp. 249–53

Chapter 11. Unemployment and Inflation

1. Describe the three major causes of unemployment. pp. 264–68
2. Explain why some unemployment is hidden. p. 268
3. Define inflation and the CPI. pp. 271–72
4. Describe three causes of inflation and explain the usage of the quantity equation. pp. 272–74
5. Explain the relationship between unemployment and inflation and use the Phillips curve to show this relationship. pp. 276–77
6. Define stagflation and relate the price level to output and employment levels by use of the aggregate supply and aggregate demand curves. pp. 277–80
7. Explain the consequences of unemployment and inflation. pp. 284–87

Chapter 12. The Economy's Output

1. Define the GNP and explain the two ways of measuring it and why they give the same result. pp. 297–301
2. List the four types of expenditures that make up the total demand for goods and services. pp. 304–6
3. Define National Income and discuss how it differs from GNP. pp. 299–300
4. Define constant dollar GNP and show how it relates to current dollar GNP. p. 301
5. Explain the Keynesian economic model and show under what conditions the output of the economy is at equilibrium. pp. 303–6
6. Define Say's Law. pp. 310–12